Lord, Make Me
an Instrument
of Your Peace

Lord, Make Me

San Damiano Books

PARACLETE PRESS
BREWSTER, MASSACHUSETTS

an Instrument
of Your Peace

THE COMPLETE PRAYERS OF
ST. FRANCIS & ST. CLARE,

WITH SELECTIONS FROM
BROTHER JUNIPER, ST. ANTHONY OF PADUA,
AND OTHER EARLY FRANCISCANS

—— Jon M. Sweeney ——

First Printing 2020
Lord, Make Me an Instrument of Your Peace: The Complete Prayers of St. Francis and St. Clare, with Selections from Brother Juniper, St. Anthony of Padua, and Other Early Franciscans
Copyright © 2020 by Jon M. Sweeney

Portions of this book were previously published in *The St. Francis Prayer Book* (2004), *The St. Clare Prayer Book* (2007), and *The St. Francis Holy Fool Prayer Book* (2017). The first remains largely unchanged; the second with deletions and additions; and the third substantially different here than originally published.

Unless otherwise noted, quotations from the Gospels and other parts of the New Testament are taken from The New Jerusalem Bible, published and copyright 1985 by Darton, Longman & Todd, Ltd., and Doubleday, a division of Random House, Inc., and used by permission of the publisher; Scripture from the Psalms taken from the Book of Common Prayer and Administration of the Sacraments and Other Rites and Ceremonies of the Church according to the use of the Episcopal Church, copyright 1979 The Church Hymnal Corp., NY; Scripture from the songs, canticles, and prophets of the Hebrew Scriptures taken from the New Revised Standard Version of the Bible, copyright © 1993 and 1989 by the Division of Christian Education of the National Council of Churches of Christ in the USA, used by permission. All rights reserved.

ISBN 978-1-64060-146-8

The Paraclete Press name and logo (dove on cross) and the San Damiano Books logo are trademarks of Paraclete Press, Inc.

Library of Congress Cataloging-in-Publication Data
Names: Sweeney, Jon M., 1967- author.
Title: Lord, make me an instrument of your peace : the complete prayers of
   St. Francis and St. Clare, with selections from Brother Juniper, St.
   Anthony of Padua, and other early Franciscans / Jon M. Sweeney.
Description: Brewster, Massachusetts : San Damiano Books, Paraclete Press,
   2020. | Summary: "This prayer book gathers the stories and words of the
   prayer life and prayers of these remarkable Christians"-- Provided by
   publisher.
Identifiers: LCCN 2019043196 | ISBN 9781640601468 (trade paperback)
Subjects: LCSH: Franciscans--Spiritual life. | Prayers. | Francis, of
   Assisi, Saint, 1182-1226. | Clare, of Assisi, Saint, 1194-1253.
Classification: LCC BX3603 .S94 2020 | DDC 242/.802--dc23
LC record available at https://lccn.loc.gov/2019043196

10 9 8 7 6 5 4 3 2 1

Published by Paraclete Press
Brewster, Massachusetts
www.paracletepress.com

Printed in the United States of America

*"My Father still goes on working,
and I am at work, too."*

—Our Lord Jesus Christ, in St. John's Gospel (5:17)

CONTENTS

INTRODUCTION

W̶e do not immediately associate Francis and Clare with prayer and praying. That is not how we typically imagine them in the world. It is easier to see them giving away their possessions, setting doves free, counseling wolves, bandaging lepers' wounds, mediating between people, begging for their bread, preaching to birds, or singing religious poetry accompanied by lute and lyre.

St. Francis, according to the most common legends, rarely sat still. St. Clare did more so, but that was probably mostly because of the convent and the grille and the conventions of the time: she couldn't be a walkabout friar.

However, they *did* sit still. And they stood. And they danced. And they fasted. And they sang. In all these ways, Francis and Clare prayed for hours each day, as did the brothers and sisters who came after them on the Franciscan way.

This prayer book gathers the stories and words of the prayer life and prayers of these remarkable Christians. Their charism was unique in its time, and it remains a reservoir and a river flowing through the centuries, reviving the life and spirit of the church and its people. May it be so for you wherever you are, wherever it finds you, and in however you incorporate these ways and words into your life for God.

Francis said to his friars, "Listen to what I say," (Acts 2:14 NRSV). "Whoever is from God hears the words of God" (John 8:47 NRSV).

St. Francis

Begin a Life of Conversion

I

THE PRAYER LIFE *of* FRANCIS OF ASSISI

II

PRAYING ALONGSIDE ST. FRANCIS
The Daily Office for Sunday Through Saturday
Morning and Evening Prayer—An Introduction
Seven Themes for Seven Days

Sunday
Monday
Tuesday
Wednesday
Thursday
Friday
Saturday

III

OCCASIONAL PRAYERS OF FRANCIS

The Lord's Prayer (Francis's expanded version)
Songs of Joy in the Morning and Evening
Prayer for Doing God's Will
Prayer for Detachment
Prayer to the Virgin Mary, *Theotokos* (Mother of God)
Prayer for Exuberant Faith
A Benediction of St. Francis
Prayer for a Rich Spiritual Life
"The Canticle of the Creatures" (Francis's Song of Joy)

IV
MORE PRAYERS

V
ABOUT PRAYER
IN THIRTEENTH-CENTURY EUROPE
The Use of Devotional Books in Francis's Day
Memorization and Prayer in the Middle Ages

THE PRAYER LIFE *of* FRANCIS OF ASSISI

First, a Story . . .

Francis and Leo Cannot Agree in Responsive Prayer

Francis was out walking one day with Brother Leo, his closest friend and companion, when it came time to pray the Divine Office. It was in the earliest days of Francis's new movement, when the brothers lived in the utmost simplicity; for this reason, and given their remote location, Francis and Leo had no books at hand when the hour for Morning Prayer had come.

Francis said to Leo, "Since we do not have a breviary with us, but it is still important that we spend time praising God, let us create something new.

"I will speak and you will answer, as I teach you. I will say 'O Brother Francis, you have done so many sins and evils in this world. You are deserving of hell.'

"And you, Leo, will respond, 'So it is, Francis, you deserve the lowest depths of hell.'"

Brother Leo nodded that he understood and gave Francis assurances of his perfect obedience. "Let us begin, Father," he agreed.

And so Francis began the new liturgy. He said, "You have done so many sins and evils in this world, Brother Francis, that you are deserving of hell."

"But God will work through you so much good," Leo replied earnestly, "that surely you will go to paradise."

"No, no, no," Francis said, "that is not right. When I say my part, you must say as I have instructed you, repeating, 'You are worthy only to be set among the cursed in the depths of hell.'" Again, in obedience, Brother Leo replied, "Willingly, Father."

This time Francis paused and painfully considered his words. After a few moments, with tears in his eyes and while pounding his heart Francis said in a much louder voice: "O Lord of heaven and earth, I have done so much evil and so many sins in this world that I am worthy only to be cursed by you!"

And Leo replied in turn, "O Brother Francis, God will do great things for you and you will be blessed above all others!"

Francis was perplexed and more than a little bit angry.

"Why do you disobey me, Brother Leo? You are to repeat as I have instructed you!"

"God knows, Father," Leo answered, "that each time I set my mind to do as you say, God then makes me say what pleases him."

How could Francis argue with this? He marveled at Leo's words, searching them for the divine purpose. Nevertheless, after some time, Francis quietly said, "I pray most lovingly that you will answer me this time as I have asked you to do." Leo agreed to try, but try as he might, again and again, he could not do as Francis wished.

Time after time, into the night, past Compline and throughout the early hours of the morning, the entreaties of Francis grew ever more passionate as Leo's joy grew ever larger. Their prayers never did match, and they never did agree, praying responsively as Francis had hoped.

Francis taught the first spiritual explorers drawn to understand and imitate his life— the way to a deeper relationship with God through prayer. He showed these men and women how to pray, he gave them words to get them started, and he insisted on the dailyness of the practice. Like the first followers of the little poor man from Assisi, Francis invites us to join him in the prayer and spirituality that punctuated his life at every turn.

Francis approached God from many directions; his prayer life demonstrates the varied ways that he intertwined himself with God, through Christ, in the power of the Holy Spirit. He maintained delicate balances, such as balancing joy and song with penitence and prostration. He prayed at times in community as a leader would conduct a band in a riotous tune, but he also used prayer as form of penitence, occasionally sentencing additional prayers to those whose minds seemed idle. His prayer life was intricate and of one piece with his broad spirituality. We might also try to strike these balances in our practices of prayer. But at the very least, we should try to pray each day, perhaps many times throughout the day, with the words and spirit of Francis.

Francis viewed prayer as a tool for overcoming pride and sinfulness. For him, it was a training of the soul and body to live in eternity and not in the world. With this in mind Francis became a champion of prayer while still a young man, and through his early experiences at prayer, he found guidance on the way to his conversion. The Spirit taught him to pray. This "inner work" never ended for Francis, as he continually saw the effects of original sin in his own life and used prayer to stamp them out.

He probably began praying in earnest in the early months of the year 1206, when he was twenty-four years old. He still lived in his father's house at this time, and it is unlikely he received much religious instruction there. Although his mother wished a deep love of God for her only son, Francis's father, Peter Bernardone, held little respect for the church. This was the time in Francis's life when he struggled finally to overcome his repulsion of lepers, and the filth and disease that they represented. In his final will and testament, written just before his death twenty years later, Francis connected his conversion to this time in his young adulthood.

Also at this critical stage in his life, Francis became sensitive for the first time to his need to spend time alone in quiet. A rowdy youth and king of many carnivals in Assisi, young Francis's turning away from carousing and revelry and turning toward solitude was another important stage of his receptivity to the Spirit. His prayer life could not have grown otherwise. He needed time alone to meet himself, and to meet God.

Now interested in religion, with basic capacities forming in him so that he could accept and understand its subtleties, Francis soon began to use prayer as an essential tool for discernment of the will of God in his life. When Bernard of Quintavalle, a wealthy man of Assisi, became the first to ask Francis what it might mean to follow him in his new spiritual work, the young saint insisted that they pray together at the bishop's house from early morning until Terce (9:00 AM). Only then would they be ready to open the Scriptures together and discover the will of God. Also early on in his religious life, Francis asked two of his most trusted friends—Brother Sylvester, the first priest to join the order, and Sister Clare, the first woman to join the movement—to pray for him, seeking God's will for his vocation. Francis could not discern for which purpose his life was intended. On the one hand, he felt drawn to a life of asceticism and contemplative prayer, like many religious before him, but on the other hand he felt called to a life among the people of Italy, preaching, ministering, and caring for them. Brother Sylvester and Sister Clare, after days of prayer on Francis's behalf, confirmed the latter as God's true desire, and Francis took this as if from God's very own lips. He believed in signs and in genuine intercession.

From the earliest days of his intentional spiritual life, Francis was committed to a daily prayer practice. Although he never viewed his new movement as a traditional monastic one (the early Franciscans were mendicant friars, quite distinct from cloistered monks), he nevertheless was a keeper of fixed-hour prayer, as it is often called in liturgical churches today. Cloistered monks, whose vocation is the contemplative life, sing or chant these prayers—mostly from the Psalms—in choir for hours on end each day. But because Francis never intended to stay put in one place for very long, daily prayer took on a different meaning in his movement. His prayers were peripatetic, and his spirituality was too.

Francis maintained a regular prayer life through the praying of the Divine Office. The word "office" used in this context is from a Latin word meaning "work." This ancient form of fixed-hour prayer, also known as the Liturgy of the Hours, or the work of God, was inherited by the early Christians from Judaism. The Hebrew psalmists and the lives of the prophets (e.g., Daniel) are full of references to fixed-hour prayer—in the morning, at noon, in the evening; one psalm even says, "Seven times a day do I praise you" (Ps. 119:164). The Divine Office is distinct from the saying of the Mass, and has always been faithfully kept not just by clergy, monks, and nuns, but also by laypeople. Francis claimed this type of prayer for his vocation, and taught his followers to practice it. Regardless of his many travels—for he was forever on the road—Francis prayed "the Hours," probably remaining the most faithful to the traditional times of morning and evening prayer.

He would pray with his brothers regardless of where he was. His first biographer, Thomas of Celano, who was also a contemporary of Francis, wrote, "When he was travelling the world on foot, he always would stop walking in order to say the Hours, and when he was on horseback he would dismount to be on the ground."[1] Many of us today find ourselves praying in the strangest of places (a stall in the restroom works well for private noontime prayers) to keep our everyday lives tuned to God's ear.

At this time, almost all prayer was spoken aloud, and at times this was difficult for Francis: "[Even when] he was suffering from diseases of the eyes, stomach, spleen, and liver, he did not want to lean against a wall or partition when he was chanting the Psalms. He always fulfilled his hours standing up straight and without a hood, without letting his eyes wander and without dropping syllables."[2] This reminds me of the elderly couple who physically struggle but determinedly make their way to the front of our church at daily Mass to receive Holy Communion.

In addition to those times when Francis would pray together with his brothers and sisters, Francis also prayed often in solitude. Contemplative prayer outside of the cloister was uncommon in Francis's day, but both Francis and many of his brothers spent hours each week alone with God. When Francis spent time alone, it was usually to find a more intimate, mystical communion with God. Perhaps, on these occasions, his reciting of the words of the prayer books and Scriptures turned into something more, as the words of the Psalms and the Gospels became resting places for Francis in the bosom of the Unknown. Francis experienced both spoken prayers and aphasic communications with God.

His favorite places to pray alone were woods, rocky caves, cliffs, and abandoned churches. Francis, with his restless spirit, easily understood the passion of the psalmists. Sometimes a trusted friend would accompany Francis on long walks to these distant places; other times, he would set out alone. When he was quiet and alone, he sometimes prayed aloud. He would often accuse himself before God, calling himself "Vain!" and "Coward!" Francis wondered aloud to God, asking many searching questions. Who was he to have "followers"? Why hadn't God found him worthy for martyrdom when he had traveled to Syria to see the Sultan? Was his whole life a mistake? Should he have married and had children? Why had he survived serious illness when others had not?

Francis came to know his own heart very well, and he accused it of every possible hint of selfishness.

Francis always returned to the most basic spiritual questions. Toward the end of his life, an eavesdropping Brother Leo overheard Francis asking plaintively, "Who are you, my dearest God? And what am I?"[3] Unlike some more famous mystics, his contemplation never steered far from his own sinfulness.

One reason for Francis's preference to pray in seclusion was his sensitivity to avoid the appearance of showing off. He wanted to heed the warning of Jesus about hypocrites: "they love to say their prayers standing up in the synagogues [and the churches!] and at the street corners for people to see them" (Matt. 6:5). Francis also took seriously the words of Christ when he instructed his disciples to go into their room and close the door to pray. Like many of the church fathers and mothers before him, Francis probably interpreted this verse both spiritually and literally. In the spiritual sense, our prayers are times when we are alone before God; our doors are shut against worldly concerns and distractions, and we spend intimate time with our Creator, our Redeemer, our Friend. In the literal sense, a closed door brings the quiet and solitude that are necessary for proper intention and attention in prayer. Francis also surely believed, as did his contemporaries, that demons want to assail us when we pray, and demons can only know our thoughts (and hence, our prayers) if we give them verbal expression. So, we should be quiet at times and passionately inward in our prayers.

He loved to pray in the middle of the night while his brothers were asleep. At these most impassioned times, the postures of prayer became important to Francis. *The Little Flowers of St. Francis*, a collection of legends and stories from Francis's life, tells often of the saint's penitent postures in contemplative prayer. He was expressive and his movements dramatic. At times, he would beat his chest while on his knees, pounding his breast again and again as if to awaken his restive heart, and at other times he would raise his hands, lifting them as to the heavens. On one such occasion, Francis was desperately seeking Christ through this sort of combination of spiritual, mental, and physical effort. "And at last he found him," the text reads, "in the secret depths of his heart. And he spoke to him reverently as to his Lord. Then he answered him as his judge. Next he entreated him as a father. Then he talked with him as with a friend."[4] What an extraordinary theology of prayer these lines represent!

Francis taught his brothers to care for their bodies with adequate food, sleep, and stretching so that "Brother Body" might never have reason to complain and say, "I can't pray for very long standing up, or I can't be cheerful when I ought to be." But then, Francis also taught his brothers, if your Brother Body will not do as it should, and it easily becomes sleepy or lazy in prayer, "You should then punish him like a beast of burden"![5]

One of the stories of Francis's nighttime prayers took place during one of his many preaching tours. He stopped on his way at a little house the brothers were using, and after joining them for the evening prayer of Compline, decided to retire early with the intent of waking in the middle of the night to pray in solitude while the other brothers slept. At this time, a young boy who had recently joined the order was staying at the house. He had heard the wonders of their master and founder and, with childlike curiosity, wanted to watch, listen, and understand more about St. Francis for himself.

Soon after Francis lay down to sleep on one of the mats on the floor, the young boy lay down closely beside him. The boy quietly and gently tied his tunic cord to the cord of Francis, so that when Francis arose in the middle of the night, as he was rumored to do, the boy would feel it. When Francis woke, he saw that he was attached to the boy. Before rising, he quietly loosed the cords, leaving the lad sound asleep. Francis then left the house silently and entered the nearby woods to pray. The boy, a short time later, awoke and saw Francis was gone. Seeing the door leading to the woods slightly ajar, he believed his master had gone there. When he drew near and spied Francis praying in a small clearing, he saw great visions of light surrounding Francis, and saints conversing with him as with a close friend. The young boy fainted, and the next he knew, Francis was carrying him in his arms, as a good shepherd does for his sheep, back to the house.

But Francis did not allow himself, or his brothers, to spend an excessive amount of time alone in contemplative prayer. He believed that there could be too much of a good thing, and that their lives were primarily intended for serving others. On one occasion, Francis confronted his friend and spiritual brother, Rufino, who had taken to contemplation so much that, over time, he had become almost mute in his love of God. He rarely spoke, and never went out to preach, as the other brothers did, for he spent all his time in quiet meditation, absorbed in the divine mysteries. One day, Francis asked Rufino to go into Assisi and preach to the people, listening for God's inspiration. Rufino answered, "Reverend Father, please pardon me and do not send me. I do not have the gift of preaching, but am only simple and ignorant." But Francis commanded Rufino to go, and because of his hesitance and disobedience insisted that he preach to the people in the utmost simplicity and humility—wearing only his breeches. Francis did not shy away from prescribing radical cures for spiritual ills. Rufino did as he was asked, but Francis soon joined him, also wearing only his breeches.

An idealist to be sure, Francis was never a perfectionist in prayer. He always allowed for human frailty before God, and we see his own doubts and weaknesses again and again, some of them remarkably simple, like our own. On one occasion, while Francis and his three closest brothers were spending the days of Lent high atop Mount Verna in Italy, Francis had trouble waking before dawn in time for morning prayers. A combination of weariness and idleness was keeping him from his spiritual work until a mother falcon sitting on her nest near his thatched roof cell began to wake him each morning. A few minutes before Matins (just before sunrise), she would make noise, waking Francis to pray. He was grateful for this outside assistance, and many legends grew up around the story of that simple bird.

Francis's praying had great joy and passion, whether he was alone or with others. But prayer, even for the great St. Francis, was not always wonderful. Not only did he, like us, find it difficult at times to get out of bed in the morning to spend time with his Creator, but Francis's prayers were not always regular and joyful. They were occasionally full of torment. Francis spent thousands of hours throughout his life in seclusion, much of it in a thunderous silence before God. Occasionally, at these times, Francis would use fasting as a part of his prayer practice, which added bodily weariness to an already intense spiritual experience. He was also sometimes lonely, feeling isolated in his vocation. Particularly in the last few years of his life, we can observe Francis's prayer life growing most intense, as he felt that his own order was separating more and more from his original ideals.

Another Story . . .

Francis and the Young Novice Who Wanted to Own a Prayer Book

One day St. Francis was sitting before a fire when a young novice drew near to speak with him again about acquiring a psalter. The novice, knowing how passionately the master felt about Brothers Minor now owning things, was nevertheless asking again for his permission to own his own prayer book.

"Then, when you have your psalter," Francis said to him, "you will want a breviary too. And when you own a breviary you will seat yourself in a pulpit like a great prelate and beckon to your companions, saying in a proud voice, 'Bring me my breviary!'"

Francis said this with great vivacity, like an actor in a play, motioning as a king would to his subjects. Then, taking up some cool ashes from the nearby fire, he smeared them on the forehead of the novice saying, "There is the breviary! There is the breviary!"

Several days later, Francis was walking up and down along the roadside not far from his cell when the same young brother came to speak to him about his psalter. He asked yet again for Francis's permission to own one.

"Very well," Francis replied reluctantly and wearily. "Go on, you have only to do what your minister tells you." (This all occurred soon after Francis had lost control of his order and Peter of Catana was the new minister-general of the Brothers Minor.) At these words, the novice hurried away, but Francis, reflecting on what he had said, called out to the friar, crying, "Wait for me!"

Francis ran quickly to catch up with the boy, saying, "Retrace your steps a little way, I beg you. Where was I when I told you to do whatever your minister told you as to the psalter?"

They retraced their steps, as Francis had requested, finding the spot along the road near Portiuncula where their brief exchange had just taken place. Falling on his knees there, Francis prostrated himself at the feet of the boy, crying, "Pardon, my brother, pardon, for what I said, for truly, he who would be a true Brother Minor ought to have nothing but his clothing!"

We see Francis's heart clearly in the story of his exchange with the young brother wanting to own a prayer book. He had an unwavering passion for Christ and knowledge from firsthand experience that it is all too easy for things to stand in the way of our full-time love of God. We, too, should examine ourselves for the obstructions that stand in our way. Most often, we have either put them there or allowed them to creep in. Even prayer books, Francis believed, such as the one you hold in your hands, can sometimes be an obstacle, rather than a ladder, to God.* We can sometimes take too much comfort in the written prayers of our books, and these can become more important to us than using these same words in our lives. Francis believed that the owning of prayer books—and even the saying of prayers themselves—are not the same as relationship and intimacy with God. They are tools for our use, but by themselves they cannot produce a passion for God.

As a passionate reformer, Francis insisted that religion not be only rote, but heartfelt and true. This little prayer book is your invitation to follow Francis on his way—a unique way, to be sure, and one that is as relevant now as it was centuries ago. Francis wanted those who followed in his footsteps be the closest of friends with God, true followers of Jesus Christ,

---

* It is also worth noting that books, before paper, were extravagantly expensive. Francis did not want his brothers to own their own books because of what books represented at that time. For example, more than two hundred years after the time of Francis, "it had been calculated that each copy of the Gutenberg Bible (641 leaves) printed on parchment required the skins of 300 sheep" (Hugh Kennedy, *Times Literary Supplement*, August 16, 2002). Francis's love for poverty and hate of pride were the two most important reasons for his strong opinion about the brothers not possessing their own books.

without need for anything else. Through Francis, we can learn prayer that is best made in community, but also the depths of prayer that is private and solitary. Both are necessary for a rich Christian life.

Prayer was to Francis as play is to a child—natural, easy, creative, and joyful. Before it became common to speak in personal terms of a relationship with God, Francis did so and made it seem natural. He was what we might call an intimate of the Divine. Like Moses on Mount Sinai and Jesus on Mount Tabor, he heard God's word to him with great clarity, and from an intimate distance. The Brothers Minor (which was Francis's preferred name for himself and his followers), whom he taught to pray, displayed a similar spirit. That is why Brother Giles, one of the first generation of Franciscans, was able to say with confidence, "He who does not know how to pray does not know God." The earliest followers of St. Francis knew from him that to know God is to pray; it was not supposed to be difficult.

Praying with Scripture

Many of Francis's prayers originated in the words of Scripture, because he found all the emotions he was feeling already expressed there so clearly. Francis memorized large portions of the Bible, and he appears to have instructed his followers to do the same. He was most familiar with the Psalms and the Gospels and quoted them from memory when dictating to one of his followers a letter or an addition to the Rule, the written instruction intended to guide the spiritual and everyday life of the friars. Such memorization was common in Francis's day.

In Francis's time, several books were used for the praying of the Divine Office. The Psalms usually were contained in their own volume, as were the Gospels. On a few occasions, Francis insisted that he and his brothers open the book of the Gospels together to discern the will of God. On one such occasion, Brother Leo opened the book three times at Francis's bidding, while the master was at prayer, and each time read passages related to the passion of Christ. Francis took this as confirmation that, as he had followed Christ in life, so he should follow Christ in some way related to his passion. It is from this experience, in part, that we have come to understand the meaning of the stigmata in Francis's life. In fact, most of his religious life was spent giving renewed meaning—and physical expression—to the words of Jesus.

The essence of the Divine Office is the words of Scripture. We all have our favorite passages of Scripture, those that seem to "speak" directly to our hearts, and Francis had many favorites. Among his favorite psalms, for instance, was this pointed one, which he attempted to put to use when he wanted Brother Leo to pray responsively with him, in the story told at the beginning of this book:

> You have rebuked the insolent; cursed are they who stray from your
> commandments! (Ps. 119:21)

Francis loved this psalm, too, and he often repeated it to his brothers to explain why they should work with their hands:

> You shall eat the fruit of your labor; happiness and prosperity shall
> be yours. (Ps. 128:2)

He often referred to a given psalm using a kind of shorthand that was common in his day, referring to it by its first line, as when he instructed the brothers to say the "Our Father" together with the "Out of the Depths" (Ps.130) for the deceased:

> Out of the depths have I called to you, O LORD;
> Lord, I hear my voice;
>   let your ears consider well the voice of my supplication. . . .
> I wait for the Lord; my soul waits for him;
>   in his word is my hope.
> My soul waits for the LORD,
>   more than watchmen for the morning,
>   more than watchmen for the morning. (Ps. 130:1, 4–5)

There was never a key moment in his life when Francis did not turn to pray. His brothers listened as he sang Psalm 142 on his deathbed:

> I cry to the LORD with my voice;
>   to the LORD I make loud supplication.
> Bring me out of prison, that I may give
>   thanks to your Name;

> when you have dealt bountifully with me,
>
> the righteous will gather around me. (Ps. 142:1, 7)

And, of course, Francis's most popular piece of writing—"The Canticle of the Creatures" (sometimes called "Canticle of Brother Sun")—was composed in the style of a Hebrew psalm. Francis prayed the Psalms in the spirit of St. Augustine, one of the four great Latin church fathers, who said, "If the psalm prays, you pray; if it sighs, you sigh; if it rejoices, rejoice; if it hopes, hope; if it fears, fear."

Next to the Psalms, the Gospels most influenced Francis's prayer life. The teachings of Jesus spoke to the heart of Francis's vocation, informing it at every turn. Francis emulated the life of Jesus in ways that we don't easily understand today. His entire adult life, in fact, was a steady conversion of his body, soul, and spirit to the ways and words of Jesus. The Gospels were the lifeblood of his prayers and spirituality.

He knew all four Gospels well, but loved Matthew's and Luke's the best, quoting from them more than twice as often as from Mark and John. He often quoted to his brothers the words of Jesus from the Gospel of Matthew, chapter 19. These were teachings of Christ for the first apostles; Francis and his brothers read them with the same sense of urgency, as they followed Christ's instructions to the letter:

> Jesus said, "If you wish to be perfect, go and sell your possessions and give the money to the poor, and you will have treasure in heaven; then come, follow me." (Matt. 19:21)

> "And everyone who has left houses, brothers, sisters, father, mother, children or land for the sake of my name will receive a hundred times as much, and also inherit eternal life." (Matt. 19:29)

Similarly, it was the words of Jesus to the first disciples that instructed the first generation of Franciscans how to grow in numbers, traveling from town to town sharing the Good News:

> "Take nothing for the journey. . . . Whatever house you enter, stay there; and when you leave let your departure be from there." . . . So they set out and went from village to village proclaiming the Good News and healing everywhere. (Matt. 9:3–6)

By following this advice, Francis's new movement spread more rapidly than anyone imagined possible.

At the same time, when too many of his countrymen were clamoring to leave everything and follow him, Francis was careful and insistent to teach that this more radical form of discipleship is not necessarily better than one where we remain as spouses, mothers, fathers, supporters of families, and members of local communities. The spirituality of St. Francis has always been available to everyone.

The following words of Jesus about servant leadership were critical to Francis's vocation. He often spoke of Matthew, chapter 20:

> Jesus called them to him and said, "You know that among the gentiles the rulers lord it over them, and great men make their authority felt. Among you this is not to happen. No; anyone who wants to become great among you must be your servant, and anyone who wants to be first among you must be your slave, just as the Son of man came not to be served but to serve, and to give him life as a ransom for many." (Matt. 20:25–28)

In addition to the Psalms and the Gospels, Francis also learned from other portions of Scripture. But not all portions of the Bible are equally represented in his written prayers and spiritual instructions. He quotes the Hebrew prophets rarely, for instance; the earliest version of his Rule contains no references to them. But in a letter that Francis composed at the end of his life to all members of the Franciscan order, its leaders, and future leaders, he adopted a prophetic voice to make himself heard clearly. At this time, Francis had lost control of his order and it was headed in directions that he felt were in opposition to its original ideals. And so, in the last few years of his life, in this open letter to all his brothers, Francis prayed like a prophet:

> If you turn to him with all your heart and with all your soul, to do what is true before him, then he will turn to you and will no longer hide his face from you. (Tob. 13:6)

If you will not listen, if you will not lay it to heart to give glory to my name, says the LORD of hosts, then I will send the curse on you and I will curse your blessings. (Mal. 2:2)

Accursed is the one who is slack in doing the work of the LORD. (Jer. 48:10)

Incline your ear, and come to me; listen, so that you may live. (Isa. 55:3)

If we listen carefully, we can hear the voices of the Hebrew prophets resounding today as Francis's voice resounded in Italy in the thirteenth century.

The epistles of St. Paul and St. John also spoke directly to Francis in his new life. For example, as Jesus did before him, Francis understood keenly that a spiritual life is ultimately found in our intentions, not only in our actions. Francis taught from this passage in the First Epistle of St. John:

We know that we have passed from death to life because we love one another. Whoever does not love abides in death. All who hate a brother or sister are murderers, and you know that murderers do not have eternal life abiding in them. We know love by this, that he laid down his life for us—and we ought to lay down our lives for one another. How does God's love abide in anyone who has the world's goods and sees a brother or sister in need and yet refuses help? (1 John 3:14–17)

The prayer life of St. Francis was fueled by regularity, and the Scriptures were a large part of what he prayed, as well as the teachings that informed how he should pray. We, too, deepen our spiritual lives and multiply our connections to our Creator when we make daily prayer a priority in our lives. Repeated words and phrases from the Scriptures, the tested rhythms of ancient liturgical hopes and confessions, and the even more mystical communion of other believers doing the same thing around the world at the same time—which is what praying the Divine Office, or fixed-hour prayer, is all about—all serve to school us in our devotion.

PRAYING ALONGSIDE ST. FRANCIS

The Daily Office for Sunday Through Saturday

Morning and Evening Prayer—An Introduction

The following weekly liturgy is derived from various sources and reflects the concerns of Francis of Assisi. Many of the words are the same that Francis prayed, and all of them are examples of the spirituality of the *Poverello*, or little poor man, from Assisi.

In his earliest Rule, Francis gave instructions to his brothers for the praying of the Divine Office. He used canticles or songs, collects, psalms, silent reflection, and the words of the Gospels themselves in his own prayer life. Similarly, in the week of daily morning and evening prayers that follow, Francis's words and ideas are our first guide.

The sequence for each day of this special morning and evening liturgy is as follows:

A. PREPARATION

B. GOSPEL SENTENCE

C. CONFESSION (as Francis instructed the brothers for each morning and evening)

D. *Silence* (intended to be not merely pauses, but minutes of contemplation)

E. SONG OR CANTICLE (inspiring words from the prophets)

F. PSALM

G. GOSPEL READING

H. *Silence*

I. PRAYERS OF THE SAINTS (and the early Franciscans)

J. COLLECT (as Francis may have prayed with his brothers)

There are many ways that you can use these days of morning and evening prayer in your own prayer life. First, they are ideal as the structure for a weeklong retreat focusing on the life and message of St. Francis. You can make such a retreat by yourself in your own home or in a group with others. Second, they are recommended as a substitute for your regular prayer practice whenever you find yourself stagnating or needing special inspiration. For some people, this sort of resurgence is needed one week a month, and for others, less frequently. Third, the prayers and readings, as they reflect the themes from Francis's own ministry, are a good devotional supplement to any academic or adult study of the saint.

Seven Themes for Seven Days

Seven themes emerge from the life of St. Francis, and each is the framework and subject for one of our days of prayer.

Day One: Following Christ—the essence of Christian spirituality, and the only purpose of Francis's own life. Francis tried to follow Christ's guidelines for discipleship exactly as the original Twelve had done.

Day Two: Disregard for Possessions—the first and most important rule for a true follower of Jesus, according to Francis. The first Franciscans held no personal possessions, and they also owned nothing in common. But it is not necessary to be a friar to keep the essence of this practice. As Francis's biographer Paul Sabatier explains, the way of St. Francis has, from its beginnings, been open to "whoever was free at heart from all material servitude."

Day Three: Peace and Care in Human Relationships—the sign of a person who has been transformed, or is becoming transformed, by the Spirit of God. As a young adult first going through the stages of conversion, Francis became sensitive in his relationships for the first time. He began to notice the outcast, give of himself to the unfortunate, deal honestly and forthrightly with the wealthy and the powerful, and use his influence to reap peace whenever and wherever he could.

Day Four: Love for All Creatures—the subject of so many legends of St. Francis. This virtue or quality is found in each of us more and more as we progress on our pilgrimage with Christ. We replace roughness toward God's creatures and Creation with a sensitivity to what is around us.

Day Five: Preaching the Good News—the primary purpose of Francis's vocation. Early in his religious life, Francis asked for intercessory prayer from Brother Sylvester and Sister Clare to ask God whether he should focus his life on contemplative work or active work. Sylvester and Clare confirmed that God's intention for Francis's vocation was to preach and teach. Francis's life was extraordinarily active and contemplative at the same time.

Day Six: Passion More Important Than Learning—a central belief of Francis. There will never be a shortage of intellectuals, but the world needs more people striving for spiritual growth and the salvation of others. Francis believed and lived that God is found more in a passionate heart than in a book.

Day Seven: Joyful Simplicity—the atmosphere of Francis's life. He surrounded his brothers, and those who he taught and cared for, with a spirit of joy for God's goodness. The essential goodness of all things, because all things are from God, is seen in simple ways, by lives lived simply. Even Francis's reaction to pain—as when he received pseudomedical treatment with fire to his face—was to find the goodness and beauty in Brother Fire, loving its goodness as he loved and revered all of God's Creation.

Morning Prayer, Sunday
(Theme/Intent: Following Christ)

PREPARATION

O Lord, open our lips and hear our prayer.
Light of the world,
shine through our lives this day.
Our mouths shall proclaim your glory.
Praise the Lord! Alleluia!

GOSPEL SENTENCE

Our Lord Jesus Christ says: You must love the Lord your God with all your heart, with all your soul, and with all your mind. This is the greatest and the first commandment. The second resembles it: You must love your neighbor as yourself. On these two commandments hang the whole Law, and the Prophets too.

—Matthew 22:37–40

CONFESSION

Have Mercy on Me, O God
(from Psalm 51)

Have mercy on me, O God, according to your loving-kindness;
    in your great compassion blot out my offenses.
Wash me through and through from my wickedness
    and cleanse me from my sin.
For I know my transgressions, and my sin is ever before me.
Create in me a clean heart, O God,
    and renew a right spirit within me.
Cast me not away from your presence
    and take not your holy Spirit from me.
Give me the joy of your saving help again
    and sustain me with your bountiful Spirit.
Deliver me from death, O God,
    and my tongue shall sing of your righteousness,
O God of my salvation.

Silence

SONG OR CANTICLE
(sung when possible; otherwise spoken aloud with feeling)

The Song of Hannah

REFRAIN

My heart exults in the LORD;

my strength is exalted in my God.

The pillars of the earth are the LORD's,

and on them he has set the world.

My heart exults in the LORD;

my strength is exalted in my God.

Those who were full have hired themselves out for bread,

but those who were hungry are fat with spoil.

The barren has borne seven, but she who has many children is forlorn.

The LORD makes poor and makes rich;

he brings low, he also exalts.

He raises up the poor from the dust;

he lifts the needy from the ash heap,

to make them sit with princes and inherit a seat of honor.

For the pillars of the earth are the LORD's,

and on them he has set the world.

My heart exults in the Lord;

my strength is exalted in my God.

The pillars of the earth are the Lord's,

and on them he has set the world.

—1 Samuel 2:1, 5, 7–8

PSALM
(chanted when possible; otherwise, spoken aloud)
My heart is firmly fixed, O God, my heart is fixed;

I will sing and make melody.

Wake up, my spirit; awake, lute and harp;

I myself will waken the dawn.

I will confess you among the peoples, O LORD;
   I will sing praises to you among the nations.
For your loving-kindness is greater than the heavens,
    and your faithfulness reaches to the clouds.
Exalt yourself above the heavens, O God,
    and your glory over all the earth.
—Psalm 108:1–5

GOSPEL READING

Hear the Word of the Lord: Jesus began to speak to them in parables once again, "The kingdom of Heaven may be compared to a king who gave a feast for his son's wedding. He sent his servants to call those who had been invited, but they would not come. Next he sent some more servants with the words, 'Tell those who have been invited: Look, my banquet is all prepared, my oxen and fattened cattle have been slaughtered, everything is ready. Come to the wedding.' But they were not interested. . . . Then he said to his servants, 'The wedding is ready; but as those who were invited proved to be unworthy, go to the main crossroads and invite everyone you can find to come to the wedding.' So these servants went out into the roads and collected together everyone they could find, bad and good alike; and the wedding hall was filled with guests. When the king came in to look at the guests he noticed one man who was not wearing a wedding garment, and said to him, 'How did you get in here, my friend, without a wedding garment?' And the man was silent. Then the king said to the attendants, 'Bind his hand and foot and throw him into the darkness outside, where there will be weeping and grinding of teeth.' For many are invited but not all are chosen."

—Matthew 22:1–5a, 8–14

Silence

PRAYERS OF THE SAINTS

Pierce, O most sweet Lord Jesus, my inmost soul with the most joyous and healthful wound of your love, and with true, calm, and most holy apostolic charity, that my soul may ever languish and melt with entire love and longing for you, may yearn for you and for your courts, may long to be dissolved and to be with you. Grant that my soul may hunger after you, the Bread of Angels, the refreshment of holy souls, our daily and super-substantial bread, having all sweetness and savor and every delightful taste.

—St. Bonaventure, minister general of the Brothers Minor

COLLECT

Blessed Holy Physician,

who heals the sick and removes the offending limb,

at home both in heaven and on earth,

save us, O Holy One,

we who are sick and ailing.

Our wounds are deep, our hearts heavy,

and your medicine heavenly.

Amen.

Evening Prayer, Sunday
(Theme/Intent: Following Christ)

PREPARATION

O Lamb of God,

   that takes away the sins of the world,

   have mercy upon us.

O Lamb of God,

   that takes away the sins of the world,

   grant us thy peace.

GOSPEL SENTENCE

Our Lord Jesus Christ says: If anyone wants to be a follower of mine, let him renounce himself and take up his cross and follow me. Anyone who wants to save his life will lose it; but anyone who loses his life for my sake will find it. What, then, will anyone gain by winning the whole world and forfeiting his life?

—Matthew 16:24–26

CONFESSION
The Our Father
Our Father in heaven, may your name be held holy,

your kingdom come, your will be done, on earth as in heaven.

Give us today our daily bread.

And forgive us our debts,

as we have forgiven those who are in debt to us.

And do not put us to the test, but save us from the Evil One.

—Matthew 6:9–13

Silence

SONG OR CANTICLE
(sung when possible; otherwise, spoken aloud with feeling)

Judith's Song of Praise

REFRAIN

For every sacrifice as a fragrant offering is a small thing.

But whoever fears the Lord is great forever.

I will sing to my God a new song.

O Lord, you are great and glorious, wonder in strength, invincible.

Let all your creatures serve you, for you spoke, and they were made.

You sent forth your spirit, and it formed them;

there is none that can resist your voice.

For the mountains shall be shaken to their foundations with the waters;

before your glance the rocks shall melt like wax.

But to those who fear you you show mercy.

For every sacrifice as a fragrant offering is a small thing,

and the fat of all whole burnt offerings to you is a very little thing;

but whoever fears the Lord is great forever.

For every sacrifice as a fragrant offering is a small thing.

But whoever fears the Lord is great forever.

—Judith 16:13–16

PSALM

(chanted when possible; otherwise, spoken aloud)

O my God, I cry in the daytime, but you do not answer;

    by night as well, but I find no rest.

Yet you are the Holy One,

    enthroned upon the praises of Israel.

Our forefathers put their trust in you;

    they trusted, and you delivered them.

They cried out to you and were delivered;

    they trusted in you and were not put to shame.

But as for me, I am a worm and no man,

    scorned by all and despised by the people.

All who see me laugh me to scorn;

    they curl their lips and wag their heads, saying,

"He trusted in the LORD; let him deliver him;

    let him rescue him, if he delights in him."

Yet you are he who took me out of the womb,

    and kept me safe upon my mother's breast.

I have been entrusted to you ever since I was born;

    you were my God when I was still in my mother's womb.

Be not far from me, for trouble is near,

    and there is none to help.

—Psalm 22:2–11

GOSPEL READING

Hear the Word of the Lord: The kingdom of Heaven is like treasure hidden in a field which someone has found; he hides it again, goes off in his joy, sells everything he owns and buys the field. Again, the kingdom of Heaven is like a merchant looking for fine pearls; when he finds one of great value he goes and sells everything he owns and buys it.

—Matthew 13:44–46

Silence

PRAYERS OF THE SAINTS

Christ, be with me, Christ within me, Christ behind me, Christ before me,
Christ beside me, Christ to win me, Christ to comfort and restore me,
Christ beneath me, Christ above me, Christ in quiet, Christ in danger,
Christ in hearts of all that love me, Christ in mouth of friend and stranger.
Amen.

—St. Patrick, apostle of Ireland

COLLECT

Glorious God our Father,
like old Simeon in the temple, our eyes have seen your salvation.
You have prepared it in the presence of all people, a light—
as we ourselves should be—a revelation to the Gentiles and
glory to your people Israel. Amen.[6]

Morning Prayer, Monday
(Theme/Intent: Disregard for Possessions)

PREPARATION

In the morning we call out to you, O Lord.
We offer our hands, our feet, our minds,
our hearts, and our souls to you this day.

GOSPEL SENTENCE

Our Lord Jesus Christ says: Do not store up treasures for yourselves on
earth, where moth and woodworm destroy them and thieves can break in
and steal. But store up treasures for yourselves in heaven. . . . For wherever
your treasure is, there will your heart be too.

—Matthew 6:19–21

CONFESSION

Have Mercy on Me, O God

(from Psalm 51)

Have mercy on me, O God, according to your loving-kindness;

    in your great compassion blot out my offenses.

Wash me through and through from my wickedness

    and cleanse me from my sin.

For I know my transgressions, and my sin is ever before me.

Create in me a clean heart, O God,

    and renew a right spirit within me.

Cast me not away from your presence

    and take not your holy Spirit from me.

Give me the joy of your saving help again

    and sustain me with your bountiful Spirit.

Deliver me from death, O God,

    and my tongue shall sing of your righteousness,

O God of my salvation.

Silence

SONG OR CANTICLE
(sung when possible; otherwise, spoken aloud with feeling)

Isaiah's Second Song

REFRAIN

    Why do you spend your money for that which is not bread,

        and your labor for that which does not satisfy?

Ho, everyone who thirsts, come to the waters;

    and you that have no money,

        come, buy and eat!

Come, buy wine and milk without money and without price.

Why do you spend your money for that which is not bread,

    and your labor for that which does not satisfy?

Listen carefully to me, and eat what is good,

    and delight yourselves in rich food.

Incline your ear, and come to me; listen, so that you may live.
Seek the LORD while he may be found,
　　call upon him while he is near.
　　　　Why do you spend your money for that which is not bread,
　　　　　　and your labor for that which does not satisfy?
—Isaiah 55:1–3, 6

PSALM
(chanted when possible; otherwise, spoken aloud)

Come, let us sing to the LORD;
　　let us shout for joy to the Rock of our salvation.
Let us come before his presence with thanksgiving
　　and raise a loud shout to him with psalms.
For the LORD is a great God, and a great King above all gods.
In his hand are the caverns of the earth,
　　and the heights of the hills are his also.
The sea is his, for he made it,
　　and his hands have molded the dry land.
Come, let us bow down, and bend the knee, and kneel
　　before the LORD our Maker.
For he is our God, and we are the people of his pasture and
　　the sheep of his hand.
Oh, that today you would hearken to his voice!
—Psalm 95:1–7

GOSPEL READING

Hear the Word of the Lord: Jesus said to them, "Watch, and be on your guard against avarice of any kind, for life does not consist in possessions, even when someone has more than he needs." Then he told them a parable, "There was once a rich man who, having had a good harvest from his land, thought to himself, 'What am I to do? I have not enough room to store my crops.' Then he said, 'This is what I will do: I will pull down my barns and build bigger ones, and store all my grain and my goods in them, and I will say to my soul: My soul, you have plenty of good things laid by for many years to come; take things easy, eat, drink, have a good time.' But God said to him, 'Fool! This very night the demand will be made for your soul; and this hoard of yours, whose will it be then?' So it is when someone stores up treasure for himself instead of becoming rich in the sight of God."

—Luke 12:15–21

Silence

PRAYERS OF THE SAINTS

O Lord, save your people, and bless your inheritance. Govern them and lift them up forever. Day by day we magnify you; we worship your name forever. Keep us this day from all sin. O Lord, have mercy on us. O Lord, show us mercy as we put our trust in you. O Lord, our hope is in you; our hope is not in vain.

—Nicetas, fifth-century bishop of Remesiana[7]

COLLECT

Most High, glorious God, enlighten the shadows of our hearts.
Grant us a right faith, a certain hope,
and perfect charity, sense, and understanding,
so that we may accomplish
your holy and true command. Amen.[8]

Evening Prayer, Monday
(Theme/Intent: Disregard for Possessions)

PREPARATION

In the evening, we call out to you, O Lord.
We offer our prayers, ourselves, to you this night.
May our words and our intentions rise up.
Incline your ear to hear us.

GOSPEL SENTENCE

Our Lord Jesus Christ says: If you wish to be perfect, go and sell your possessions and give the money to the poor, and you will have treasure in heaven; then come, follow me.—Matthew 19:21

CONFESSION

The Our Father

Our Father in heaven, may your name be held holy,

your kingdom come, your will be done, on earth as in heaven.

Give us today our daily bread.

And forgive us our debts,

as we have forgiven those who are in debt to us.

And do not put us to the test, but save us from the Evil One.

—Matthew 6:9–13

Silence

SONG OR CANTICLE
(sung when possible; otherwise, spoken aloud with feeling)

Isaiah's Song for Deliverance

REFRAIN

Sing praises to the LORD, for he has done gloriously;

let this be known in all the earth.

Surely God is my salvation; I will trust, and will not be afraid,

for the LORD GOD is my strength and my might;

he has become my salvation.

With joy you will draw water from the wells of salvation.

And you will say on that day:

Give thanks to the LORD, call on his name;

make known his deeds among the nations;

proclaim that his name is exalted.

Sing praises to the LORD, for he has done gloriously;

let this be known in all the earth.

Sing praises to the LORD, for he has done gloriously;

let this be known in all the earth.

—Isaiah 12:2–5

PSALM
(chanted when possible; otherwise, spoken aloud)

Be joyful in the LORD, all you lands;

> serve the LORD with gladness

> and come before his presence with a song.

Know this: The LORD himself is God;

> he himself has made us and we are his;

> we are his people and the sheep of his pasture.

Enter his gates with thanksgiving; go into his courts with praise;

> give thanks to him and call upon his Name.

For the LORD is good; his mercy is everlasting;

> and his faithfulness endures from age to age.

—Psalm 100

GOSPEL READING

Hear the Word of the Lord: Then Jesus said to his disciples, "In truth I tell you, it is hard for someone rich to enter the kingdom of Heaven. Yes, I tell you again, it is easier for a camel to pass through the eye of a needle than for someone rich to enter the kingdom of Heaven." When the disciples heard this they were astonished. "Who can be saved, then?" they said. Jesus gazed at them. "By human resources," he told them, "this is impossible; for God everything is possible."

—Matthew 19:23–26

Silence

PRAYERS OF THE SAINTS

Lord, you are not seen except by the pure of heart. I seek by reading and meditating what is true purity of heart and how it may be had, so that with its help I may know you, if only a little. Lord, for long have I meditated in my heart, seeking to see your face. It is the sight of you, Lord, that I have sought; and all the while in my meditation the fire of longing, the desire to know you more fully, has increased. . . . So give me, Lord, some pledge of what I hope to inherit, at least one drop of heavenly rain with which to refresh my thirst, for I am on fire with love. Amen.

—*Guigo the Carthusian*[9]

COLLECT

Blessed Lady Poverty,

hidden from the eyes of the world, a pearl priceless and beautiful.

Guide us, our Lady, we your simple ones, for the road is difficult

and the gate at the end is narrow. Amen.[10]

Morning Prayer, Tuesday
(Theme/Intent: Peace and Care in Human Relationships)

PREPARATION

Blessed Jesus,

heaven and earth praise you.

You are worthy of every praise and honor.

Children of God, praise the Lord.

We are all God's children.

Praise! Praise!

GOSPEL SENTENCE

Our Lord Jesus Christ says: I give you a new commandment: love one another; you must love one another just as I have loved you. It is by your love for one another, that everyone will recognize you as my disciples.

—John 13:34–35

CONFESSION

Have Mercy on Me, O God

(from Psalm 51)

Have mercy on me, O God, according to your loving-kindness;

    in your great compassion blot out my offenses.

Wash me through and through from my wickedness

    and cleanse me from my sin.

For I know my transgressions, and my sin is ever before me.

Create in me a clean heart, O God,

    and renew a right spirit within me.

Cast me not away from your presence

    and take not your holy Spirit from me.

Give me the joy of your saving help again

and sustain me with your bountiful Spirit.

Deliver me from death, O God,

and my tongue shall sing of your righteousness,

O God of my salvation.

Silence

SONG OR CANTICLE
(sung when possible; otherwise, spoken aloud with feeling)

Tobit's Hymn for Repentance

REFRAIN

Exalt God in the presence of every living being,

because he is our lord and he is our God.

Blessed be God who lives forever,

because his kingdom lasts throughout all ages.

For he afflicts, and he shows mercy; he leads down to Hades

in the lowest regions of the earth, and he brings up from

the great abyss, and there is nothing that can escape his hand.

Acknowledge him before the nations, O children of Israel;

for he has scattered you among them.

He has shown you his greatness even there.

Exalt him in the presence of every living being, because he

is our Lord and he is our God; he is our Father and he is God forever.

He will afflict you for your iniquities,

but he will again show mercy on all of you.

He will gather you from all the nations

among whom you have been scattered.

If you turn to him with all your heart and with all your soul,

to do what is true before him, then he will turn to you

and will no longer hide his face from you.

Exalt God in the presence of every living being,

because he is our lord and he is our God.

—Tobit 13:1–6a

PSALM
(chanted when possible; otherwise, spoken aloud)

As the deer longs for the water-brooks, so longs my soul for you, O God.
My soul is athirst for God, athirst for the living God;
> when shall I come to appear before the presence of God?

My tears have been my food day and night,
>> while all day long theysay to me,
> "Where now is your God?"

I pour out my soul when I think on these things:
> how I went with the multitude and led them into the house of God,

With the voice of praise and thanksgiving,
>> among those who keep holy-day.

Why are you so full of heaviness, O my soul?
> and why are you so disquieted within me?

Put your trust in God; for I will yet give thanks to him,
> who is the help of my countenance, and my God.

—Psalm 42:1–7

GOSPEL READING

Hear the Word of the Lord: Jesus knew that the Father had put everything into his hands, and that he had come from God and was returning to God, and he got up from table, removed his outer garments and, taking a towel, wrapped it round his waist; he then poured water into a basin and began to wash the disciples' feet and to wipe them with the towel he was wearing. . . . When he had washed their feet and put on his outer garments again he went back to the table. "Do you understand," he said, "what I have done to you? You call me Master and Lord, and rightly; so I am. If I, then, the Lord and Master, have washed your feet, you must wash each other's feet. I have given you an example so that you may copy what I have done to you."

—John 13:3–5, 12–15

Silence

PRAYERS OF THE SAINTS

Christian, learn from Christ how you ought to love Christ. Learn a love that is tender, wise, strong; love with tenderness, not passion, wisdom, not foolishness, and strength, lest you become weary and turn away from the love of the Lord. . . . Let your love be strong and constant, neither yielding to fear nor cowering at hard work. Let us love affectionately, discreetly, intensely. We know that the love of the heart, which is affectionate, is sweet indeed, but liable to be led astray if it lacks the love of the soul. Amen.

—St. Bernard of Clairvaux[11]

COLLECT

Abba, Father,

cleanse our hearts of sin this day, reminding us that

love is more powerful than knowledge or judgment.

Fill our weak vessels with the fruits of righteousness,

through Jesus Christ, for your glory and honor.

Amen.[12]

Evening Prayer, Tuesday
(*Theme/Intent: Peace and Care in Human Relationships*)

PREPARATION

O Christ, have mercy upon us. O Christ, save us from our sins.

Our mouths shall proclaim your praise.

Praise the Lord! Alleluia!

GOSPEL SENTENCE

Our Lord Jesus Christ says: So always treat others as you would like them to treat you; that is the Law and the Prophets.

—Matthew 7:12

CONFESSION
The Our Father
Our Father in heaven, may your name be held holy,

your kingdom come, your will be done, on earth as in heaven.

Give us today our daily bread.

And forgive us our debts,

as we have forgiven those who are in debt to us.

And do not put us to the test, but save us from the Evil One.

—Matthew 6:9–13

Silence

SONG OR CANTICLE
(sung when possible; otherwise, spoken aloud with feeling)

Tobit's Hymn of Blessing

REFRAIN

My soul blesses the Lord, the great King!

Happy are those who love you,

and happy are those who rejoice in your prosperity.

Happy also are all people who grieve with you

because of your afflictions;

for they will rejoice with you and witness all your glory forever.

My soul blesses the Lord, the great King!

For Jerusalem will be built as his house for all ages.

How happy I will be if a remnant of my descendants should survive

to see your glory and acknowledge the King of heaven.

My soul blesses the Lord, the great King!

—Tobit 13:14–16a

PSALM
(chanted when possible; otherwise, spoken aloud)

Hallelujah!

Praise the LORD, O my soul!

I will praise the LORD as long as I live;

I will sing praises to my God while I have my being.

Put not your trust in rulers, nor in any child of earth,

for there is no help in them.

When they breathe their last, they return to earth,

and in that day their thoughts perish.

Happy are they who have the God of Jacob for their help!

whose help is in the LORD their God;

Who made heaven and earth, the seas, and all that is in them;

who keeps his promise for ever;

Who gives justice to those who are oppressed,

and food to those who hunger.

The LORD sets the prisoners free;

the LORD opens the eyes of the blind;

the LORD lifts up those who are bowed down;

The LORD loves the righteous; the LORD cares for the stranger;

he sustains the orphan and widow,

but frustrates the way of the wicked.

The LORD shall reign for ever,

your God, O Zion, throughout all generations.

Hallelujah!

—Psalm 146

GOSPEL READING

Hear the Word of the Lord: Jesus called the disciples to him and said, "You know that among the gentiles the rulers lord it over them, and great men make their authority felt. Among you this is not to happen. No; anyone who wants to become great among you must be your servant, and anyone who wants to be first among you must be your slave, just as the Son of man came not to be served but to serve, and to give his life as a ransom for many."

—Matthew 20:25–28

Silence

PRAYERS OF THE SAINTS
Holy and blessed One,
help the spring of radiant love that fills our hearts to gush forth.
Jesus in our hearts, Jesus in our mouths,
Jesus in our ears, Jesus in our eyes,
Jesus in our hands,
as we make our way in the world. Amen.
—Brother Thomas of Celano[13]

COLLECT
Almighty and merciful God,
You know the desires of our hearts;
our greatest desire is to love you more completely.
We also yearn to know our neighbor,
to be your presence to both friends and strangers.
Show us your light and your wisdom,
through Jesus Christ our Lord.
Amen.

Morning Prayer, Wednesday
(Theme/Intent: Love for All Creatures)

PREPARATION
O Lord, our shepherd:
You revive our soul, you guide our path,
and save us from death each day.
We always want to be in your company.

GOSPEL SENTENCE
Our Lord Jesus Christ says: It is the spirit that gives life, the flesh has
nothing to offer. The words I have spoken to you are spirit and they are life.
—John 6:63

CONFESSION

Have Mercy on Me, O God

(from Psalm 51)

Have mercy on me, O God, according to your loving-kindness;
in your great compassion blot out my offenses.
Wash me through and through from my wickedness
and cleanse me from my sin.
For I know my transgressions, and my sin is ever before me.
Create in me a clean heart, O God,
and renew a right spirit within me.
Cast me not away from your presence
and take not your holy Spirit from me.
Give me the joy of your saving help again
and sustain me with your bountiful Spirit.
Deliver me from death, O God,
and my tongue shall sing of your righteousness,
O God of my salvation.

Silence

SONG OR CANTICLE

(sung when possible; otherwise, spoken aloud with feeling)

Sing a New Song

REFRAIN

Sing to the LORD a new song, his praise from the end of the earth!
Let the sea roar and all that fills it, the coastlands and their inhabitants.
Let the desert and its towns lift up their voice,
the villages that Kedar inhabits;
let the inhabitants of Sela sing for joy,
let them shout from the tops of the mountains.
Let them give glory to the LORD, and declare his praise in the coastlands.
But now thus says the LORD, he who created you, O Jacob,
he who formed you, O Israel:

Do not fear, for I have redeemed you;
    I have called you by name, you are mine.
When you pass through the waters, I will be with you;
    and through the rivers, they shall not overwhelm you;
        when you walk through fire you shall not be burned,
        and the flame shall not consume you.
For I am the Lord your God, the Holy One of Israel, your Savior.
        Sing to the Lord a new song, his praise from the end of the earth!
—Isaiah 42:10–12; 43:1–3a

PSALM
(chanted when possible; otherwise, spoken aloud)

How dear to me is your dwelling, O Lord of hosts!
My soul has a desire and longing for the courts of the Lord;
    my heart and my flesh rejoice in the living God.
The sparrow has found her a house and the swallow a nest where
    she may lay her young; by the side of your altars,
O Lord of hosts, my King and my God.
Happy are they who dwell in your house!
    they will always be praising you.
Happy are the people whose strength is in you!
    whose hearts are set on the pilgrims' way.
Those who go through the desolate valley will find it a place of springs,
    for the early rains have covered it with pools of water.
They will climb from height to height,
    and the God of gods will reveal himself in Zion.
Lord God of hosts, hear my prayer; hearken, O God of Jacob.
—Psalm 84:1–7

GOSPEL READING

Hear the Word of the Lord: Seeing the crowds, he went onto the mountain. And when he was seated his disciples came to him. Then he began to speak. This is what he taught them:

How blessed are the poor in spirit: the kingdom of Heaven is theirs.

Blessed are the gentle: they shall have the earth as inheritance.

Blessed are those who mourn: they shall be comforted.

Blessed are those who hunger and thirst for uprightness: they shall have
their fill.

Blessed are the merciful: they shall have mercy shown them.

Blessed are the pure in heart: they shall see God.

Blessed are the peacemakers: they shall be recognised as children
of God.

Blessed are those who are persecuted in the cause of uprightness:
the kingdom of Heaven is theirs.

—Matthew 5:1–10

Silence

PRAYERS OF THE SAINTS

The most wondrous thought of all is: In this dreadful deed of the Passion
committed against the Innocent One, he furnished an example of
patience; he taught the truth to those who slew him, and with cries and
tears did pray to the Father for them, and in return for this greatest of
sins (for which the whole world and human nature deserved to perish),
he bestowed on them the greatest benefits. By the pain and suffering they
inflicted on him he saved them from pain and suffering. He opened the
gates of Paradise to those who crucified him and to all others, reconciling
them to the Father, and such grace did he obtain for us that we are to
become the Sons of God. Amen.

—Blessed Angela of Foligno[14]

COLLECT

Most powerful,

holy, lofty,

supreme God:

You are good, most good, the supreme good!

You alone we give praise, glory,

Thanks, honor, and all good!

Amen.

Amen!

So be it.

So be it![15]

Evening Prayer, Wednesday
(Theme/Intent: Love for All Creatures)

PREPARATION

Almighty and everlasting God, at evening, and morning, and noonday, we humbly ask your majesty that you would drive from our hearts the darkness of sins and make us to come to the true Light, which is Christ, through Jesus Christ our Lord.[16]

GOSPEL SENTENCE

Our Lord Jesus Christ says: I am the living bread which has come down from heaven. Anyone who eats this bread will live for ever; and the bread that I shall give is my flesh, for the life of the world.

—John 6:51

CONFESSION

Trisagion, an ancient Lenten prayer
(said three times)

Holy God,

Holy and Mighty,

Holy Immortal One,

Have mercy upon us.

Silence

SONG OR CANTICLE
(sung when possible; otherwise, spoken aloud with feeling)

Song of the Three Young Men

REFRAIN

Bless the Lord, all the Lord's creation:

praise and glorify him for ever!

Let the earth bless the Lord: praise and glorify him for ever!

Bless the Lord, mountains and hills, praise and glorify him for ever!

Bless the Lord, springs of water, seas and rivers, whales and everything

that moves in the waters, praise and glorify him for ever!

Bless the Lord every kind of bird, praise and glorify him for ever!

Bless the Lord, all animals wild and tame,

praise and glorify him for ever!

Bless the Lord, all the human race: praise and glorify him for ever!

Bless the Lord, all the Lord's creation:

praise and glorify him for ever!

—Daniel 3:57, 74–82

PSALM

(chanted when possible; otherwise, spoken aloud)

O LORD, I call to you; come to me quickly;

hear my voice when I cry to you.

Let my prayer be set forth in your sight as incense,

the lifting up of my hands as the evening sacrifice.

Set a watch before my mouth, O LORD, and guard the door of my lips;

let not my heart incline to any evil thing.

My eyes are turned to you, LORD God; in you I take refuge;

do not strip me of my life.

—Psalm 141:1–3, 8

GOSPEL READING

Hear the word of the Lord: Jesus said, "You are salt for the earth. But if salt loses its taste, what can make it salty again? It is good for nothing, and can only be thrown out to be trampled under people's feet. You are light for the world. A city built on a hill-top cannot be hidden. No one lights a lamp to put it under a tub; they put it on the lamp-stand where it shines for everyone in the house. In the same way your light must shine in people's sight, so that, seeing your good works, they may give praise to your Father in heaven."

—Matthew 5:13–16

Silence

PRAYERS OF THE SAINTS

Sweet, incomparable love, you are Christ. You are love that joins friends who fight; love that anoints wounds and cures them; love that pardons those who offend you and crown with glory those who know how to humble themselves.

Sweet and delicate love, you are the uncreated Divine. You make the seraphim flame with your glory; you make cherubim, apostles, and martyrs happy; you draw prophets from the devil's net. We have such thirst for you, sweet love, and may it never be satisfied. Amen.

—Brother Jacopone of Todi[17]

COLLECT

O Holy One,

whose Son is our Good Shepherd,

watching for us when we stray,

keeping us close at hand, we pray:

Show us the way of gentleness,

love, and care for all of your creatures,

that we may see your Spirit, and heed its holy presence,

in all things created by your hand. Amen.

Morning Prayer, Thursday
(*Theme/Intent: Preaching the Good News*)

PREPARATION

Make us, O Lord, to flourish like pure lilies
in the courts of your house, and to show to the faithful
the fragrance of good works and the example of a godly life,
through your mercy.[18]

GOSPEL SENTENCE

Our Lord Jesus Christ says: Come to me, all you who labour and are over-
burdened, and I will give you rest. Shoulder my yoke and learn from me,
for I am gentle and humble in heart, and you will find rest for your souls.
—Matthew 11:28–29

CONFESSION

Have Mercy on Me, O God
(*from Psalm 51*)

Have mercy on me, O God, according to your loving-kindness;
  in your great compassion blot out my offenses.
Wash me through and through from my wickedness
  and cleanse me from my sin.
For I know my transgressions, and my sin is ever before me.
Create in me a clean heart, O God,
  and renew a right spirit within me.
Cast me not away from your presence
  and take not your holy Spirit from me.
Give me the joy of your saving help again
  and sustain me with your bountiful Spirit.
Deliver me from death, O God,
  and my tongue shall sing of your righteousness,
O God of my salvation.

Silence

SONG OR CANTICLE
(sung when possible; otherwise, spoken aloud with feeling)

God's Calling

REFRAIN

A new heart I will give you,

and a new spirit I will put within you.

I will take you from the nations, and gather you from all the countries,

and bring you into your own land.

I will sprinkle clean water upon you, and you shall be clean from all

your uncleannesses, and from all your idols I will cleanse you.

A new heart I will give you, and a new spirit I will put within you;

and I will remove from your body the heart of stone and

give you a heart of flesh.

I will put my spirit within you, and make you follow my statutes

and be careful to observe my ordinances.

Then you shall live in the land that I gave to your ancestors;

and you shall be my people, and I will be your God.

A new heart I will give you,

and a new spirit I will put within you.

—Ezekiel 36:24–28

PSALM

(chanted when possible; otherwise, spoken aloud)

The earth is the Lord's and all that is in it,

the world and all who dwell therein.

For it is he who founded it upon the seas

and made it firm upon the rivers of the deep.

"Who can ascend the hill of the Lord?

and who can stand in his holy place?"

"Those who have clean hands and a pure heart, who have not pledged

themselves to falsehood, nor sworn by what is a fraud.

They shall receive a blessing from the Lord

and a just reward from the God of their salvation."

Such is the generation of those who seek him,
   of those who seek your face, O God of Jacob.
—Psalm 24:1–6

GOSPEL READING

Hear the Word of the Lord: As they travelled along they met a man on the road who said to him, "I will follow you wherever you go." Jesus answered, "Foxes have holes and the birds of the air have nests, but the Son of man has nowhere to lay his head." Another to whom he said, "Follow me," replied, "Let me go and bury my father first." But he answered, "Leave the dead to bury their dead; your duty is to go and spread the news of the kingdom of God." Another said, "I will follow you, sir, but first let me go and say good-bye to my people at home." Jesus said to him, "Once the hand is laid on the plough, no one who looks back is fit for the kingdom of God."

   —Luke 9:57–62

Silence

PRAYERS OF THE SAINTS

In the mighty power of God, who is both God and human, and in every place—for his power extends everywhere—the faithful must be empowered by the four Evangelists, pondering God's precepts and filled with virtuous prudence, so that they may understand from where they've come and what they will become. For God is fire, and his angels, from time to time, announce to humankind his miracles and the wonders of his throne. They are burning spirits, who shine before his face and who are so on fire in their love for him that they desire nothing other than what he wishes. Amen.

   —St. Hildegard of Bingen[19]

COLLECT

The Agnus Dei

O Lamb of God,
> that takes away the sins of the world,
> have mercy upon us.

O Lamb of God,
> that takes away the sins of the world,
> have mercy upon us.

O Lamb of God,
> that takes away the sins of the world,
> grant us thy peace.

Evening Prayer, Thursday
(Theme/Intent: Preaching the Good News)

PREPARATION

Blessed Lord, anoint our lips;
seal them with your holy touch;
breathe fire into our quiet hearts,
that we may praise you,
and sing your praises to the world.

GOSPEL SENTENCE

Our Lord Jesus Christ says: Look, I am sending you out like sheep among
wolves; so be cunning as snakes and yet innocent as doves.
> —Matthew 10:16

CONFESSION

The Our Father

Our Father in heaven, may your name be held holy,
your kingdom come, your will be done, on earth as in heaven.
Give us today our daily bread.
And forgive us our debts,
as we have forgiven those who are in debt to us.
And do not put us to the test, but save us from the Evil One.
> —Matthew 6:9–13

Silence

SONG OR CANTICLE
(sung when possible; otherwise, spoken aloud with feeling)

The Spirit of God at Work

REFRAIN

The LORD has anointed me;

and sent me to bring good news to the oppressed.

The spirit of the LORD GOD is upon me,

because the LORD has anointed me;

he has sent me to bring good news to the oppressed,

to bind up the brokenhearted,

to proclaim liberty to the captives, and release to the prisoners;

to proclaim the year of the LORD's favor,

and the day of vengeance of our God;

to comfort all who mourn; to provide for those who mourn in Zion—

to give them a garland instead of ashes, the oil of gladness

instead of mourning, the mantle of praise instead of a faint spirit.

They will be called oaks of righteousness,

the planting of the LORD, to display his glory.

For as the earth brings forth its shoots, and as a garden causes what

is sown in it to spring up, so the LORD GOD will cause righteousness

and praise to spring up before all the nations.

The LORD has anointed me;

and sent me to bring good news to the oppressed.

—Isaiah 61:1–3, 11

PSALM

(chanted when possible; otherwise, spoken aloud)

LORD, remember David, and all the hardships he endured;

How he swore an oath to the LORD

  and vowed a vow to the Mighty One of Jacob:

"I will not come under the roof of my house,

    nor climb up into my bed;

I will not allow my eyes to sleep, nor let my eyelids slumber;

Until I find a place for the LORD,

    a dwelling for the Mighty One of Jacob."

Arise, O LORD, into your resting-place, you and the ark of your strength.

Let your priests be clothed with righteousness;

  let your faithful people sing with joy.

For your servant David's sake,

    do not turn away the face of your Anointed.

—Psalm 132:1–5, 8–10

GOSPEL READING

Hear the Word of the Lord: Jesus said to the twelve disciples: "What I say to you in the dark, tell in the daylight; what you hear in whispers, proclaim from the housetops. Do not be afraid of those who kill the body but cannot kill the soul; fear him rather who can destroy both body and soul in hell. Can you not buy two sparrows for a penny? And yet not one falls to the ground without your Father knowing. Why, every hair on your head has been counted. So there is not need to be afraid; you are worth more than many sparrows. So if anyone declares himself for me in the presence of human beings, I will declare myself for him in the presence of my Father in heaven."

—Matthew 10:27–32

Silence

PRAYERS OF THE SAINTS

O wondrous condescension of the divine mercy for us! How boundless the depths of God's love, which sacrificed a Son to ransom a slave! Yet God does not withhold the gifts of his compassion, but still protects with continual care the vineyard his right hand has planted. Even at the eleventh hour, God has sent workers to cultivate it, root out briars and thorns with hoe and plowshare. These men and women have cut back the overgrown branches and pulled up the brambles and shallow-rooted offshoots so that the vines might produce sweet fruit. Such fruit, when purified in the winepress of endurance, can be stored in the cellar of eternity. Amen.

—Pope Gregory IX, friend and advisor to St. Francis[20]

COLLECT

Grant your servants, O God, to be set on fire with your Spirit,
strengthened by your power, illuminated by your splendor,
filled with your grace, and to go forward by your aid.
Give us, O Lord, a right faith, perfect love, true humility.
Grant, O Lord, that there may be in us simple affection, brave
patience, persevering obedience, perpetual peace, a pure mind,
a right and clean heart, a good will, a holy conscience, spiritual
compunction, spiritual strength, a life unspotted and upright;
and after having finished our course, may we be happily enabled
to enter into your kingdom. Amen.

—Gallican Sacramentary

Morning Prayer, Friday
(Theme/Intent: Passion More Important Than Learning)

PREPARATION

Christ, have mercy upon us.
Christ, save us from our sins.
Your love has no bounds,
and neither shall ours, with your help.
You are the lamp for our path and
the light within us.

GOSPEL SENTENCE

Our Lord Jesus Christ says: I have come to bring fire to the earth, and how I wish it were blazing already!

—Luke 12:49

CONFESSION

Have Mercy on Me, O God

(from Psalm 51)

Have mercy on me, O God, according to your loving-kindness;
> in your great compassion blot out my offenses.

Wash me through and through from my wickedness
> and cleanse me from my sin.

For I know my transgressions, and my sin is ever before me.

Create in me a clean heart, O God,
> and renew a right spirit within me.

Cast me not away from your presence
> and take not your holy Spirit from me.

Give me the joy of your saving help again
> and sustain me with your bountiful Spirit.

Deliver me from death, O God,
> and my tongue shall sing of your righteousness,

O God of my salvation.

Silence

SONG OR CANTICLE
(sung when possible; otherwise, spoken aloud with feeling)

Isaiah's Song for Righteousness

REFRAIN

Come, let us walk in the light of the LORD!

In days to come the mountain of the LORD's house shall be established
> as the highest of the mountains, and shall be raised above the hills; all the nations shall stream to it.

Many peoples shall come and say, "Come, let us go up to the mountain
> of the LORD, to the house of the God of Jacob;
> that he may teach us his ways and that we may walk in his paths."

For out of Zion shall go forth instruction,
    and the word of the LORD from Jerusalem.
He shall judge between the nations, and shall arbitrate for many peoples;
they shall beat their swords into plowshares, and their spears into
    pruning hooks; nation shall not lift up sword against nation,
    neither shall they learn war any more.
O house of Jacob, come, let us walk in the light of the LORD!
    Come, let us walk in the light of the LORD!
—Isaiah 2:2–5

PSALM

(chanted when possible; otherwise, spoken aloud)

Blessed are you, O LORD; instruct me in your statutes.
With my lips will I recite all the judgments of your mouth.
I have taken greater delight in the way of your decrees than in all
    manner of riches.
I will meditate on your commandments, and give attention to your ways.
My delight is in your statutes; I will not forget your word.
Deal bountifully with your servant, that I may live and keep your word.
Open my eyes, that I may see the wonders of your law.
I am a stranger here on earth; do not hide your commandments from me.
—Psalm 119:12–19

GOSPEL READING

Hear the Word of the Lord: Jesus said: "What comparison, then, can I find
for the people of this generation? What are they like? They are like children
shouting to one another while they sit in the market place: 'We played the
pipes for you, and you wouldn't dance; we sang dirges, and you wouldn't
cry.' For John the Baptist has come, not eating bread, not drinking wine,
and you say, 'He is possessed.' The Son of man has come, eating and drinking, and you say, 'Look, a glutton and a drunkard, a friend of tax collectors
and sinners.' Yet wisdom is justified by all her children."
    —Luke 7:31–35

Silence

PRAYERS OF THE SAINTS

Give me, O Lord, pure lips, a clean and innocent heart, humility, courage, patience. Give me the Spirit of wisdom and understanding, the Spirit of counsel and strength, the Spirit of knowledge and godliness, and of the fear of God. Help me to always seek your face with all of my heart, all of my soul, and all of my mind. Grant me to have a contrite and humble heart in your presence. Most high, eternal, and ineffable Wisdom, drive away from me the darkness of blindness and ignorance. Most high and eternal Strength, deliver me. Most high and eternal Light, illuminate me. Most high and infinite Mercy, have mercy on me. Amen.

—Gallican Sacramentary

COLLECT

Good Shepherd and Guardian of our souls,

we adore you.

We adore you in Spirit and in truth.

Let us not lose heart,

except to make more room for you

in our hearts. Amen.[21]

Evening Prayer, Friday
(Theme/Intent: Passion More Important Than Learning)

PREPARATION

Blessed Holy One, Lover of my youth,

draw me after you, and I will come.

I long for your affection,

your embrace and your kiss.

You are Most Beautiful, my Beloved;

I will sing your praises.

GOSPEL SENTENCE

A reading from the Gospel according to Luke: And now a lawyer stood up and, to test Jesus, asked, "Master, what must I do to inherit eternal life?" He said to him, "What is written in the Law? What is your reading of it?" He replied, "You must love the Lord your God with all your heart, with all your soul, with all your strength, and with all your mind, and your neighbor as yourself." Jesus said to him, "You have answered right, do this and life is yours."

—Luke 10:25–28

CONFESSION
Trisagion, an ancient Lenten prayer
(said three times)
Holy God,
Holy and Mighty,
Holy Immortal One,
Have mercy upon us.

Silence

SONG OR CANTICLE
(sung when possible; otherwise, spoken aloud with feeling)

Jeremiah's Song of Hope

REFRAIN
You are in the midst of us; we set our hope on you.
You, O LORD, are in the midst of us,
    and we are called by your name; do not forsake us!
We acknowledge our wickedness, O LORD,
the iniquity of our ancestors, for we have sinned against you.
Do not spurn us, for your name's sake;
    do not dishonor your glorious throne;
    remember and do not break your covenant with us.
We set our hope on you.
    You are in the midst of us; we set our hope on you.
—Jeremiah 14:9b, 20–21, 22b

PSALM
(chanted when possible; otherwise, spoken aloud)

In you, O LORD, have I taken refuge; let me never be put to shame:
    deliver me in your righteousness.
Incline your ear to me; make haste to deliver me.
Be my strong rock, a castle to keep me safe, for you are my crag and
    my stronghold; for the sake of your Name, lead me and guide me.

Take me out of the net that they have secretly set for me, for you are
my tower of strength.

Into your hands I commend my spirit,

for you have redeemed me, O LORD, O God of truth.

—Psalm 31:1–5

GOSPEL READING

Hear the Word of the Lord: So I say to you: "Ask, and it will be given to
you; search, and you will find; knock, and the door will be opened to you.
For everyone who asks receives; everyone who searches finds; everyone
who knocks will have the door opened. What father among you, if his
son asked for a fish, would hand him a snake? Or if he asked for an egg,
hand him a scorpion? If you then, evil as you are, know how to give your
children what is good, how much more will the heavenly Father give the
Holy Spirit to those who ask him!"

—Luke 11:9–13

Silence

PRAYERS OF THE SAINTS

"Lord hear my prayer" (Ps. 60:2) that my soul may not collapse (Ps.
83:3) under your discipline (Ps. 54:2), and may not suffer exhaustion in
confessing to you your mercies, by which you have delivered me from all
my evil ways. Bring to me a sweetness surpassing all the seductive delights
which I pursued. Enable me to love you with all my strength that I may
clasp your hand with all my heart.

—St. Augustine of Hippo[22]

COLLECT

Guide us in your way, O Christ,

and mercifully show the fountain of wisdom to our thirsting minds;

that we may be free from sorrowful heaviness,

and may drink in the sweetness of life eternal. Amen.[23]

Morning Prayer, Saturday
(Theme/Intent: Joyful Simplicity)

PREPARATION

O Holy Christ, our shepherd, we bleat before you.

O Holy Ghost, our inspiration, we dance before you.

O Holy One,

even our foolishness brings you praise.

GOSPEL SENTENCE

Our Lord Jesus Christ says: Can any of you, however much you worry, add one single cubit to your span of life? And why worry about clothing? Think of the flowers growing in the fields; they never have to work or spin; yet I assure you that not even Solomon in all his royal robes was clothed like one of these.

—Matthew 6:27–29

CONFESSION

Have Mercy on Me, O God
(from Psalm 51)

Have mercy on me, O God, according to your loving-kindness;

in your great compassion blot out my offenses.

Wash me through and through from my wickedness

and cleanse me from my sin.

For I know my transgressions, and my sin is ever before me.

Create in me a clean heart, O God,

and renew a right spirit within me.

Cast me not away from your presence

and take not your holy Spirit from me.

Give me the joy of your saving help again

and sustain me with your bountiful Spirit.

Deliver me from death, O God,

and my tongue shall sing of your righteousness,

O God of my salvation.

Silence

SONG OR CANTICLE
(sung when possible; otherwise, spoken aloud with feeling)

A Song for the Messiah

REFRAIN

Those who lived in a land of deep darkness—

on them light has shined.

The people who walked in darkness have seen a great light;

those who lived in a land of deep darkness—on them light has shined.

You have multiplied the nation, you have increased its joy;

they rejoice before you as with joy at the harvest,

as people exult when dividing plunder.

For the yoke of their burden, and the bar across their shoulders,

the rod of their oppressor, you have broken as on the day of Midian.

For all the boots of the tramping warriors and all the garments rolled in

blood shall be burned as fuel for the fire.

For a child has been born for us, a son given to us;

authority rests upon his shoulders;

and he is named Wonderful Counselor,

Mighty God, Everlasting Father, Prince of Peace.

His authority shall grow continually, and there shall be endless peace

for the throne of David and his kingdom.

He will establish and uphold it

with justice and with righteousnessfrom this time onward and

forevermore.

The zeal of the LORD of hosts will do this.

Those who lived in a land of deep darkness—

on them light has shined.

—Isaiah 9:2–7

PSALM

(chanted when possible; otherwise, spoken aloud)

Give thanks to the Lᴏʀᴅ and call upon his Name;
    make known his deeds among the peoples.
Sing to him, sing praises to him, and speak of all his marvelous works.
Glory in his holy Name; let the hearts of those who seek the Lᴏʀᴅ rejoice.
Search for the Lᴏʀᴅ and his strength; continually seek his face.
—Psalm 105:1–4

GOSPEL READING

Hear the Word of the Lord: By now it was getting very late, and his disciples came up to him and said, "This is a lonely place and it is getting very late, so send them away, and they can go to the farms and villages round about, to buy themselves something to eat." He replied, "Give them something to eat yourselves." They answered, "Are we to go and spend two hundred denarii on bread for them to eat?" He asked, "How many loaves have you? Go and see." And when they had found out they said, "Five, and two fish." Then he ordered them to get all the people to sit down in groups on the green grass, and they sat down on the ground in squares of hundreds and fifties. Then he took the five loaves and the two fish, raised his eyes to heaven and said the blessing; then he broke the loaves and began handing them to his disciples to distribute among the people. He also shared out the two fish among them all. They all ate as much as they wanted. They collected twelve basketfuls of scraps of bread and pieces of fish.

—Mark 6:35–43

Silence

PRAYERS OF THE SAINTS

Let there be no doubt about your possession of the kingdom of heaven. Let there be no hesitation among you! For you already possess a promise of a future inheritance and have received the pledge of the Spirit. Signed with the seal of Christ's glory, you respond in everything, by his grace, like those of that first school which he established upon coming into the world. For what they did in his presence, you have thoroughly begun to do in his absence.

—attributed to Caesar of Speyer[24]

COLLECT

Heavenly Father, by your blessed Holy Spirit, lead us.

Ghost of God, show us the way.

Guide us to your orchards of luscious fruit: love, joy, peace, patience, gentleness, goodness, faith, meekness, temperance, and these will be our law. Amen.[25]

Evening Prayer, Saturday
(*Theme/Intent: Joyful Simplicity*)

PREPARATION

Let us praise the divine mysteries of our faith.

Our joy rests in God and all of God's glory.

Beneath what troubles our hearts, our lives,

we are simple, we are God's.

GOSPEL SENTENCE

Our Lord Jesus Christ says: It is not anyone who says to me, "Lord, Lord," who will enter the kingdom of Heaven, but the person who does the will of my Father in heaven.

—Matthew 7:21

CONFESSION

THE OUR FATHER

Our Father in heaven, may your name be held holy,

your kingdom come, your will be done, on earth as in heaven.

Give us today our daily bread.

And forgive us our debts,

as we have forgiven those who are in debt to us.

And do not put us to the test, but save us from the Evil One.

—Matthew 6:9–13

Silence

SONG OR CANTICLE
(sung when possible; otherwise, spoken aloud with feeling)

The Lord Will Shine on You

REFRAIN

Your light has come,

and the glory of the LORD has risen upon you.

Arise, shine; for your light has come,

and the glory of the LORD has risen upon you.

For darkness shall cover the earth, and thick darkness the peoples;

but the LORD will arise upon you.

Violence shall no more be heard in your land, devastation or destruction

within your borders;

you shall call your walls Salvation, and your gates Praise.

The sun shall no longer be your light by day, nor for brightness shall

the moon give light to you by night; but the LORD will be your

everlasting light, and your God will be your glory.

Your sun shall no more go down, or your moon withdraw itself;

For the LORD will be your everlasting light,

and your days of mourning shall be ended.

Your light has come,

and the glory of the Lord has risen upon you.

—Isaiah 60:1–2, 18–20

PSALM
(chanted when possible; otherwise, spoken aloud)

Behold now, bless the LORD, all you servants of the LORD,
    you that stand by night in the house of the LORD.
Lift up your hands in the holy place and bless the LORD;
    the LORD who made heaven and earth bless you out of Zion.
—Psalm 134

GOSPEL READING

Hear the Word of the Lord: In the course of their journey Jesus came to a village, and a woman named Martha welcomed him into her house. She had a sister called Mary, who sat down at the Lord's feet and listened to him speaking. Now Martha, who was distracted with all the serving, came to him and said, "Lord, do you not care that my sister is leaving me to do the serving all by myself? Please tell her to help me." But the Lord answered, "Martha, Martha," he said, "you worry and fret about so many things, and yet few are needed, indeed only one. It is Mary who has chosen the better part, and it is not to be taken from her."
—Luke 10:38–42

Silence

PRAYERS OF THE SAINTS

Do not be daunted immediately by fear and run away from the road that leads to salvation. It is bound to be narrow at the outset. But as we progress in this way of life and in faith, we shall run on the path of God's commandments, our hearts overflowing with the inexpressible delight of love. Amen.
—St. Benedict of Nursia, Prologue to the Rule[26]

COLLECT

O Lord God, Light of the faithful,
Strength of those who labor,
the Resting Place for those who have died:

Grant us a tranquil night free from worry,
and after quiet sleep may we, by your bounty,
at the return of light,
be given new activity by the Holy Spirit,
once again to give thanks to you.
Amen.[27]

OCCASIONAL PRAYERS OF FRANCIS

The Lord's Prayer
(FRANCIS'S EXPANDED VERSION)

The following expanded version of one of our most familiar prayers was written by St. Francis. *The Mirror of Perfection*, a compilation of stories about him, many of them written by his beloved friend Brother Leo, relates in the eighty-second chapter that Francis taught this long, beautiful version of the Lord's Prayer to his brothers.

OUR FATHER,
Most Holy, our Creator and Redeemer, our Savior and our Comforter.
WHO ART IN HEAVEN:
Together with the angels and the saints, giving them light so that they may
     have knowledge of you, because you, Lord, are Light; inflaming them
     so that they may love, because you, Lord, are Love; living continually
     in them and filling them so that they may be happy, because you, Lord,
     are the supreme good, the eternal good, and it is from you that all good
     comes, and without you there is no good.
HALLOWED BE THY NAME.
May our knowledge of you become ever clearer, so that we may realize the
     width and breadth of your blessings, the steadfastness of your prom-
     ises, the sublimity of your majesty, and the depth of your judgments.
THY KINGDOM COME,
So that you may reign in us by your grace and bring us to your kingdom,
     where we will see you clearly, love you perfectly, be blessed in your
     presence, and enjoy you forever.
THY WILL BE DONE IN EARTH AS IT IS IN HEAVEN:
So that we may love you with our whole heart by always thinking of you;
     directing our whole intention with our whole mind toward you and

seeking your glory in everything; spending all our powers and affections of soul and body with all our strength in the service of your love alone. May we also love our neighbors as ourselves, encouraging them to love you as best we can, rejoicing at the good fortune of others, just as if it were our own, and sympathizing with their misfortunes, giving offense to no one.

GIVE US THIS DAY OUR DAILY BREAD,

Your own beloved Son, our Lord Jesus Christ, so to remind us of the love he showed for us and to help us understand and appreciate it and everything that he did or said or suffered.

AND FORGIVE US OUR TRESPASSES,

In your infinite mercy, and by the power of the passion of your Son, our Lord Jesus Christ, together with the merits and the intercession of the Blessed Virgin Mary and all your saints.

AS WE FORGIVE THOSE WHO TRESPASS AGAINST US,

And if we do not forgive perfectly, Lord, make us do so, so that we may indeed love our enemies out of our love for you, and pray fervently to you for them, never returning evil for evil, anxious only to serve everybody in you.

AND LEAD US NOT INTO TEMPTATION.

Neither hidden or obvious, sudden or unforeseen.

BUT DELIVER US FROM EVIL—

Present, past, or to come. Amen.

Songs of Joy in the Morning and Evening

Francis refined "The Canticle of the Creatures" over the course of several years. He and his companions would sing it from time to time to cheer themselves up, to bless the creatures of the earth, or simply to praise God. Its themes show Francis to be carefully tuned to the world around him, in loving relationship to the many aspects of God. While this complete prayer is reproduced in its entirety below (see pp. 76–77), here are two songs derived from Francis's Canticle for morning and evening.

A Song in the Morning

Glory to God, source of all being;
to you belong praise, glory, honor,
and all blessing!
Blessed be our Lord and all of the creatures.
Bless Brother Sun,
who brings us the day, brings us the light.
Illumine our day, make bright our way!
Brother Sun never fails,
shining with great splendor.
Glory to God, source of all being. Amen.

A Song in the Evening

Glory to God, source of all things;
to you belong praise, glory, honor,
and all blessing!
Praised be God for Sister Death of the Body;
we cannot escape her.
Blessed are they who walk by God's holy will,
for the second death
has no power to do them harm.
Bless the Lord for creating Sister Death.
Glory to God, source of all things. Amen.

Prayer for Doing God's Will

The authors of *The Legend of the Three Companions*, another one of the early biographical documents written about St. Francis, first recorded this brief prayer spoken by the young saint as he kneeled in the old ruined church of San Damiano before the crucifix that would later become famous for "speaking" to him, telling him what to do. It is the earliest prayer of Francis that we have handed down to us.

Most High
and glorious God,
enlighten the darkness of my heart
and give me
truer faith,
more certain hope,
and perfect charity,
sense and knowledge
of you,
so that I may carry out
your holy and true command
for my life.

Prayer for Detachment

The Poverello beautifully combined in his spirituality a love for the Creation
and all its manifestations with a traditional mystic's love for detachment
from everything but God. In John of the Cross and John Cassian we see
only the latter; in Dante we see only the former; in Francis's life these two
seemingly incompatible facets of spiritual understanding seem as easy parts
of a whole. Where "The Canticle of the Creatures" is his song for God's
many-splendored Creation, the following prayer shows Francis turning his
face straight toward heaven, although with metaphors very much from
earth. (The early fourteenth-century leader of the "Spiritual" Franciscans,
Ubertino of Casale, attests to this prayer's authenticity, but some contemporary scholars disagree.)

O Lord Jesus Christ,
I pray you that the fiery and honey-sweet
power of your love may detach my soul
from everything under heaven,
so that I may die for love of your love,
who out of love for your people
did die on the tree of the cross. Amen.[28]

Prayer to the Virgin Mary, Theotokos
(Mother of God)

Francis's devotion to Mary was deeply felt throughout his adult life. The images used here—handmaid, mother, spouse—each correspond in Mary's ministry to one of the persons of the Trinity.

> Holy Virgin Mary,
> There is none like you among all women on earth.
> You are the daughter and handmaid of
> the Most High King and Father of Heaven.
> You are the mother of our most holy Lord Jesus Christ.
> You are the spouse of the Holy Spirit.
> Pray for us, with Saint Michael the Archangel and all
> the powers of heaven and all the saints,
> to your most holy and beloved Son,
> Our Lord and Master.
> Glory to the Father and to the Son,
> and to the Holy Spirit. Amen.

Prayer for Exuberant Faith

The penultimate chapter in the first version of Francis's Rule is a long prayer of 165 lines. The first half chronicles the basic tenets of the Apostles' Creed and asks for the perseverance of all Christians in faith. The second half is by far the more lovely and moving. It articulates the exuberant faith that Francis desired for himself and his brothers; it builds a beautiful momentum from beginning to end. This version is an adaptation from the original.

> I.
> With our whole heart, soul, mind, strength,
> and fortitude;
> with our whole understanding, powers, effort,
> affection, and feeling;
> with every desire and wish,

let us love the Lord our God
who gives each of us our body, our soul, our life;
who creates, redeems, and saves us by mercy alone;
who does all good for us, the miserable, wretched,
rotten, and ungrateful.

II.
Let us desire nothing else, want nothing else,
delight in nothing else,
except our Creator, Redeemer, and Savior
who alone is good; who alone is holy.
Let nothing hinder, separate, or come between us.
Wherever we are, in every place, hour,
and time of day,
let us continually, truly, and humbly hold in
our heart and love the Most High,
Trinity and Unity, Father, Son, and Holy Spirit.

III.
Creator of all, Savior of all,
we believe in, hope in, and love you.
Unchangeable, invisible,
unspeakable, unfathomable,
you alone are most gentle, most lovable,
most delightful, and totally desirable
above all others! Amen.

A Benediction of St. Francis

Taken from the same chapter of Francis's Rule as are the prayers immediately
above, we also have this beautiful benediction penned by the saint.

Now, wherever we are,
and in every place,
and at every hour,

throughout each time of each day,
may all of us honestly and humbly believe,
holding in our hearts
to love, honor, adore,
serve, praise, bless, glorify,
exalt, magnify, and give thanks
to the Most High and Eternal God,
Trinity and Unity. Amen.

Prayer for a Rich Spiritual Life

The following prayer, written by Francis late in life, is probably the best summary we have of his spiritual concerns. In praying this prayer, we can draw on the spirit of Francis of Assisi in our attempt to live a meaningful life before God.

In the manuscript tradition of his writings, "Almighty, eternal, just, and merciful God" is often appended to the letter that Francis wrote to the Franciscan brothers, its leaders, and future leaders, laying out his priorities for the order beyond his death. It is most likely for that reason—and simply because of the beauty and completeness of it—that these words encompass all of Francis's spiritual priorities.

Almighty, eternal, just, and merciful God,
grant to us miserable ones the grace to do for you
what we know you want us to do.
Give us always to desire what pleases you.
Inwardly cleansed, interiorly illumined
and enflamed with the fire of the Holy Spirit,
may we be able to follow in the footprints
of your beloved Son, our Lord Jesus Christ,
and attain to you, Most High, by your grace alone,
who in perfect Trinity and simple Unity
lives and reigns and is glorified as God almighty,
forever and ever. Amen.[29]

"The Canticle of the Creatures"
(FRANCIS'S SONG OF JOY)

"The Canticle of the Creatures" is Francis's most popular prayer with the exception of "Lord, Make Me an Instrument of Thy Peace," which was not actually composed by him. (See part 4, below.) The Canticle is a song to be sung; the brothers sang it for Francis at many crisis times in his life and the early life of the Franciscan movement. It sustained them and is remarkable for its affirmation of the elements of God's Creation.

Francis wrote this popular prayer song after a period of self-doubt, ill health, and despondency. In *The Road to Assisi: The Essential Biography of St. Francis*, Paul Sabatier explains what happened to the saint after he wrote "The Canticle of the Creatures":

> Joy had returned to Francis, joy as deep as ever. For a whole week he put aside his breviary and passed his days in repeating "The Canticle of the Sun."
>
> During a night of sleeplessness he heard a voice saying to him, "If you had faith as a grain of mustard seed, you would say to this mountain, 'Be removed from here,' and it would move away." Was not the mountain his sufferings, the temptation to murmur and despair? "Be it, Lord, according to your word," Francis replied with all his heart, and immediately he felt that he was delivered.
>
> Francis might have perceived that the mountain had not greatly changed its place, but for several days he turned his eyes away from it and had been able to forget its existence.
>
> For a moment he thought of summoning to his side Brother Pacifico, the king of verse, to retouch his canticle. His idea was to attach to him a certain number of friars who would go with him from village to village, preaching. After the sermon they would sing the hymn of the sun, and they were to close by saying to the gathered crowd, "We are God's jugglers. We desire to be paid for our sermon and our song. Our payment will be that you persevere in penitence."
>
> "Is it not in fact true," Francis would add, "that the servants of God are really like jugglers, intended to revive the hearts of men and lead them into spiritual joy?"

The Francis of the old raptures was back—the layman, the poet, the artist.[30]

"The Canticle of the Creatures" represented many great things in Francis's life: Francis saw it as a gift from God, a recovery from his deeply felt self-doubts, and a revelation of what role he and his brothers were to play in the lives of the people they encountered. The joy of this simple song is unmatched. The earthiness—and the sanctifying of the earthy everydayness of life that comes by repeating it—was essential for him. Its influence in the early days of the Franciscan movement was great, as was its influence in the earliest moments of vernacular literature in Italy. This was Francis of Assisi's favorite of his prayers.

O most high, almighty, good Lord God,
to you belong praise, glory, honor, and all blessing!
Praised be my Lord God with all your creatures,
and especially our Brother Sun,
who brings us the day and who brings us the light.
Fair is he and shines with a very great splendor:
O Lord, he signifies you to us!
Praised be you, Most High, for Sister Moon and the Stars,
You set them in the heavens, making them so
bright, luminous, and fine.
Praised be my Lord for our Brother Wind,
and for air and cloud, calms and all weather
through which you uphold life in all creatures.
Praised be my Lord for our Sister Water,
who is very useful to us and humble
and precious and clean.
Praised be my Lord for our Brother Fire,
through whom you give us light in the darkness;
and he is bright and pleasant and very mighty
and strong.
Praised be my Lord for our Mother Earth,

who does sustain us and keep us,
and brings forth many fruits and flowers
of many colors, and grass.
Praised be my Lord for all those who pardon one
another for your sake,
and who endure weakness and tribulation;
blessed are they who peaceably endure, for you,
O most High, shall give them a crown.
Praised be my Lord for our Sister Death of the Body,
from whom no one can escape.
Woe to those who die in mortal sin.
Blessed are they who are found walking by your
most holy will, for the second death shall have no
power to do them harm.
Praise and bless the Lord, and give thanks to him
and serve him with great humility.

MORE PRAYERS

Saint Francis very often prayed by heart, which means that the words of prayers like those that follow reverberated inside of him. He memorized them, or he simply remembered them as a result of repetition, so that their words could be easily on his lips, and so that in mystical ways, they would pray themselves for him, inside of him, like our heart, which also beats involuntarily.

We can do the same. Here are some basic prayers for learning by heart. Each has its origins in the early centuries of the Christian church and is today found in various forms throughout the world.

Collect for Purity
Almighty God, to you all hearts are open,
all desires known,
and from you no secrets are hid:
Cleanse the thoughts of our hearts
by the inspiration of your Holy Spirit,
that we may perfectly love you,
and worthily magnify your holy Name;
through Jesus Christ our Lord. Amen.[31]

The Doxology
Glory be to the Father, and to the Son,
and to the Holy Spirit.
As it was in the beginning,
is now, and ever shall be,
world without end. Amen.

A Prayer to Our Lady

O Mother of God,
we take refuge in your loving care.
Let not our plea to you pass unheeded
in the trials that confront us, but deliver us from danger.
For you alone are truly pure; you alone are truly blessed.

The Jesus Prayer

Lord Jesus Christ, Son of God,
have mercy on me, a sinner.

IMPORTANT SAINTS' DAYS

St. Francis and St. Clare

Throughout the year, the church calendar includes various kinds of feast days. Some feast days are for the purpose of remembering the lives of saints; they are a time to celebrate the life of a saint on the day that marks his or her death.

August 11

Traditional Prayer for the Feast Day of St. Clare

O God, whose blessed Son became poor that we through his poverty might be rich: Deliver us, we pray, from an inordinate love of this world, that, inspired by the devotion of your servant Clare, we may serve you with singleness of heart, and attain to the riches of the age to come; through Jesus Christ our Lord, who lives and reigns with you, in the unity of the Holy Spirit, one God, now and ever. Amen.

(See Part Two for many more prayers by and about St. Clare.)

October 4

Traditional Prayer for Animals for the Feast Day of St. Francis

God our heavenly Father, you created the world to serve humanity's needs and to lead them to you. By our own fault we have lost the beautiful relationship we once had with all your Creation. Help us to see that by restoring our relationship with you we will also restore it with all your Creation. Give us the grace to see all animals as gifts from you and to treat them with respect for they are your creation. We pray for all animals who are suffering as a result of our neglect. May the order you originally established be once again restored to the whole world through the intercession of the Glorious Virgin Mary, the prayers of St. Francis and the merits of your Son, Our Lord Jesus Christ, who lives and reigns with you, now and forever. Amen.

❈ ❈ ❈

ABOUT PRAYER
IN THIRTEENTH-CENTURY EUROPE

The Use of Devotional Books in Francis's Day

The small devotional book of today had its beginnings in Europe in the centuries before St. Francis. As early as the eighth and ninth centuries, many examples were common, including Psalters (collections of the 150 Psalms from the Bible) with additional prayers; illuminated, or illustrated, editions of the Gospels with additional creeds and litanies of saints; breviaries for reciting the Divine Office; and emerging in Francis's century was the primer, or Book of Hours, which focused primarily on the spirituality of the Blessed Virgin. All these devotional tools reflected the efforts of laypeople desiring to pray each day in ways similar to monks and nuns.

Francis wanted the spirituality of the cloister to be available to people everywhere. In fact, at the end of most of his writings, he encouraged his friars and others to make copies, adding, "Let those who keep this writing with them, and those who make copies of it to distribute and share with others, know that they will be greatly blessed by God." He wanted to publish the good news that he was preaching and teaching.

We know that Francis used books from time to time, but they must have been very spare indeed. It is impossible to imagine books with ornamentation—gold gilded edges, elegant illuminations—allowed by the Poverello in the chapel of Portiuncula, in the convent of San Damiano, with the brothers on the cliffs of La Verna, in the simple abodes of Rivo-Torto, or in the Carceri, those damp caves that he loved so much. This was a man who believed that the simple handling of coins was a sin for a friar married to Poverty. The personal owning of books represented to Francis both extravagance and arrogance.

These early devotional books were actually handbound manuscripts, often illuminated with beautiful colors and designs. Such books were usually owned or commissioned by wealthy patrons. For example, copies of the Gospels were fairly common in the Middle Ages and highly valued by those lucky enough to possess one. Cuthbert, the seventh-century bishop of Lindisfarne, was buried with his Gospel of John; the mystical—and valuable—text was found enclosed in his coffin.[32]

But we also know that Francis used prayer books. Books were sometimes available in the community of friars for spiritual purposes. If Francis ever used a prayer book for private devotions, it was probably small and well-worn. It was surely borrowed or given to his young order secondhand, a copy previously owned by a wealthy monastery, discarded for the very plainness that attracted the newly converted son of Bernardone. It may have had beechwood boards, making it lighter and more portable than the oak wood boards commonly used for bound manuscripts in England in Francis's day.

The pages of devotional books were made of parchment—sheepskin, to be exact—because paper was not introduced widely in Italy until after the time of St. Francis. The boards—the rough equivalent of what we refer to as "hardcovers" today—were covered with animal skin, usually goat, calf, or sheep. We can imagine that the use of animal products added to Francis's displeasure with owning books. As he turned the pages, searching for the words of David to express his latest anguish or triumph, he would have felt the roughness of one side of each page, where the hair of the animal had originally been, and the comparative smoothness on the other where the flesh had been.

Finally, Thomas of Celano, friend and first biographer of St. Francis, wrote, "[Francis] always fulfilled his hours standing up straight and without a hood, without letting his eyes wander and without dropping syllables," revealing an important difference in public and private prayer from Francis's time to our own: silent reading was uncommon until about the time of Francis. When Thomas writes that his master did not drop syllables, he knows this because, in Francis's day, even "private" prayer was public in the sense that it was spoken aloud. Imagine what it was like for Brother Leo and the other early Franciscans to listen in!

Memorization and Prayer in the Middle Ages

Children, knowledge is a treasury and your heart is its strongbox.
—Hugh of St. Victor, in his treatise on the art of memory titled
De Tribus Maximis Circumstantiis Gestorum

> He sometimes read the Sacred Books, and whatever he once put
> into his mind, he wrote indelibly in his heart. His memory took
> the place of books, because, if he heard something once, it was not
> wasted, as his heart would mull it over with constant devotion.
> He said this was the fruitful way to read and learn, rather than to
> wander through a thousand treatises.
> —*Thomas of Celano*, in his second biography of St. Francis[33]

The primary function of learning in medieval Europe, before the growth of the first universities in the twelfth and thirteenth centuries, was to teach moral lessons. For this reason, people read, or learned to read, primarily to memorize. At a time when philosophy was rediscovered and seen as useful only in its service to theology and to the church, reading was seen as useful only in its helpfulness to memorization and morality.

Memorization—the last remnant of which can still be found in some of our Sunday schools—was commonplace in ways that are hard to understand today. The Middle Ages inherited various intricate techniques for memorizing words on a page, dating from the days of Cicero in ancient Rome. These teachings were passed from teacher to student, and they appeared in various written treatises on the subject by Cicero, Aristotle, Albertus Magnus—the early Dominican and teacher of Thomas Aquinas—and many others.

Large portions of the written word were committed to memory by creating pictures in the mind, background scenes on which the words— or images used to represent categories of words—were projected. These mental pictures were then rehearsed over and over until they could be remembered flawlessly. The most common image used to describe a good memory was a wax tablet or seal, a good image for the sort of indelible impression that was intended.

Writing, too, was a tool for memorization. Practicing letters, words, and sentences on a tablet was seen as perhaps the best of all possible methods for training the memory. As the psalmist who urges us, "Remember the word of the Lord," the child learning to write did so as moral practice, inscribing on the heart.

Finally, memory was intended to come to the service of good rhetoric (speechmaking) and persuasion. Some of Francis's contemporaries even saw divine origins to persuasive speech, for otherwise, how would Lucifer have convinced the other angels in heaven to follow him?[34] Francis probably understood this connection, and his persuasiveness as a speaker was legendary. Just as he turned secular music to sacred ends, Francis also used the techniques of Cicero to preach the Good News.

❋ TWO ❋
St. Clare

Listen for God's Leading

I

THE PRAYER LIFE OF ST. CLARE OF ASSISI

II

PRAYING ALONGSIDE ST. CLARE

The Daily Office for Sunday Through Saturday
Morning and Evening Prayer—An Introduction
Seven Themes for Seven Days

Sunday

Monday

Tuesday

Wednesday

Thursday

Friday

Saturday

III

OCCASIONAL PRAYERS OF ST. CLARE

On the Loveliness of Christ

On Faithfulness to Ideals

Three More Collects for Faithfulness

The Office of the Five Wounds of Christ

For an Increase in Franciscan Spiritual Values

Clare's Blessings

From Clare's Final Words

IV
OTHER PRAYERS

V
SOURCES FOR LITERARY AND HISTORICAL CONTEXT
A Very Brief Life of St. Agnes of Rome
Sister Clare: A "Little Play," by Laurence Housman

THE PRAYER LIFE OF ST. CLARE OF ASSISI

B y all accounts, she was an attractive and lively girl, smart and strong-willed. Her conversion to religious life culminated one night as she snuck away from her parents' home on the eastern edge of Assisi and joined St. Francis and the friars at Portiuncula, a tiny chapel, down in the valley below town. She was eighteen years old and had spent several years questioning her family's ideas of who she should marry and who she would become. She chose to run away—and run toward—the enigmatic Francis, who had upset the town several years before with his similar conversion.†

But just as St. Clare began her religious life dramatically, the next four-plus decades saw her spend most of her time in prayer. She was like a mother to her sisters, counseling them why and how to pray, and helping them with their questions about the spiritual life. She possessed a quiet power that was respected by all who came to know her. She communicated often with popes, cardinals, and women and men around Europe about what it means to be Christian. Clare of Assisi was the most important woman of her day, even though she spent most of her life behind bars.

The bars were known as a grille, which separated Clare and her sisters both symbolically and physically from all visitors who would come to their little convent just outside Assisi. Even the priest who would hear their confessions and administer the sacraments was separated by the grille from the Poor Clares.

It is behind that grille that Clare found her true freedom in Christ—a freedom to explore a relationship with God that was unencumbered by societal expectations. She used prayer books, and she memorized many of her prayers, and the book you hold in your hands now would probably embarrass her, but she would also understand exactly how to use it.

---

† See "*Sister Clare:* A 'Little Play,'" on pages 181–86, for a dramatic rendering of that first night.

We pick up prayer books when we realize that we need something to stimulate our devotion to God. For many of us, prayer is our lifeboat, but we still find ourselves treading water from time to time. The unique vision and spiritual depth of St. Clare's prayers and prayer life will hopefully open for you new opportunities and paths for knowing God.

Clare's prayers are very rarely collected in books. She is often over-shadowed by her more famous friend and mentor, St. Francis. Evelyn Underhill once referred to Clare as "the hidden spring" of Franciscan spirituality, which is an apt description because Clare's wisdom was a spring for Francis and the first generation of Franciscans, and it is only in recent years that we have come to really discover it.[1]

She is a different sort of saint from the ones we may be accustomed to spending time with. Her life and spirituality bring something different to a life of faith that is both relevant today, and unique among her more famous contemporaries.

By outward appearances, her life was drab compared to the colorful lives of women such as Catherine of Siena and Hildegard of Bingen. Catherine scolded popes and emperors, and Hildegard composed mystical music and theological texts. Both women had a wide range of interests and influence in the world of politics and power, in contrast to Clare, whose life was mostly hidden except to her spiritual brothers and sisters.

St. Clare's stature has also been hampered by the pious descriptions that grew up around her legends. This began with the biography that Thomas of Celano wrote just after her death as part of the process of canonizing her. Every writer since the 1250s has had to make decisions about what is history in Thomas's accounts and what is simply good storytelling in the life of a saint. Many misinterpretations have persisted through the centuries, and sometimes writers have made her sound so pure as to become more angelic than human.

For example, Father Cuthbert wrote these saccharine sentences in his study of St. Clare about ninety years ago: "One must be grossly lacking in spiritual perception not to recognize in the story of her life . . . the pure spirituality which was the atmosphere in which her mind and heart had their being. In her it is evident no ordinary earthliness found place, but all was consecrated by a purity staid with the constant vision and love of the heavenly life."[2] He would like us to believe that Clare never faced temptation, never doubted her vocation, and that human emotions such as anger, frustration, boredom, and sadness failed to affect her prayer life. The opposite was true, which is why Clare speaks so profoundly to us today.

Twenty-seven years separated Francis's and Clare's deaths. In other words, she had better than a quarter century to live out the ideals of Francis in her own ways. The two great saints of Assisi shared much in common: they each began their religious lives with dramatic gestures of separation from worldly values and self-conscious identification with the person of Christ—but Clare's subsequent spirituality became strong, wise, and quiet in ways that differentiate her from her mentor. Where Francis usually sought to jolt people into understanding truth directly and experientially, Clare grew slowly and deeply into wisdom. As a result, it takes more time and patience to learn from Clare than it does from Francis.

She and her first sisters in religious life were bound by the traditional vow of stability, and in contrast to Francis and the first friars, stability meant a cloistered life. The life of Clare was completely centered on a small community of women in the former Assisan church of San Damiano. For forty-one years, Clare lived almost every moment of life within the walls of that church-turned–leper hospital–turned-monastery. The prospect of such a circumspect existence has caused one writer to recently refer to San Damiano as "Clare's *Prison*."[3] But it wasn't so.

Despite society's ideas about the roles of women, who were seen as the "second sex," inferior to men, Clare formed a way of Christian living that was deepened through separation from men, and most of society around her. Spiritual formation went on behind that grille, and it was women transformed who then went out into the world to help the sick, give to the poor, pray for the needs of others, and found new houses for more women to do the same.

Francis himself desired that Clare spend most of her days within the monastery; he believed that her calling was different from his own. In that era, men and women outside of religious orders did not mingle unless they were married or blood relations. Men did not visit with women unless a chaperone was present; men did not even look upon women unless their intentions were clearly stated; and the men and women of the Franciscan movement could not work side by side.

However, in that era when women outside marriage and cloister were usually regarded merely as temptations to men, Clare became a not-so-hidden spring to the men around her: Francis, and the other friars who came to rely on her after Francis's death, as well as cardinals and even popes. As one contemporary Poor Clare sister has described it, "[Clare's] conscience was formed by a theology which viewed women as embodiments of evil inclined to lust and sensuality." She overcame society's expectations for her and became one of the most important religious leaders of her day.

Clare and Francis Side by Side

Francis of Assisi was peripatetic in his spirituality and in his prayer life. He was God's juggler, an innovator, passionate, creative personality, and these qualities come through in the few descriptions and depictions left to us. He was small, strong, and always on the move. G. K. Chesterton explains,

> All his life was a series of plunges and scampers; darting after the beggar, dashing naked into the woods, tossing himself into the strange ship, hurling himself into the Sultan's tent and offering to hurl himself into the fire. In appearance he must have been like a thin brown skeleton autumn leaf dancing eternally before the wind; but in truth it was he that was the wind.[4]

These qualities carried over into Francis's life of prayer. In many respects, Francis "made it up as he went along," as one might say today—which is what made the early years of his movement creative and energizing for thousands of converts. We know from the wonderful collection of tales, *The Little Flowers*, that in the early days Francis would sometimes gather his followers together and ask them with fervor to open their mouths as the Spirit of God so moved them. Thus was their simple prayer session composed of the movings of the Spirit like a Quaker Friends meeting might be today. On one such occasion, after each had spoken as the Spirit prompted him, Francis summarized: "Dear brothers, give thanks to God, who has willed that by the mouths of babes should be revealed the treasures of heavenly wisdom."

In Clare's heart were the ideals that made Francis's bold actions in the world make sense. As Francis and the friars were walking all over Italy and Europe, Clare and the sisters were deepening the same sense of excitement and enthusiasm, primarily among and within themselves, and in their local settings. Many communities of Poor Clares were formed beyond Assisi, including one in Florence headed by Clare's sister, Agnes, but Clare always remained put. Clare's depth and constancy of prayer gave rise to an interior life that was different from Francis—which expresses itself in Clare's prayers. She became known throughout Italy as a woman of profound wisdom. As the cleric who wrote the papal bull for Clare's canonization explained it, "Clare was concealed, yet her life was revealed; Clare kept silence, yet her reputation cried aloud; she was hidden in a cell, but known throughout the towns."[5]

The spirit of Clare's written prayers is as full of joy and charity as Francis's, but Clare's prayer life was also more rooted in community and all its challenges. One imagines that Francis would have been a difficult companion: coming and going at all hours, changing direction and priorities often and at an instant, never thinking about the future. Indeed, he would have made a lousy husband except to Lady Poverty! But Clare was different. She was a deep, ready source of wisdom—a well to Francis's river. Clare developed a form of Franciscan spirituality that was true to the spirit of Francis, while deepening it in various, new directions.

Even the daily work of her hands showed Clare as one who brought spiritual strength to others who were more visible. From the first days, every Franciscan was to have manual work of some kind, in addition to prayer and other activities. Behind the walls of San Damiano, Clare's work was embroidery. She embroidered fine altar cloths—the kind that are used during the Mass on the high altar and on which the host is set. This is the sort of work that St. Francis would have never done himself, but upon which he surely relied. Tradition also has it that Clare created the cloth-shoes for Francis's tender feet after he was blessed with the stigmata.

It was during these extended periods of silence, manual work, and care for the needs of others that St. Clare became famous for intercessory prayer. Her intercessions were highly valued by popes, cardinals, the friars, and St. Francis himself. All these men would send word to Clare, asking for her intercession and, often, for her received wisdom. She also had a unique ability to bring joy to others. Clare did this for Francis when he rediscovered the gift of song in her garden at San Damiano. It was the last time that they were together, as Francis stopped for a time at San Damiano on his way to Rieti to see a physician. Clare made a special place for him in her garden, and it was in that place and spirit that Francis broke out of a depression that was ailing him and wrote his famous vernacular song, "The Canticle of the Creatures."

Clare was also the first woman to write her own Rule for religious life. Before her—and even for much of her own religious life—men wrote the Rules for women. The Dominican sisters, who were closest to the Poor Clares both geographically and chronologically, had rules against laughing in choir, or making someone else laugh; eating without permission of the abbess; any subtle rebellion in word or deed; and much more. Penalties for breaking these rules were spelled out in detail. Flogging was common, as was being required to humiliate oneself by eating bread and water while kneeling before the rest of the community. In contrast, Clare's Rule was a disappointment to the disciplinarians. She sent the message to her sisters and to the church authorities who approve monastic rules—not that Franciscans were not serious or strict (because Francis and Clare could be both)—that to be a Franciscan was a decision made each day, voluntarily for Christ. The spiritual life is not a path of renunciations.

Clare's life of prayer is perhaps best illumined by a metaphor of yeast and bread first suggested by Christ in the Gospel of Matthew, and then repeated by Evelyn Underhill a century ago. In *The School of Charity*, Underhill explains,

> The leavening of meal must have seemed to ancient men a profound mystery, and yet something on which they could always depend. Just so does the supernatural enter our natural life, working in the

hiddenness, forcing the new life into every corner and making the dough expand. If the dough were endowed with consciousness, it would not feel very comfortable while the yeast was working. Nor, as a rule, does our human nature feel very comfortable under the transforming action of God.[6]

Sometimes we don't stand still long enough to know the creative action of God working in us through prayer as yeast works in dough. Clare did.

The "hiddenness" of Clare was the very source of her wisdom and strength. Her spirituality is full of subtlety and understanding of the difficulties of being Christian, but she paves the way for us through the habits of a deliberate life of prayer—one where we don't do all the work ourselves, but it is as if the human body remains the same size just as Christ begins to leaven and take fuller shape within it.

Clare's Life of Prayer

In the legends passed down to us about Clare, there are many stories of her prayer life as a child. With all hagiographical texts, we should take these stories with a slight grain of salt, but nevertheless, they can at least point us in the right directions of understanding how and why and where she prayed.

Modeling St. Clare's *Life* after those of other great saints, Thomas of Celano portrays her childhood as devout, sober, and full of distinction from those around her. We have no stories of Clare that depict her childhood as anything approaching typical; she appears to have been one of those children that is serious from the start. Thomas writes that "she delighted in attending holy prayer regularly" and "little by little attained a heavenly life." He compares her to the Desert Fathers and Mothers of ancient, Christian tradition when he writes that Clare did not have access to rosary beads as a girl, and so she counted her Our Fathers by casting pebbles aside one by one. She "attached little value to worldly objects," Thomas explains, and "wore a hair shirt underneath her small, precious clothes." All these references are ways that medieval writers would tell the story of one of their contemporaries in the terms of, and with allusions to, the lives of previous saints. In fact, when Thomas writes about Clare on her deathbed, he compares her to the Virgin Mary. He says that the suffering of Clare's last days was like what Simeon had prophesied to Mary about the Christ child: "Look, he is destined for the fall and for the rise of many in Israel, destined to be a sign that is opposed—and a sword will pierce your soul too."[7]

It is in Clare's adolescence that we first come to see who she would become as a woman of God. Unlike the unquestioning child of Thomas of Celano's early storytelling, Clare shows signs of being a contrarian teenager, full of doubts and questions. There were times when she disobeyed her parents as well as her priest and bishop. Her conversion, in fact, relies on this sort of willful disobedience.

Clare did not want to follow the traditional course of a girl from a good family: marriage and children. She observed the conversion of St. Francis, and began listening to the Holy Spirit, who had other plans for her life. How it must have surprised and possibly disappointed her parents when she turned away from what they had planned for her! Clare's conversion—on that first night flight to Portiuncula—actually began the morning beforehand, on Palm Sunday, 1212. That morning, during an elaborate and traditional service with all of Assisi in attendance, Clare distinguished herself from all the other girls in town by refusing to show herself as an eligible woman waiting for the proper marriage match and blessing. She refused to stand to present herself to the bishop for his blessing, as was the fashion of all unmarried girls in town on that special day. This rebuff would have been felt by her parents, as well, who were probably embarrassed by it. At that point, Clare's tender jaw was surely and firmly set, matching a mind and heart already looking in another direction.

Thus began the religious life of Clare. It was the stuff of great films. But then what followed were four quiet decades of deepening experience in prayer. For Clare, it was necessary to leave the secular world to truly live in the spiritual world. The same is not true for all of us today. For many of us, these spiritual riches are ready and waiting, regardless of where we find ourselves and where we live.

There are other, little details about Clare's manners and methods of praying that are helpful to understand at the outset of our own praying with her. For instance, Thomas of Celano tells us that Clare often sought the solitude of praying alone late into the night, after the last evening office of Compline. She cried often while praying, which was not unusual for medieval mystics.

Thomas also explains that Clare was like a mother to her spiritual sisters. She would sometimes wake up early and would quietly, through the lighting of the lamps and other more subtle means, arouse the younger sisters to pray with her. On other occasions, Clare would intentionally wake up first and rouse the house by ringing a bell for all the sisters to come to the first office of prayer. Thomas adds this commentary: "There was no place for timidity, no place for idleness, where a quick reproof prodded lazy souls to prayer and service of the Lord." She acted unreservedly as her sisters' spiritual mother when it came to teaching them about prayer. Similarly, when one of her sisters needed healing, she would lay herself at the sister's feet and attempt to caress away the pain as a good mother might do.

Clare also practiced visual meditation, a common practice during the late Middle Ages. We have accounts of her doing this in various ways. At times, she would imagine as she lay prostrate facedown on the floor that she was kissing Jesus's feet. Later, Thomas says that she meditated on the cross to such a degree that she felt the devil strike her on the jaw. And at another time, she spent twenty-four hours in a meditative state, feeling as if she was nailed to the cross with Christ; she finally had to be roused by one of her sisters at San Damiano, who used Francis's injunction that Clare may not go a day without food of some kind, to bring her back to her senses.

In her meditative practices, Clare also prayed at times a series of short prayers taught to her by Francis called "The Office of the Five Wounds of Christ" (see pp. 164-65 below). It is easy to imagine Clare visualizing herself with Jesus in the Garden of Gethsemane, determined to stay awake and pray with him, but also crying beside him. She would have easily understood the poignant African American spiritual "Were You There When They Crucified My Lord?"

The Foundation for Clare's Prayers

Her life of prayer was built upon a varied foundation. Saints are always constructing on the spiritual work of those saints who have gone before them. For Clare, the building blocks were the teachings of Francis, the Old and New Testaments, and the Office of the Feast of St. Agnes of Rome (a fourth-century martyr), whose life and example were meaningful to Clare's understanding of women's spirituality in an age when men so clearly dominated most aspects of everyday life.[8] It was in the spirit of St. Agnes that Clare was fond of quoting from Matthew 13:

> The kingdom of heaven is like treasure hidden in a field, which a man found and covered up; then in his joy he goes and sells all that he has and buys that field. Again, the kingdom of heaven is like a merchant in search of fine pearls, who, on finding one pearl of great value, went and sold all that he had and bought it.

The primary sources for understanding the spirituality and prayer life of Clare are relatively few. Most importantly, we have her writings: four letters written to Agnes of Prague (the daughter of the king of Bohemia who refused arranged marriages to both Emperor Frederick II and King Henry III of England in order to become a Poor Clare in Prague), and one other letter to a woman of influence who chose the religious life (Ermentrude of Bruges); Clare's Rule and Testament; and her final blessing, as recorded by Thomas of Celano in *The Legend of St. Clare*.[9] In total, Clare's writings amount to twenty-two pages in the most recent, authoritative edition.[10]

Another essential component to Clare's prayer life was the repetition of praying the Divine Hours each day. This ancient form of prayer was inherited from ancient Judaism by the first Christians. The Hebrew psalmists were fond of praying what are sometimes called "the Hours" at fixed times throughout the day; as Psalm 119 says, "Seven times a day do I praise you." Clare and her sisters were faithful keepers of these Hours.

She prayed the Divine Hours more regularly than did her friend Francis. Francis was committed to praying the Hours, in the manner of monks, but his spirituality was also one of continual pilgrimage following

Christ, like a friar, and as such, he sometimes found it difficult to keep to the regularity of the practice. Clare would not have had that problem.

Clare was also probably better educated than Francis. We know that her mother was deeply religious herself, sometimes traveling on pilgrimages to major sites in Europe, and we know that Clare's family was wealthy, offering more educational opportunities and more encouragement at home than Francis would have enjoyed. Her writings show great subtlety as well as a thorough knowledge of Latin. She—and many of her spiritual sisters—would have prayed the Psalter in Latin, its ancient phrases forming the backbone of a religious life. Certain key verses were known by all baptized Christians, even the uneducated, in the same way that nursery rhymes were once known by our parents. Just as a child of the last century might have gone to bed with "I see the moon, and the moon sees me; God bless the moon, and God bless me"—so, too, in Clare's day, many children would associate phrases from the Psalms with the end of the day: "I will bless the Lord who gives me counsel; my heart teaches me, night after night" (16:7). Similarly, as children a generation ago may have woken up to "Donkey, donkey, old and gray, open your mouth and gently bray. Lift your ears and blow your horn to wake the world this sleepy morn"— children in Clare's family home would have known "Be joyful in the Lord, all you lands; serve the Lord with gladness and come before his presence with a song" (100:1), as the way to rise in the morning.

Late medieval religious life was rich with the rhythms and phrasings of psalms, and so were Clare's prayers. Psalm 51, for example, was used most every day as a prayer of confession (as it is in the weekly liturgy that follows), and Psalm 8 each Christmas. The Scriptures were read and prayed in Latin, and Latin was much better known to the spiritually minded at that time than was the vernacular. Francis actually created some of the first vernacular songs and prayers to God, and is credited by scholars as the very first Italian poet for his famous song, "The Canticle of the Creatures."

Like Francis, Clare knew the importance of spiritual reading, and many of her prayers resemble those of great saints who came before her. What confused Francis and Clare was how to read for spiritual guidance and edification without becoming too dependent on prayer books. Both

Francis and Clare must have known St. Jerome's early medieval instruction against idleness in the religious life: "Be sure to always have holy reading at hand. Look at it when sleep steals upon you and let the sacred page hold up your drooping head." But both Francis and Clare were hesitant to own prayer books; they both believed that books could too often become crutches to real spiritual learning and engagement in daily life. There are many stories of Francis urging his brother friars not to own their own books, and Clare seems to have carried on this tradition after his death. "*I* am a breviary! *I* am a breviary!" Francis once urged a young novice, in a fruitless attempt to convince him that books are not so much for owning as they are for changing one's life.

While in medieval culture prayer books often became merely decorative or used superstitiously or perfunctorily, the purer purpose that Francis and Clare called people toward was the prayer of the heart. The words of books—more than the object, the book—speak to this sort of prayer in the heart that matters. In England during Clare's era, it was common for a woman to own a copy of the *Life of St. Margaret* simply because expectant women were instructed to clutch the book to their breast during childbirth for protection from harm.[11] It was also common for upper-class women to be read to, rather than to read on their own. Chaucer's character Criseyde, for instance, listens with other ladies to tales of Thebes in *Troilus and Criseyde*. Similarly, elaborate Books of Hours would sit on the tables of ladies' dressing rooms, and the ladies would hear edifying words from them read aloud while they were dressing. A woman of Clare's standing in the community most likely said her prayers aloud far more often than she read them. So-called aural reading was once considered a refined substitution for visual reading. But also, both women and men of the Middle Ages believed that to say prayers out loud was one further step toward speaking with, and praying to, the heart. Clare was always praying aloud with her sisters, reminding herself all the while of the truth of prayer-words.

Above All, Jesus

One of the most important features of St. Clare's prayer life was her absorption in the person of Jesus. Clare's life with Christ was a love story of the highest order. She never fell in love with St. Francis—as novels and Hollywood have supposed—but she did fall in love with Jesus. As many other medieval women mystics would later do, Clare spoke often of Jesus in language that might today only be reserved for the words used between physical lovers; it is language that reminds us of the Song of Songs from the Hebrew Scriptures and the ways in which love between lovers can be metaphors for the relationship with Christ. Francis had earlier taken as his "spouse" Lady Poverty, and so Clare's marriage to Christ made perfect sense within her own religious context.

However, as Clare speaks of loving Jesus, she also speaks of loving God the Father, and of the Holy Spirit's love within her. Her expressions of love for and marriage with Christ differ from those of later mystics in this regard. Clare's prayer, inasmuch as it was mystical, was always Trinitarian, focused on the full Christian understanding of God in three persons. This is important to note simply because other medieval mystics were sometimes excessive in one or another direction.

Clare always speaks of God as Trinity and views her relationship to God in Christ through the love felt within by the Holy Spirit. Francis was the one who initially set Clare on this course. In his guidelines for Clare and her sisters—published for posterity by Clare herself in chapter six of her Rule—Francis explains that the relationship of Clare to Christ should be as "daughter and servant," and it is the Holy Spirit who is likened to her spouse. Francis emphasizes that love for the poor Christ of the Cross is deepened in us by the coming of the Holy Spirit as the unifying force of God the Father's love and the church.

Clare echoed these words of Francis again and again, in varying metaphor, as she instructed Agnes of Prague. With glorious language, Clare uses the following allusions to the Trinity at the beginning of the fourth letter to Agnes:

To her who is . . . bride of the Lamb . . . servant of Chris . . . hand-maid of His handmaids . . . may you sing a new song . . . before the throne of God the Father and follow the Lamb wherever He goes . . . I delight with you in the joy of the Holy Spirit.

Blessed Angela of Foligno, a prominent Third Order Franciscan, echoed the Franciscan idea of understanding the marriage to Christ through the Holy Spirit. She recorded having heard these words from God once while on the road between Spello and Assisi: "I am the Holy Spirit, who has come to you to bring you consolation as you have never before tasted. I will be within you and very few of those who are with you will be able to perceive it. I will keep you company and will speak with you at all times. . . . Bride and daughter, you are sweet to Me."[12]

The mystic is as uncommon in Christianity today as it was in Clare's day. But the goals of the mystic are the goals of faith, even when they are expressed in language that is more vivid and pictorial than we might normally be accustomed to. In the last century, Teilhard de Chardin once prayed, "When you stretched out nets to imprison me . . . thrilled with greater joy than when you offered me wings . . . the only element I hanker after in your gifts is the fragrance of your power over me, and the touch of your hand upon me . . . what exhilarates us human creatures more than freedom . . . is the joy of finding and surrendering . . . the rapture of being possessed."[13] Such is the mystical goal of any Christian, and it fairly represents how Clare felt about Jesus.

The Wisdom of Meditation

We know that Clare spent hours most days in prayer, as did Francis. Much of this prayer was contemplative, not vocal. Clare spent little time asking God for things or favors in her prayers. Instead, she spent time *with* Christ, in a quiet, listening relationship that is in itself without words. Most of what Clare would have called prayer we today would simply call meditation, or contemplative prayer, or Centering Prayer.

Contemplative life was an important part of her dedication to poverty. Both she and Francis sought to be voluntarily poor in terms of money and other resources, and they also worked to be poor in spirit, as Jesus described this way of poverty in the Sermon on the Mount. Part of this sort of poverty involved meeting Christ in the simplest, most bare and direct of ways.

There was plenty of spiritual teaching about meditation at this time in Assisi and elsewhere. In fact, several years after the death of Clare, Bonaventure, who was then the minister general of the Franciscans, wrote to the Poor Clares with advice in these subtle matters. He urged them to "descend" into prayer through stillness and meditation in ways that Clare had already understood:

> Return to yourself; enter into your heart; ponder what you were, are, should have been, called to be; . . . meditate in your heart; let your spirit brood. Plow this field, work on yourself; strive for freedom within, the freedom that leads to relationship with God, realizing that God will never force us to love him; . . . if you are not able to understand (and accept) your own self, you will not be able to understand (or accept) what is beyond you.[14]

It is clear that Clare spent a great deal of time in contemplation with God because she frequently spoke of these sorts of techniques in her writings. In the third letter to Agnes, for instance, Clare urged her:

> Place your mind before the mirror of eternity.
> Place your soul in the brilliance of heaven.
> Place your heart in the figure of the divine substance.
> Transform your entire self into the image of the Godhead so that
>   you too may feel and taste the hidden sweetness that
>   God has reserved for his lovers.

She adds a certain poetry to the theological teachings that would come later from Bonaventure. These are the specific instructions from one experienced meditator to another, offering paths of contemplative reflection, each of which one might spend days on end (or longer!) pursuing.

Clare was a down-to-earth mystic. Her power of concentration was intense, but hers was a mysticism that had feet and intelligence, in addition to heart. Her always-practical mystic voice often stands in contrast to those of other, medieval mystics.

The Power of Intercession

Her prayer life was often focused on intercession for the needs of others. These were times when she would appeal to God for the physical, spiritual, and emotional needs of those around her. Naturally, these occasions are not well chronicled, but we know that Clare's prayers resulted in many answers to prayer. We know that Francis often asked Clare's advice in serious matters and for her prayers on his behalf. One story from *The Little Flowers* explains how Francis was doubting his vocation. He was drawn to a life of contemplation and wondering whether he was supposed to live more like a hermit. Francis counseled with Clare and with Father Sylvester, the first priest to join the order and also a renowned contemplative, asking them to pray to God on his behalf, and asking God for guidance in the matter of Francis's vocation. Both Sylvester and Clare returned the verdict that Francis was doing as God wanted of him—just as Christ had wanted of the first disciples—to practice his vocation in and among the people of his town and beyond.

Pope Gregory IX, too, was said to rely on Clare implicitly, regarding her intercession on his behalf as a chief source of God's wisdom for his life. Some early texts say that Pope Gregory would often write a letter to Clare, explaining his trial or need, and that he would later tangibly experience her spiritual help.

Most importantly, Clare helped her sisters and was the mother of prayer at San Damiano. They turned to her daily for spiritual nourishment in the same way that women in various parts of the world still visit a well each day for water. For them, Clare was a well of wisdom. Her wisdom was hard-won over many trials, decisions, and hours spent forming the habit of words and patterns of communicating with God. She was a deep well, a reservoir of faith and sustenance for other people. We often turn to the saints as intercessors for us to God, and Clare is indeed the saint whom many turn to frequently. Her spirituality matches the metaphor of a well, just as an ever-moving river may best capture St. Francis. In her meditation and her prayer, Clare went down deep and often, listening for God's leading.

PRAYING ALONGSIDE ST. CLARE

Clare wrote at the end of her first letter to Agnes of Prague, "Farewell in the Lord, and pray for me!" So, too, we may pray for Clare, and Clare prays for us. But most importantly in this little book, we may pray *with* Clare.

Her words of prayer can at times be deceptively simple. There are different layers at which most prayers may be used and understood. Scripture works the same way. One writer describes the varied ways that we can read the Psalms that goes back to the late Middle Ages by explaining that the words are "shallow enough for lambs to paddle in [and] deep enough for elephants to swim."[15] Lambs and elephants! Imagine the feet of each animal and the body weight resting on those feet. The same prayer may provide a shallow pool of easy understanding on one occasion, and a deep lake of exploration on another. That is why Clare believed it profits us to pray the same words again and again. Clare's prayers work this way—in more than one way—and in the prayer section of this book we will pray with Clare, focusing on both aspects, the lamb and the elephant. As you pray with Clare, look for the simplicity of her message, but also for the subtleties and complexities of her understandings of God.

Clare's writings are full of Scripture quotes and references. She was drawn to both lamb and elephant passages in the Old and New Testaments. In her prayer life, she would have repeated and ruminated on certain phrases and words over and over again, in her mind, and on her lips. She also peppered her writings with Scripture, and to understand her prayers more thoroughly, we need to look at those passages that were most dear to her.

Praying with the Prophets

Clare ruminates and prays often from what are called The wisdom writings of the Hebrew Scriptures, including Song of Songs, Lamentations, and Proverbs. These books have been a profound source of language for many saints over the ages, particularly in looking for the right words to express love for God, sorrow in the difficulties of life, and disappointment at what seems unfair.

The extended love poem known as Song of Songs was interpreted allegorically in ancient Judaism as symbolic of the "spousal" love possible between God and human, and this method of understanding the Hebrew book of love was adopted by Clare and others. The following passages from Song of Songs were alluded to by Pope Gregory IX in a letter to Clare and all the sisters at San Damiano in 1228, two years after St. Francis's death.

Let him kiss me with the kisses of his mouth!
For your love is better than wine, your anointing oils are fragrant,
    your name is perfume poured out;
therefore the maidens love you.

Scarcely had I passed them, when I found him whom my soul loves.
I held him, and would not let him go
until I brought him into my mother's house,
and into the chamber of her that conceived me.[16]

But just as she prayed to God at times like a lover, Clare also sometimes prayed with the prophet Jeremiah, calling the people of God, who were behaving like adulterers, back to holiness. Loving words of devotion were mixed with serious words of challenge in the prayer of Clare. This is one of the ways that her prayers can be like both lambs and elephants.

Lamentations, or the book of Israel's sorrow, was also important to St. Clare's prayers. These two passages from Lamentations stand out in Clare's fourth letter to St. Agnes of Prague as most meaningful:

Is it nothing to you, all you who pass by?
Look and see if there is any sorrow like my sorrow,
which was brought upon me,
which the LORD inflicted on the day of his fierce anger.

The thought of my affliction and my homelessness
  is wormwood and gall!
My soul continually thinks of it and is bowed down within me.

Praying with the Psalms

Also from the Old Testament, the Psalms formed the real backbone of
the daily prayers of St. Clare. They were prayed every day from before
dawn until usually after dusk. Traditionally, on Fridays, Clare would have
prayed Psalm 22, feeling that she was being crucified along with Christ:
"My God, my God, why have you forsaken me? and are so far from my
cry and from the words of my distress?" And Psalm 51 was the basis for
a daily confession of one's sins, and also became the subject of a dramatic
demonstration by St. Francis before the women of San Damiano. The
little poor man was asked to preach the Word of God to the women, and
instead of a more traditional address, the dramatic saint made a circle of
ashes around himself, poured more ashes on his head, and sat down. After
a short while, Francis stood and recited the complete psalm as his only
sermon.

Sometimes, Clare turned to different psalms than those Francis turned
to. Psalm 45 was particularly meaningful to Clare:

Kings' daughters stand among the ladies of the court;
  on your right hand is the queen, adorned with the gold of Ophir.
"Hear, O daughter; consider and listen closely;
  forget your people and your father's house.
The king will have pleasure in your beauty;
  he is your master; therefore do him honor.
The people of Tyre are here with a gift;

the rich among the people seek your favor."
All glorious is the princess as she enters;
    her gown is cloth-of-gold.
In embroidered apparel she is brought to the king;
    after her the bridesmaids follow in procession.[17]

It is easy to imagine that Clare would have viewed her life through the lens of such a psalm. Two years after her death, Thomas of Celano immortalized Clare's life by comparing her time on earth to the words of Psalm 68:13: "you shall be like a dove whose wings are covered with silver, whose feathers are like green gold," adding that that silver dove built a nest in the cleft of rock that was San Damiano and raised up a community there.[18]

Praying with the Gospels

Like Francis before her, Clare was always looking at Jesus's earthly life as her example for what to do and who to become. She read and quoted from the Gospels more than any other Scripture. Also like Francis, Clare quoted most often from Matthew's Gospel out of the canonical four. In the first letter to Agnes of Prague, as Clare gives advice on the religious life, she quotes or alludes to Matthew no less than ten times. She instructs Agnes to store up treasures in heaven rather than on earth, to love poverty and serve God rather than money, to know the kingdom of heaven by being poor and humble in spirit, and to seek only those treasures that can never be stolen—and those are just the references from Matthew chapters 5 and 6.

Clare also appreciated this passage from Matthew, chapter 19, where Jesus speaks to Peter, saying, "Everyone who has left houses, brothers, sisters, father, mother, children or land for the sake of my name will receive a hundred times as much, and also inherit eternal life." She patterned her life after this teaching, and she instructed others to do likewise.

In addition to Matthew, she prayed frequently with passages from Luke and John but never from Mark. To ask her sisters to own spiritual books only when it was absolutely necessary, Clare referenced Luke 9:3, "Take nothing for the journey: neither staff, nor haversack, nor bread, nor money; and do not have a spare tunic." To explain why she often neglected her physical body, she quoted Matthew 6:34: "So do not worry about tomorrow: tomorrow will take care of itself." The Gospels were very dear to Clare and to the life of the Poor Clares.

Praying with St. Paul

Finally, Clare reflected in prayer and in her letters on the various letters of St. Paul to the first churches. Both Clare and Francis believed that their thirteenth-century spiritual movement was a return to the way of living that marked the earliest Christians. Clare begins her *Testament* by echoing Paul's advice to the first Christians in Corinth: "Consider your own call, brothers and sisters."[19]

Several themes from St. Paul were essential to the prayers of Clare. She reflected, for instance, that a vocation was something never to be concluded; conversion was a lifelong process. Also, the promises of following Christ were an abundant life of joy and meaning. In her *Testament*, Clare quoted from the Second Letter of Paul to the Corinthians: "For you know the generous act of our Lord Jesus Christ, that though he was rich, yet for your sakes he became poor, so that by his poverty you might become rich."[20] The Franciscan vocation could be summarized in that one verse.

The Daily Office for Sunday Through Saturday

Morning and Evening Prayer—An Introduction

The following weekly liturgy is derived from various sources and reflects the concerns of St. Clare of Assisi. Many of the words are the same that Clare prayed, and all of them are examples of the spirituality of the first Franciscans. In chapter 3 of her Rule, Clare urged all the sisters who could read to celebrate the Divine Office according to the same custom as the Franciscan men. And so, the twice-daily weekly portion of the Divine Office below reflects how Clare may have prayed morning and evening prayer with her sisters, and also repeats many of the words and phrases that were dear to them.

The sequence for each day of this special morning and evening liturgy is as follows:

A. PREPARATION (a very simple prayer of intention)

B. GOSPEL SENTENCE (the brevity of these passages can be profound, as Clare said, like "eating the fruit of a bountiful tree")[21]

C. *Silence* (more than a moment; a minute or more)

D. CONFESSION

E. FIRST READING (a canticle from the Hebrew Prophets or New Testament Epistles)

F. PSALM

G. GOSPEL READING

H. *Silence* (again)

I. PRAYERS OF THE SAINTS (that Clare may have prayed, or written by early Franciscans)

J. COLLECT (as Clare may have prayed with her sisters)

There are various ways that you may choose to use these morning and evening prayers in your own devotional life. First, they form a special prayer book for your daily life as you walk along with St. Clare and pray into the themes that formed her own spiritual life. If you do have a prayer book you use daily, there are other ways to pray with this book. Perhaps you wish to focus your prayer time, praying with Clare for a special weekend focus or weeklong spiritual retreat focusing on the life and message of St. Clare.

The Divine Hours of prayer have, from their earliest beginnings in the ancient synagogue, been intended for group use; so you may wish, in addition, to pray these short liturgies together with others in a group devoted to learning more about Clare of Assisi. Otherwise, as you pray alone, know that you are not truly alone. You join with thousands of Poor Clares around the world both past and present who have prayed similar words, as well. For them and for us, daily prayer is a means of beginning anew each day.

Second, if you already have a prayer practice and a prayer book, this book's offering of a week of special prayers may be a substitute for your regular practice. You may wish to make a special prayer week with Clare, finding some fresh inspiration by praying closely with Clare. It is natural to come to these points in our spiritual lives, and feel the necessity of books such as this one.

Third, while I hope that these prayers become a personal and daily prayer ritual for many, it may also appeal to those may wish to pray in community, in study groups of St. Clare, or even in academic settings. There is no way to really understand the "little plant," as she called herself, without enjoining her spiritual life, themes, and the very words of her prayers.

Seven Themes for Seven Days

Seven themes emerge from the life and writings of St. Clare, and each provides a framework and subject for one of our seven days of prayer.

Day One—Embracing Christ Quoting Paul's Letter to the Romans, Clare wrote in her second letter to Agnes of Prague praising her, "You have offered yourself as a holy and pleasing sacrifice" to God. All Christians are called to do this, whether or not we make a vow of celibacy in a religious life. What could be more true? For Clare, this embrace—or marriage—was total, and it was also Trinitarian. As mentioned above, according to the "Form of Life" written by St. Francis for the sisters, Francis said that the sisters were married to the Holy Spirit. "By divine inspiration you have made yourselves daughters of the most High . . . the heavenly Father, and taken the Holy Spirit as your spouse." The emphasis is on unity with God as Trinity. Elsewhere, in her second letter to Agnes of Prague, Clare describes Francis as an imitator of God the Father. And in her *Testament*, Clare refers to Francis as one who imitated Christ to the point of following his very footprints. All these ideals of embracing God boil down to seeing oneself entirely in the mirror of Christ, through the aid of the Holy Spirit's leading, and by so doing to see our true selves.

Day Two—Purity Clare was not pure as if she put on a gown and clothed herself in righteousness. Following Christ is never that simple, even for saints. Purity was a many-sided pursuit for Clare, and it is an essential aspect of any Christian striving for sanctity in daily life. Virginal purity was part of her identity, as she followed in the steps of earlier saints such as St. Agnes of Rome (see pp. 178–79). But purity has many other sides, both for us and in the prayers of Clare.

Purity is not about being a "young virgin" or going to bed supperless or being "lily white"—as suggested in romantic images from a John Keats poem about St. Agnes—but it is, for St. Clare and for us, about a kind of holiness that happens when we " . . . require / Of Heaven with upward eyes for all that [we] desire."

Sometimes, purity can be quite measurable and straightforward, such as sexual purity. But purity of the heart is different; only God knows how we are doing there. For St. Clare, purity was never a series of negatives: *Thou shalt not* . . . For Clare, purity was a state of devotedness to God, renewed each day. In purity came single-mindedness and clarity, as well as freedom.

Day Three—Walking the Path of Conversion For both Francis and Clare, the path of conversion was lifelong and daily at the same time. Each of them advocated what we would call today voluntary poverty. In practical terms, they found that simplicity and joy were most essential for life, and neither were to be found in things. Clare believed that a follow-er of Christ needed to continually evaluate oneself and strip away those encumbrances that kept one from seeing Christ most clearly. The fewer the things that we need, the more we are liberated to become who we are meant to become in Christ.

In chapter 6 of her Rule, Clare preserved Francis's final blessing for the sisters, a simple paragraph, which goes like this:

> I, little brother Francis, follow the life and poverty of our most exalted Lord Jesus Christ as well as his most holy Mother, and to persevere in this life until the end. I ask you, my sisters, and I encourage you to live always in this holy life and poverty. Keep careful watch and never depart from it by reason of the contrary teaching of any person.

It was advice full of foreboding, as Francis's movement was torn by those who overturned the founder's commitment to poverty soon after his death. But Clare intended to preserve it for her and her sisters, and she was the guardian of the original Franciscan ideals for the quarter century that she lived after Francis's death.

Day Four—Listening with the Heart We all live messy lives, which is usually what causes us to pray. Clare leads us through many steps of faith that help us to find our focus once again. So far, we have approached God who embraces us, paid careful attention to the purity of our lives, and focused ourselves on the ongoing path of conversion. Each of these themes serves to bolster our spirits, and deepen our attention, in the process of praying in everyday life. Now, we are ready to follow Clare into this fourth stage of listening with the heart.

She speaks most eloquently on this theme in her third letter to St. Agnes. A heart must always be converted since it naturally leans toward the world. Clare tells Agnes that "the crafty enemy" (which is a combination of the devil and worldly vanity) "infatuates the human heart." But through conversion we become as Jesus said in the parable, a treasure hidden in a field. The human heart becomes a place of hidden, quiet treasure. God knows its qualities, to be sure, and we gradually do, as well. Such is the process of what theologians call sanctification.

In the second letter to Agnes, Clare urges her to "gaze, consider, contemplate, and desire" to imitate Jesus. These are very slow activities, and the primary goal of this imitation is to listen for the word of God in our lives. This sort of prayer is not always an activity of the mind, as if we only concentrate ourselves toward God. Sometimes, we listen best for God when we do some simple act of obedience, show love to our neighbor, do a simple act of piety with quiet intention, or carry out a simple task that we know we are supposed to do. This is what Clare means by turning listening into seeing—opening our eyes to what we may not normally see around us—and then action. In all these things, we are praying and developing a heart more like Christ. So Clare listens with the heart in the same sense that the apostle Paul understands when he writes to the fledgling church in Philippi: "This is my prayer, that your love may overflow more and more with knowledge and full insight."[22]

Day Five—Adoring Christ Both Francis and Clare were visual people; they learned by seeing. Eyes were windows to the soul, and images of Christ could be windows to seeing God. In an icon, when we see Christ, Christ may also see us.

Clare also believed that the eyes have a special, spiritual function in the body. Looking was akin to touching. That is how Clare believed the eyes work in the body as she adored God through her eyes. Gazing on Christ was the way to see with *his* eyes, and a way to begin to see our true selves as he sees us.

Clare's writings are abundant with metaphors and allusions that show the visual ways that she adored Christ. For example, she wrote, "Happy, indeed, is she to whom it is given to drink at this sacred banquet so that she might cling with her whole heart to Him whose beauty all the blessed hosts of heaven unceasingly admire."[23] This is the language of metaphor and adoration. Such perspective is possible from silence—a habit of Clare's that Francis did not really share. She was like Christian mystics throughout history who have spent long periods in solitude contemplating their Lord. This is similar to what we saw on Day Four, with Clare writing to Agnes to urge her to "gaze, consider, contemplate, and desire" Jesus. It is imaginative; it is visual; it is real. A more recent Christian mystic, who lived decades in India, said similarly, with adoration, "I receive him who is pure Gift."[24]

She taught her sisters to adore Christ in tangible ways, as well. Prayer, for Clare, brought Christ closer. Through the heartfelt words of prayer, Christ is adored in speech. When an icon is used in prayer, Christ is brought closer with the eyes. And caring for the sick and the poor and the stranger (as the Poor Clares often did) were tangible ways of adoring Christ, taking prayer to the next step, following the teaching of Jesus from Matthew chapter 25: "In truth I tell you, in so far as you did this to one of the least of these brothers of mine, you did it to me."

Only a loving, faithful, and creative God would expect such creative responses from human beings in prayer—standards that Clare felt to be entirely within range of the possibility of human experience. Like Velveteen rabbits, we become more authentically real the more that we touch, feel, are felt, love, and are loved.

Day Six—True Discipleship Clare thought vividly about Jesus before she ever prayed. The image of following his footprints closely, first mentioned in Scripture,[25] was repeated by Clare several times. She imagined herself quite literally walking behind Jesus, doing as he did on earth.

For her, one of the most important ways of being a disciple of Jesus was to pray. Many of Clare's prayers were modeled after the ways that Jesus prayed. At various times and in different ways, Clare spent days and nights in the "desert" in prayer; she went alone in the "garden" to pray; she even wished that her sisters would stay awake more often and pray with her; and she instructed her sisters how to pray the Our Father.

Clare measured her faithfulness to Christ, and to Francis, through a determined life of prayer. The stories about Clare are full of anecdotes that show her praying the Canonical Hours in choir, praying while eating, praying while working, and rising in the middle of the night to pray, prompted by the Holy Spirit to do so.

We also know from the tales of Francis that he wished nothing more than that the Poor Clares, and Clare herself, would illuminate the world with their faithfulness. Clare's name means "light" in Italian, and the image of light surrounds her legend. When Francis and Brother Leo were walking outside at night, it was common for Francis to compare Clare's life of prayer to the brightest stars and to the full moon.

We often consider true discipleship to be something similar to business for the kingdom: it is where we go, what activities we do, and the like. But for some Christians, prayer is the primary vocation. And for all of us, a brilliant and devoted life of prayer is a kind of true discipleship that illuminates the world for Christ.

Day Seven—Redefining Family Both Francis and Clare turned away from their earthly families in dramatic fashion to follow Christ. The drama of those memorable scenes was not accidental. Francis and Clare believed that discipleship to Christ meant making difficult decisions about our lives. We often feel the difficulty of these decisions most acutely when they affect our families. There are times when we must be away from a spouse, children, parents, and other loved ones to do what is God's work for us in the world. Francis and Clare wanted to refocus our attention on these ways that the family of God is larger than our own families.

We are not all called to a vowed life, as Sts. Francis and Clare were, but we *are* all called to a life of discipleship. We are called to a life that redefines what it means to be family in ways that Jesus explained two millennia ago.

In Matthew 5, Jesus quotes the Jewish commandments and then adds to them. He modifies an "eye for eye and tooth for tooth" with "Give to anyone who asks you, and if anyone wants to borrow, do not turn away." Jesus tells his followers, "You have heard how it was said, 'You will love your neighbor and hate your enemy.' But I say this to you, love your enemies and pray for those who persecute you; so that you may be children of your Father in heaven."

The saints from Assisi intended to redefine—as Jesus had before them—what it means to be a sister, brother, mother, and father. Just as the apostle Paul defined true love for the first time in his First Letter to the Corinthians, Jesus defined family and neighbor in ways that had never been fully understood. He taught that the prisoner, the outcast, and the unwanted are our brothers and sisters. We should find new ways to show love to them, to show them that they, too, are part of the family of God. Francis and Clare intended to do nothing less than turn the world upside down. We most often imagine them with birds, and flowers, and rabbits, and calmed wolves by their sides—and that is part of what it means to live in God's new creation—but we may also pray with Francis and Clare as prophetic voices for the transformation of human relationships.

Morning Prayer, Sunday
(Theme/Intent: Embracing Christ)

PREPARATION

Heavenly Father, we have offered ourselves as a holy and pleasing sacrifice to you. Make us mindful of our commitment of our whole selves every morning, every noontime, every evening. Only one thing is necessary and it is you.

Amen.[26]

GOSPEL SENTENCE

Our Lord Jesus Christ says: I am the way, and the truth, and the life. No one comes to the Father except through me. If you know me, you will know my Father also. From now on you do know him and have seen him.

—John 14:6–7

Silence

CONFESSION

Have mercy on me, O God, according to your loving-kindness;
   in your great compassion blot out my offenses.
Wash me through and through from my wickedness
   and cleanse me from my sin.
For I know my transgressions,
   and my sin is ever before me.
Against you only have I sinned
   and done what is evil in your sight.
And so you are justified when you speak
   and upright in your judgment.
Indeed, I have been wicked from my birth,
   a sinner from my mother's womb.
For behold, you look for truth deep within me,
   and will make me understand wisdom secretly.
   —Psalm 51:1–7

FIRST READING

My beloved speaks and says to me: "Arise, my love, my fair one, and come away; for now the winter is past, the rain is over and gone. The flowers appear on the earth; the time of singing has come, and the voice of the turtledove is heard in our land. The fig tree puts forth its figs, and the vines are in blossom; they give forth fragrance. Arise, my love, my fair one, and come away.

—Song of Solomon 2:10–13

PSALM

Deus, Deus meus

O God, you are my God; eagerly I seek you;
    my soul thirsts for you, my flesh faints for you,
    as in a barren and dry land where there is no water.
Therefore I have gazed upon you in your holy place,
    that I might behold your power and your glory.
For your loving-kindness is better than life itself;
    my lips shall give you praise.
So will I bless you as long as I live
    and lift up my hands in your Name.
My soul is content, as with marrow and fatness,
    and my mouth praises you with joyful lips,
When I remember you upon my bed,
    and meditate on you in the night watches.
For you have been my helper,
    and under the shadow of your wings I will rejoice.
My soul clings to you;
    your right hand holds me fast.
May those who seek my life to destroy it
    go down into the depths of the earth;
Let them fall upon the edge of the sword,
    and let them be food for jackals.
But the king will rejoice in God;
    all those who swear by him will be glad;
    for the mouth of those who speak lies shall be stopped.

—Psalm 63

GOSPEL READING

Hear the Word of the Lord: Jesus said, "Do not store up treasures for yourselves on earth, where moth and woodworm destroy them and thieves can break in and steal. But store up treasures for yourselves in heaven, where neither moth nor woodworm destroys them and thieves cannot break in and steal. For wherever your treasure is, there will your heart be too. The lamp of the body is the eye. It follows that if your eye is clear, your whole body will be filled with light."

—Matthew 6:19–22

Silence

PRAYERS OF THE SAINTS

I would die gladly of love
if I could.
I have seen clearly with my own eyes
Him whom I love
standing in my soul.
The bride who takes her Lover in—
never needs to go very far.

—Mechthild of Magdeburg (d. ca. 1282)[27]

Keep Doing What You Are Doing

What you are doing, may you keep on doing and do not stop.
But with swiftness, agility, and unswerving feet,
may you go forward with joy and security
knowing that you are on the path of wisdom and happiness.
Believe nothing, and agree with nothing
that will turn you away from this commitment.
Nothing should be allowed to prevent you
from offering yourself to the Most High in the perfection
to which the Spirit of God has called you.
Amen.

—Clare of Assisi[28]

Evening Prayer, Sunday
(Theme/Intent: Embracing Christ)

PREPARATION

O Holy One,

our strength is in you.

May your Holy Spirit

direct and rule our hearts in all ways

today

through Jesus Christ our Lord.

Amen.

GOSPEL SENTENCE

Our Lord Jesus Christ says: I am the bread of life. No one who comes to
me will ever hunger; no one who believes in me will ever thirst.

—John 6:35

Silence

CONFESSION

Have mercy on me, O God, according to your
  loving-kindness;
    in your great compassion blot out my offenses.
Purge me from my sin, and I shall be pure;
    wash me, and I shall be clean indeed.
Make me hear of joy and gladness,
    that the body you have broken may rejoice.
Hide your face from my sins
    and blot out all my iniquities.
Create in me a clean heart, O God,
    and renew a right spirit within me.
Cast me not away from your presence
    and take not your holy Spirit from me.
Give me the joy of your saving help again
    and sustain me with your bountiful Spirit.

I shall teach your ways to the wicked,
  and sinners shall return to you.
Deliver me from death, O God,
  and my tongue shall sing of your righteousness,
  O God of my salvation.
Open my lips, O Lord,
  and my mouth shall proclaim your praise.
Had you desired it, I would have offered sacrifice,
  but you take no delight in burnt-offerings.
The sacrifice of God is a troubled spirit;
  a broken and contrite heart, O God, you will not despise.
Be favorable and gracious to Zion,
  and rebuild the walls of Jerusalem.
—Psalm 51:1, 8–19

FIRST READING

There came a voice from the throne saying: "Praise our God, all you his servants, you that fear him, both small and great!" And I heard what sounded like a vast throng, like the sound of a mighty torrent or of great peals of thunder, and they cried: "Hallelujah! The Lord our God, sovereign over all, has entered on his reign! Let us rejoice and shout for joy and pay homage to him, for the wedding day of the Lamb has come! His bride has made herself ready, and she has been given fine linen, shining and clean, to wear." The angel said to me, "Write this: 'Happy are those who are invited to the wedding banquet of the Lamb!'" He added, "These are the very words of God."
  —Revelation 19:5–9 (REB)

PSALM
Ecce nunc
Behold now, bless the LORD, all you servants of the LORD,
  you that stand by night in the house of the LORD.
Lift up your hands in the holy place and bless the LORD;
  the LORD who made heaven and earth
  bless you out of Zion.
—Psalm 134

GOSPEL READING

Hear the Word of the Lord: In the beginning was the Word: the Word was with God and the Word was God. He was with God in the beginning. Through him all things came into being, not one thing came into being except through him. What has come into being in him was life, life that was the light of men; and light shines in darkness, and darkness could not overpower it. . . . The Word was the real light that gives light to everyone; he was coming into the world. He was in the world that had come into being through him, and the world did not recognize him. He came to his own and his own people did not accept him. But to those who did accept him he gave power to become children of God, to those who believed in his name who were born not from human stock or human desire or human will but from God himself. The Word became flesh, he lived among us, and we saw his glory.

—John 1:1–5, 9–14a

Silence

PRAYERS OF THE SAINTS

Soul of Christ, make me holy,

Body of Christ, be my salvation.

Blood of Christ, let me drink your wine.

Water flowing from the side of Christ, wash me clean.

Passion of Christ, strengthen me.

Kind Jesus, hear my prayer;

hide me within your wounds

and keep me close to you.

Defend me from the evil enemy.

Call me at my death

to the fellowship of your saints,

so that I may sing your praise with them

through all eternity. Amen.

—A Prayer to the Redeemer from the Roman Missal

COLLECT

Devote yourself to all that you desire,

the most prized possession above all other things;

that is,

the spirit of the Lord

and the work of God.

Amen.

Morning Prayer, Monday
(Theme/Intent: Purity)

PREPARATION

As the saints have turned to you,

again and again, for centuries,

we turn to you today,

again and again.

Our truer self awaits.

Our truer self awaits.

GOSPEL SENTENCE

Our Lord Jesus Christ says: The kingdom of heaven is like treasure hidden in a field, which a man found and covered up; then in his joy he goes and sells all that he has and buys that field. Again, the kingdom of heaven is like a merchant in search of fine pearls, who, on finding one pearl of great value, went and sold all that he had and bought it.

—Matthew 13:44–46

Silence

CONFESSION

(from Psalm 51)

Have mercy on me, O God, according to your loving-kindness;

in your great compassion blot out my offenses.

Wash me through and through from my wickedness

and cleanse me from my sin.

For I know my transgressions,
  and my sin is ever before me.
Against you only have I sinned
  and done what is evil in your sight.
And so you are justified when you speak
  and upright in your judgment.
Indeed, I have been wicked from my birth,
  a sinner from my mother's womb.
For behold, you look for truth deep within me,
  and will make me understand wisdom secretly.
—Psalm 51:1–7

FIRST READING

I appeal to you therefore, brothers and sisters, by the mercies of God, to present your bodies as a living sacrifice, holy and acceptable to God, which is your spiritual worship. Do not be conformed to this world, but be transformed by the renewing of your minds, so that you may discern what is the will of God—what is good and acceptable and perfect. . . . Let love be genuine; hate what is evil, hold fast to what is good; love one another with mutual affection; outdo one another in showing honor. Do not lag in zeal, be ardent in spirit, serve the Lord. Rejoice in hope, be patient in suffering, persevere in prayer.
  —Romans 12:1–2, 9–12

PSALM

How great is your goodness, O LORD!
which you have laid up for those who fear you;
which you have done in the sight of all
for those who put their trust in you.
You hide them in the covert of your presence from those
who slander them;
you keep them in your shelter from the strife of tongues.
Blessed be the Lord!
for he has shown me the wonders of his love in a
  besieged city.

Yet I said in my alarm,
"I have been cut off from the sight of your eyes."
Nevertheless, you heard the sound of my entreaty
when I cried out to you.

Love the LORD, all you who worship him;
the LORD protects the faithful,
but repays to the full those who act haughtily.

Be strong and let your heart take courage,
all you who wait for the LORD.
—Psalm 31:19–24

GOSPEL READING

Hear the Word of the Lord: Jesus told them [a] parable but they failed to understand what he was saying to them. So Jesus spoke to them again: "In all truth I tell you, I am the gate of the sheepfold. All who have come before me are thieves and bandits, but the sheep took no notice of them. I am the gate. Anyone who enters through me will be safe: such a one will go in and out and will find pasture. The thief comes only to steal and kill and destroy. I have come so that they may have life and have it to the full. I am the good shepherd: the good shepherd lays down his life for his sheep. . . .

"I am the good shepherd; I know my own and my own know me, just as the Father knows me and I know the Father; and I lay down my life for my sheep. And there are other sheep I have that are not of this fold, and I must lead these too. They too will listen to my voice, and there will be only one flock, one shepherd."
—John 10:6–11, 14–16

Silence

PRAYERS OF THE SAINTS

Fear not, my daughter, He told me,
I am medicine that heals all, heart and soul.
The sins of your eyes, which looked at vain and hurtful things, and
   delighted in things other than God.

Your ears, which listened to slander, insults, lies and blasphemies.

Your tongue, which ran on about the same.

Your mouth and throat, which delighted too much in food and drink.

Your neck, which you have held with anger and pride.

Your hands, that have touched and embraced many things that you
    shouldn't have.

And your heart, too often sad, covetous, and angry.

Fear not, my daughter, He told me,

I am medicine that heals all, heart and soul.[29]

—Blessed Angela of Foligno (d. 1309)

Traditional Collect for the Feast of St. Agnes

Almighty, eternal God,

You choose what the world considers weak

to put the worldly power to shame.

May we who celebrate the birth of Saint Agnes into eternal joy

be loyal to the faith she professed.

Grant this through our Lord Jesus Christ, Your Son,

who lives and reigns with You and the Holy Spirit,

one God, for ever and ever.

Amen.

Evening Prayer, Monday
(Theme/Intent: Purity)

PREPARATION

Now, remember: It is God

who set you apart

before you were born,

calling your name,

revealing his Son to you,

so that you might say it again

to every human being.[30]

GOSPEL SENTENCE

Our Lord Jesus Christ says: Your light must shine in people's sight, so that, seeing your good works, they may give praise to your Father in heaven.

—Matthew 5:16

Silence

CONFESSION

Have mercy on me, O God, according to your loving-kindness;
    in your great compassion blot out my offenses.
Purge me from my sin, and I shall be pure;
    wash me, and I shall be clean indeed.
Make me hear of joy and gladness,
    that the body you have broken may rejoice.
Hide your face from my sins
    and blot out all my iniquities.
Create in me a clean heart, O God,
    and renew a right spirit within me.
Cast me not away from your presence
    and take not your holy Spirit from me.
Give me the joy of your saving help again
    and sustain me with your bountiful Spirit.
I shall teach your ways to the wicked,
    and sinners shall return to you.
Deliver me from death, O God,
    and my tongue shall sing of your righteousness,
    O God of my salvation.
Open my lips, O Lord,
    and my mouth shall proclaim your praise.
Had you desired it, I would have offered sacrifice,
    but you take no delight in burnt-offerings.
The sacrifice of God is a troubled spirit;
    a broken and contrite heart, O God, you will not despise.
Be favorable and gracious to Zion,
    and rebuild the walls of Jerusalem.

—Psalm 51:1, 8–19

FIRST READING

The Canticle of the Three Young Men

Let the earth bless the Lord: praise and glorify him for ever!

Bless the Lord, mountains and hills, praise and glorify him for ever!

Bless the Lord, every plant that grows, praise and glorify him for ever!

Bless the Lord, springs of water, praise and glorify him for ever!

Bless the Lord, seas and rivers, praise and glorify him for ever!

Bless the Lord, whales, and everything that moves in the waters, praise and glorify him for ever!

Bless the Lord, every kind of bird, praise and glorify him for ever!

Bless the Lord, all animals wild and tame, praise and glorify him for ever!

Bless the Lord, all the human race: praise and glorify him for ever!

Bless the Lord, O Israel, praise and glorify him for ever!

Bless the Lord, priests, praise and glorify him for ever!

Bless the Lord, his servants, praise and glorify him for ever!

Bless the Lord, spirits and souls of the upright, praise and glorify him for ever!

Bless the Lord, faithful, humble-hearted people, praise and glorify him for ever!

—Daniel 3:74–87 (NJB)

PSALM

Dominus regit me

The LORD is my shepherd;
    I shall not be in want.

He makes me lie down in green pastures
    and leads me beside still waters.

He revives my soul
    and guides me along right pathways for his Name's sake.

Though I walk through the valley of the shadow of death,
    I shall fear no evil;
        for you are with me;
        your rod and your staff, they comfort me.

You spread a table before me in the presence of those
  who trouble me;
    you have anointed my head with oil,
    and my cup is running over.
Surely your goodness and mercy shall follow me all the days
  of my life,
    and I will dwell in the house of the LORD for ever.
—Psalm 23

GOSPEL READING

Hear the Word of the Lord: Jesus said, "Pay attention to the parable of the sower. When anyone hears the word of the kingdom without understanding, the Evil One comes and carries off what was sown in his heart: this is the seed sown on the edge of the path. The seed sown on patches of rock is someone who hears the word and welcomes it at once with joy. But such a person has no root deep down and does not last; should some trial come, or some persecution on account of the word, at once he falls away. The seed sown in thorns is someone who hears the word, but the worry of the world and the lure of riches choke the word and so it produces nothing. And the seed sown in rich soil is someone who hears the word and understands it; this is the one who yields a harvest."

—Matthew 13:19–23a

Silence

PRAYERS OF THE SAINTS

Eternal God, on you I have depended since my mother's womb; you my soul has loved with all of its strength, and to you I dedicated my body and my soul from childhood. Remember me in your kingdom, for I have been crucified with you. Do not let the abyss of death separate me from your chosen ones, and do not allow the accuser to stand in my way. Forgive me all of my sins so that my soul may be received in your sight, blameless as your Son. Amen.

—St. Macrina the Younger (d. 379)[31]

A Collect for the Ladies of San Damiano

Live always in truth, so that you may die in obedience.

Do not look longingly at life lived outside, for the Spirit is better.

In love, use discernment, and all that the Lord gives you.

When weighed down by illness, or wearied: bear it all in peace and
contentment.

For you will one day sell all weariness at a high price and you will be
crowned a queen in heaven with the Virgin Mary. Amen.[32]

—St. Francis of Assisi

Morning Prayer, Tuesday
(Theme/Intent: Walking the Path of Conversion)

PREPARATION

As the deer longs for the water-brooks,
so longs my soul for you, O God.

—Psalm 42:1

GOSPEL SENTENCE

Our Lord Jesus Christ says: For wherever your treasure is, that is where
your heart will be too.

—Luke 12:34

Silence

CONFESSION

Have mercy on me, O God, according to your loving-kindness;
in your great compassion blot out my offenses.

Wash me through and through from my wickedness
and cleanse me from my sin.

For I know my transgressions,
and my sin is ever before me.

Against you only have I sinned
and done what is evil in your sight.

And so you are justified when you speak
    and upright in your judgment.
Indeed, I have been wicked from my birth,
    a sinner from my mother's womb.
For behold, you look for truth deep within me,
    and will make me understand wisdom secretly.
—Psalm 51:1–7

FIRST READING

Now the Lord is the Spirit, and where the Spirit of the Lord is, there is freedom. And all of us, with unveiled faces, seeing the glory of the Lord as though reflected in a mirror, are being transformed into the same image from one degree of glory to another; for this comes from the Lord, the Spirit.
    —2 Corinthians 3:17–18

PSALM

Beati immaculati

Happy are they whose way is blameless,
    who walk in the law of the LORD!
Happy are they who observe his decrees
    and seek him with all their hearts!
Who never do any wrong,
    but always walk in his ways.
You laid down your commandments,
    that we should fully keep them.
Oh, that my ways were made so direct
    that I might keep your statutes!
Then I should not be put to shame,
    when I regard all your commandments.
I will thank you with an unfeigned heart,
    when I have learned your righteous judgments.
I will keep your statutes;
    do not utterly forsake me.
—Psalm 119:1–8

GOSPEL READING

Hear the Word of the Lord: Jesus said, "Why do you call me, 'Lord, Lord' and not do what I say? Everyone who comes to me and listens to my words and acts on them—I will show you what such a person is like. Such a person is like the man who, when he built a house, dug, and dug deep, and laid the foundations on rock; when the river was in flood it bore down on that house but could not shake it, it was so well built. But someone who listens and does nothing is like the man who built a house on soil, with no foundations; as soon as the river bore down on it, it collapsed; and what a ruin that house became!"

—Luke 6:46–49

Silence

PRAYERS OF THE SAINTS

Lord and protector, you are our redemption. Direct our minds by your gracious presence, and watch over our paths with guiding love; so that, among the snares that lie hidden in the path where we walk, we may pass onward with hearts fixed on you; so that by the track of faith we may come to be where you would have us to be. Amen.

—Mozarabic Sacramentary

Collect

May the Lord make you a gardener
among the vines,
pulling weeds, aerating soil,
tending to the needs of both the roots and leaves.
The vines will flourish and grow,
giving forth their fragrance,
spreading their bounty in the light.
May it be so. Amen.[33]

Evening Prayer, Tuesday
(Theme/Intent: Walking the Path of Conversion)

PREPARATION

Author of eternal light,
shed continual day on we who watch for you,
so that our lips may praise you,
our lives may bless you, and
our meditations may glorify you,
through Christ our Lord. Amen.
—Sarum Breviary

GOSPEL SENTENCE

Our Lord Jesus Christ says: You are salt for the earth. But if salt loses its
taste, what can make it salty again? You are light for the world. A city build
on a hill-top cannot be hidden.
—Matthew 5:13a, 14

Silence

CONFESSION

Have mercy on me, O God, according to your loving-kindness;
  in your great compassion blot out my offenses.
Purge me from my sin, and I shall be pure;
  wash me, and I shall be clean indeed.
Make me hear of joy and gladness,
  that the body you have broken may rejoice.
Hide your face from my sins
  and blot out all my iniquities.
Create in me a clean heart, O God,
  and renew a right spirit within me.
Cast me not away from your presence
  and take not your holy Spirit from me.
Give me the joy of your saving help again
  and sustain me with your bountiful Spirit.

I shall teach your ways to the wicked,
 and sinners shall return to you.
Deliver me from death, O God,
 and my tongue shall sing of your righteousness,
 O God of my salvation.
Open my lips, O Lord,
 and my mouth shall proclaim your praise.
Had you desired it, I would have offered sacrifice,
 but you take no delight in burnt-offerings.
The sacrifice of God is a troubled spirit;
 a broken and contrite heart, O God, you will not despise.
Be favorable and gracious to Zion,
 and rebuild the walls of Jerusalem.
—Psalm 51:1, 8–19

FIRST READING

May you be made strong with all the strength that comes from his glorious power, and may you be prepared to endure everything with patience, while joyfully giving thanks to the Father, who has enabled you to share in the inheritance of the saints in the light. He has rescued us from the power of darkness and transferred us into the kingdom of his beloved Son, in whom we have redemption, the forgiveness of sins. He is the image of the invisible God, the firstborn of all creation; for in him all things in heaven and on earth were created, things visible and invisible, whether thrones or dominions or rulers or powers—all things have been created through him and for him. He himself is before all things, and in him all things hold together.
—Colossians 1:11–17

PSALM

Domine, non est

O LORD, I am not proud;

    I have no haughty looks.

I do not occupy myself with great matters,

    or with things that are too hard for me.

But I still my soul and make it quiet,

    like a child upon its mother's breast;

    my soul is quieted within me.

O Israel, wait upon the LORD,

    from this time forth for evermore.

—Psalm 131

GOSPEL READING

Hear the Word of the Lord: Jesus took with him Peter and James and his brother John and led them up a high mountain by themselves. There in their presence he was transfigured: his face shone like the sun and his clothes became as dazzling as light. And suddenly Moses and Elijah appeared to them; they were talking with him. Then Peter spoke to Jesus. "Lord," he said, "it is wonderful for us to be here; if you want me to, I will make three shelters here, one for you, one for Moses and one for Elijah." He was still speaking when suddenly a bright cloud covered them with shadow, and suddenly from the cloud there came a voice which said, "This is my Son, the Beloved; he enjoys my favour. Listen to him." When they heard this, the disciples fell on their faces, overcome with fear. But Jesus came up and touched them, saying, "Stand up, do not be afraid." And when they raised their eyes they saw no one but Jesus.

—Matthew 17:1–8

Silence

PRAYERS OF THE SAINTS

Let us rise up without delay! The scriptures challenge us with these words: "You know what time it is, how it is now the moment for you to wake from sleep." Let us open our eyes to the light that transfigures everything; let us clear our ears for the sound of God's voice that cries out to us each day: "Oh, that today you would hearken to his voice! Harden not your hearts."

—St. Benedict of Nursia (d. 550)[34]

COLLECT

May you have tremendous joy, obtaining the one thing
    worth desiring,
but remain surprised by God, with awe for God's gift in you.
Be an essential co-worker in the heavenly field,
    a co-creator in the work of God,
a support for the Body of Christ. Amen.[35]

Morning Prayer, Wednesday
(Theme/Intent: Listening with the Heart)

PREPARATION

Almighty God, unto whom all hearts are open, all desires known, and from whom no secrets are hid: cleanse the thoughts of our hearts by the inspiration of thy Holy Spirit, that we may perfectly love you, and worthily magnify your holy name, through Jesus Christ our Lord. Amen.

—Gregorian Sacramentary

GOSPEL SENTENCE

Our Lord Jesus Christ says: Whoever holds to my commandments and keeps them is the one who loves me; and whoever loves me will be loved by my Father, and I shall love him and reveal myself to him.

—John 14:21

Silence

CONFESSION

Have mercy on me, O God, according to your loving-kindness;
  in your great compassion blot out my offenses.
Wash me through and through from my wickedness
  and cleanse me from my sin.
For I know my transgressions,
  and my sin is ever before me.
Against you only have I sinned
  and done what is evil in your sight.
And so you are justified when you speak
  and upright in your judgment.
Indeed, I have been wicked from my birth,
  a sinner from my mother's womb.
For behold, you look for truth deep within me,
  and will make me understand wisdom secretly.
—Psalm 51:1–7

FIRST READING

Now the Lord is the Spirit, and where the Spirit of the Lord is, there is freedom. And all of us, with unveiled faces, seeing the glory of the Lord as though reflected in a mirror, are being transformed into the same image from one degree of glory to another; for this comes from the Lord, the Spirit.
  —2 Corinthians 3:17–18

PSALM

Retribue servo tuo

Deal bountifully with your servant,
  that I may live and keep your word.
Open my eyes, that I may see
  the wonders of your law.
I am a stranger here on earth;
  do not hide your commandments from me.
My soul is consumed at all times
  with longing for your judgments.

You have rebuked the insolent;
   cursed are they who stray from your commandments!
Turn from me shame and rebuke,
   for I have kept your decrees.
Even though rulers sit and plot against me,
   I will meditate on your statutes.
For your decrees are my delight,
   and they are my counselors.

   My soul cleaves to the dust;
   give me life according to your word.
I have confessed my ways, and you answered me;
   instruct me in your statutes.
Make me understand the way of your commandments,
   that I may meditate on your marvelous works.
My soul melts away for sorrow;
   strengthen me according to your word.
Take from me the way of lying;
   let me find grace through your law.
I have chosen the way of faithfulness;
   I have set your judgments before me.
I hold fast to your decrees;
   O LORD, let me not be put to shame.
I will run the way of your commandments,
   for you have set my heart at liberty.
—Psalm 119:17–32

GOSPEL READING

Hear the Word of the Lord: Jesus said, "My sheep hear my voice. I know them, and they follow me. I give them eternal life, and they will never perish. No one will snatch them out of my hand. What my Father has given me is greater than all else, and no one can snatch it out of the Father's hand."

   —John 10:27–29

Silence

PRAYERS OF THE SAINTS

O God, in whom is the well of life, and

in whose light we may see light:

increase in us, we ask, the shine of divine knowledge,

that we may reach your fountain.

Impart to our thirsting souls the drink of life, and

restore to our darkened minds the light of heaven.

—Mozarabic Sacramentary

COLLECT

May Holy Wisdom

rise like a fine mist among us.

She is the radiance that reflects

eternal light,

and a mirror of the working of God.

She is one,

and makes all things new,

entering holy souls

making them the friends of God. Amen.[36]

Evening Prayer, Wednesday
(Theme/Intent: Listening with the Heart)

PREPARATION

For God alone my soul in silence waits;

from him comes my salvation.

—Psalm 62:1

GOSPEL SENTENCE

Our Lord Jesus Christ says: Blessed are those who have not seen and yet believe.

—John 20:29

Silence

CONFESSION

Have mercy on me, O God, according to your loving-kindness;
  in your great compassion blot out my offenses.
Purge me from my sin, and I shall be pure;
  wash me, and I shall be clean indeed.
Make me hear of joy and gladness,
  that the body you have broken may rejoice.
Hide your face from my sins
  and blot out all my iniquities.
Create in me a clean heart, O God,
  and renew a right spirit within me.
Cast me not away from your presence
  and take not your holy Spirit from me.
Give me the joy of your saving help again
  and sustain me with your bountiful Spirit.
I shall teach your ways to the wicked,
  and sinners shall return to you.
Deliver me from death, O God,
  and my tongue shall sing of your righteousness,
  O God of my salvation.
Open my lips, O Lord,
  and my mouth shall proclaim your praise.
Had you desired it, I would have offered sacrifice,
  but you take no delight in burnt-offerings.
The sacrifice of God is a troubled spirit;
  a broken and contrite heart, O God, you will not despise.
Be favorable and gracious to Zion,
  and rebuild the walls of Jerusalem.
—Psalm 51:1, 8–19

FIRST READING

Hear the word of the LORD, O nations, and declare it in the coastlands far away; say, "He who scattered Israel will gather him, and will keep him as a shepherd a flock." For the LORD has ransomed Jacob, and has redeemed him from hands too strong for him. They shall come and sing aloud on the height of Zion, and they shall be radiant over the goodness of the LORD, over the grain, the wine, and the oil, and over the young of the flock and the herd; their life shall become like a watered garden, and they shall never languish again. Then shall the young women rejoice in the dance, and the young men and the old shall be merry. I will turn their mourning into joy, I will comfort them, and give them gladness for sorrow. I will give the priests their fill of fatness, and my people shall be satisfied with my bounty, says the LORD.

—Jeremiah 31:10–14

PSALM

Quemadmodum

As the deer longs for the water-brooks,
    so longs my soul for you, O God.
My soul is athirst for God, athirst for the living God;
    when shall I come to appear before the presence of God?
My tears have been my food day and night,
    while all day long they say to me,
    "Where now is your God?"
I pour out my soul when I think on these things:
    how I went with the multitude and led them into the house of God,
With the voice of praise and thanksgiving,
    among those who keep holy-day.
Why are you so full of heaviness, O my soul?
    and why are you so disquieted within me?
Put your trust in God;
    for I will yet give thanks to him,
    who is the help of my countenance, and my God.

—Psalm 42:1–7

GOSPEL READING

Hear the Word of the Lord: Jesus said, "I say to you: Ask, and it will be given to you; search, and you will find; knock, and the door will be opened to you. For everyone who asks receives; everyone who searches finds; everyone who knocks will have the door opened. What father among you, if his son asked for a fish, would hand him a snake? Or if he asked for an egg, hand him a scorpion? If you then, evil as you are, know how to give your children what is good, how much more will the heavenly Father give the Holy Spirit to those who ask him!"

—Luke 11:9–13

Silence

PRAYERS OF THE SAINTS

I would like the angels of Heaven to be among us. I would like an abundance of peace. I would like vessels full of charity and rich treasures of mercy. I would like cheerfulness to preside over all people, and I would like Jesus to be present. I would like the three Marys of illustrious renown to be with us, and I would like the friends of Heaven to be gathered around us from all over and forever. Amen.

—St. Brigid (d. 525)

COLLECT

Now, in the name of God,
who chose you and set you apart
from the time when you were in
your mother's womb, and by His grace
revealed his Son to you:
Preach with your lives,
and when necessary,
use words.
Amen.[37]

Morning Prayer, Thursday
(Theme/Intent: Adoring Christ)

PREPARATION

I bend my knee
to the Father of our Lord Jesus Christ.
Through the prayers of our glorious
Virgin Mary, Christ's holy mother,
and of our blessed father Francis and all of the saints,
may the Lord who has given us
such a good beginning
increase the gift and the blessing
and our final perseverance together.
Amen.
—Clare of Assisi[38]

GOSPEL SENTENCE

Our Lord Jesus Christ says: How blessed are the poor in spirit: the kingdom of Heaven is theirs. Blessed are the pure in heart: they shall see God.
—Matthew 5:3, 8

Silence

CONFESSION

Have mercy on me, O God, according to your loving-kindness;
    in your great compassion blot out my offenses.
Wash me through and through from my wickedness
    and cleanse me from my sin.
For I know my transgressions,
    and my sin is ever before me.
Against you only have I sinned
    and done what is evil in your sight.
And so you are justified when you speak
    and upright in your judgment.

Indeed, I have been wicked from my birth,
   a sinner from my mother's womb.
For behold, you look for truth deep within me,
   and will make me understand wisdom secretly.
—Psalm 51:1–7

FIRST READING

Of this gospel I have become a servant according to the gift of God's grace that was given me by the working of his power. . . . For this reason I bow my knees before the Father, from whom every family in heaven and on earth takes its name. I pray that, according to the riches of his glory, he may grant that you may be strengthened in your inner being with power through his Spirit, and that Christ may dwell in your hearts through faith, as you are being rooted and grounded in love. I pray that you may have the power to comprehend, with all the saints, what is the breadth and length and height and depth, and to know the love of Christ that surpasses knowledge, so that you may be filled with all the fullness of God.
   —Ephesians 3:7, 14–19

PSALM

Hide your face from my sins
   and blot out all my iniquities.
Create in me a clean heart, O God,
   and renew a right spirit within me.
Cast me not away from your presence
   and take not your holy Spirit from me.
Deliver me from death, O God,
   and my tongue shall sing of your righteousness,
   O God of my salvation.
Open my lips, O Lord,
   and my mouth shall proclaim your praise.
Had you desired it, I would have offered sacrifice,
   but you take no delight in burnt-offerings.
—Psalm 51:10–12, 15–17

GOSPEL READING

Hear the Word of the Lord: Now as they went on their way, he entered a certain village, where a woman named Martha welcomed him into her home. She had a sister named Mary, who sat at the Lord's feet and listened to what he was saying. But Martha was distracted by her many tasks; so she came to him and asked, "Lord, do you not care that my sister has left me to do all the work by myself? Tell her then to help me." But the Lord answered her, "Martha, Martha, you are worried and distracted by many things; there is need of only one thing. Mary has chosen the better part."

—Luke 10:39–42a (NRSV)

Silence

PRAYERS OF THE SAINTS

Pierce my soul, sweet Lord Jesus, with the most joyous and wholesome wound of your love, and with calm, true, and holy love. Make my soul to languish and melt with love and longing for you, yearn for you and for your courts, longing to be dissolved with you. May my heart always hunger after and feed on you. May it always thirst for you, the fountain of life, of all wisdom and knowledge, of eternal light, a torrent of pleasure, the house of God. You alone will be my hope, my confidence, riches, delight, pleasure, joy, rest, peace, sweetness, food, luxury, refuge, help, wisdom, and treasure. In you will my soul and heart ever be fixed and firm, immovable. Amen.

—St. Bonaventure (d. 1274)

COLLECT

Holy One,
fill us with reverence and joy,
as your spirit withdraws
little by little
from what is worldly to a more fiery longing for God.
And may we turn away from the fleeting things
that keep us from drawing near
to the solid land of prayer.[39]

Evening Prayer, Thursday
(Theme/Intent: Adoring Christ)

PREPARATION

Incline your merciful ears, Lord,
and illuminate the darkness of our hearts by the light
of your visitation.
Amen.
—Gelasian Sacramentary

GOSPEL SENTENCE

Our Lord Jesus Christ says: God is spirit, and those who worship must
worship in spirit and truth.
—John 4:24

Silence

CONFESSION

Have mercy on me, O God, according to your loving-kindness;
  in your great compassion blot out my offenses.
Purge me from my sin, and I shall be pure;
  wash me, and I shall be clean indeed.
Make me hear of joy and gladness,
  that the body you have broken may rejoice.
Hide your face from my sins
  and blot out all my iniquities.
Create in me a clean heart, O God,
  and renew a right spirit within me.
Cast me not away from your presence
  and take not your holy Spirit from me.
Give me the joy of your saving help again
  and sustain me with your bountiful Spirit.
I shall teach your ways to the wicked,
  and sinners shall return to you.
Deliver me from death, O God,
  and my tongue shall sing of your righteousness,
  O God of my salvation.

Open my lips, O Lord,
  and my mouth shall proclaim your praise.
Had you desired it, I would have offered sacrifice,
  but you take no delight in burnt-offerings.
The sacrifice of God is a troubled spirit;
  a broken and contrite heart, O God, you will not despise.
Be favorable and gracious to Zion,
  and rebuild the walls of Jerusalem.
—Psalm 51:1, 8–19

FIRST READING

For wisdom is more mobile than any motion; because of her pureness she pervades and penetrates all things. For she is a breath of the power of God, and a pure emanation of the glory of the Almighty; therefore nothing defiled gains entrance into her. For she is a reflection of the working of God, and an image of his goodness.
  —Wisdom of Solomon 7:24–26

PSALM

Conserva me, Domine

Protect me, O God, for I take refuge in you;
    I have said to the LORD, "You are my Lord,
    my good above all other."
All my delight is upon the godly that are in the land,
    upon those who are noble among the people.
O LORD, you are my portion and my cup;
    it is you who uphold my lot.
My boundaries enclose a pleasant land;
    indeed, I have a goodly heritage.
I will bless the LORD who gives me counsel;
    my heart teaches me, night after night.
I have set the LORD always before me;
    because he is at my right hand I shall not fall.
My heart, therefore, is glad, and my spirit rejoices;
    my body also shall rest in hope.

For you will not abandon me to the grave,

> nor let your holy one see the Pit.

You will show me the path of life;

> in your presence there is fullness of joy,

> and in your right hand are pleasures for evermore.

—Psalm 16:1–2, 5–11

GOSPEL READING

Hear the Word of the Lord: Jesus said, "Do not let your hearts be troubled. You trust in God, trust also in me. In my Father's house there are many places to live in; otherwise I would have told you. I am going now to prepare a place for you, and after I have gone and prepared you a place, I shall return to take you to myself, so that you may be with me where I am. You know the way to the place where I am going."

—John 14:1–4

Silence

PRAYERS OF THE SAINTS

I adore, I venerate, I glory in the holy cross, and in our merciful Lord and what he has done for us. By you, hell is spoiled; its mouth is closed to the redeemed. By you, demons are afraid, restrained, and defeated. By you, the whole world is renewed and made beautiful.

—St. Anselm (d. 1109)[40]

Collect
O God,
unworthy servants of Christ as we are,
may we sing a new song
in the presence of your holy presence
before your very throne,
and follow the Lamb of God
wherever he goes.
Amen.[41]

Morning Prayer, Friday
(Theme/Intent: True Discipleship)

PREPARATION

Most loving God, you set me apart before I was born and called me through grace. You revealed your blessed Son to me, so that I might bless you.[42]

GOSPEL SENTENCE

Our Lord Jesus Christ says: No one can be the slave of two masters: he will either hate the first and love the second, or be attached to the first and despise the second.

—Matthew 6:24a

Silence

CONFESSION

Have mercy on me, O God, according to your loving-kindness;
    in your great compassion blot out my offenses.
Wash me through and through from my wickedness
    and cleanse me from my sin.
For I know my transgressions,
    and my sin is ever before me.
Against you only have I sinned
    and done what is evil in your sight.
And so you are justified when you speak
    and upright in your judgment.
Indeed, I have been wicked from my birth,
    a sinner from my mother's womb.
For behold, you look for truth deep within me,
    and will make me understand wisdom secretly.
—Psalm 51:1–7

FIRST READING

Let the same mind be in you that was in Christ Jesus, who, though he was in the form of God, did not regard equality with God as something to be exploited, but emptied himself, taking the form of a slave, being born in human likeness. And being found in human form, he humbled himself and became obedient to the point of death—even death on a cross. Therefore God also highly exalted him and gave him the name that is above every name, so that at the name of Jesus every knee should bend, in heaven and on earth and under the earth, and every tongue should confess that Jesus Christ is Lord, to the glory of God the Father.

—Philippians 2:5–11

PSALM

Deus deorum

The LORD, the God of gods, has spoken;
> he has called the earth from the rising of the sun to
> its setting.
Out of Zion, perfect in its beauty,
> God reveals himself in glory.
Our God will come and will not keep silence;
> before him there is a consuming flame,
> and round about him a raging storm.
He calls the heavens and the earth from above
> to witness the judgment of his people.
"Gather before me my loyal followers,
> those who have made a covenant with me
> and sealed it with sacrifice."
Let the heavens declare the rightness of his cause;
> for God himself is judge.
"Offer to God a sacrifice of thanksgiving
> and make good your vows to the Most High.
Call upon me in the day of trouble;
> I will deliver you, and you shall honor me."

—Psalm 50:1–6, 14–15

GOSPEL READING

Hear the Word of the Lord: When Jesus saw the crowd all about him he gave orders to leave for the other side. One of the scribes then came up and said to him, "Master, I will follow you wherever you go." Jesus said, "Foxes have holes and the birds of the air have nests, but the Son of man has nowhere to lay his head." Another man, one of the disciples, said to him, "Lord, let me go and bury my father first." But Jesus said, "Follow me, and leave the dead to bury their dead." And when he got into the boat, his disciples followed him. A windstorm arose on the sea, so great that the boat was being swamped by the waves; but he was asleep. And they went and woke him up, saying, "Lord, save us! We are perishing!" And he said to them, "Why are you afraid, you of little faith?" Then he got up and rebuked the winds and the sea; and there was a dead calm. They were amazed, saying, "What sort of man is this, that even the winds and the sea obey him?"

—Matthew 8:18–27

Silence

PRAYERS OF THE SAINTS
"Make Your Prayer Like a Mother"
A prayer is surely a mother when it conceives virtues by the love of God, and brings them forth in the love of neighbors. Where do you show love, faith, hope, and humility? In prayer.

Mental prayer is the motherhood of prayer. By mental prayer the soul receives the reward for the labors she underwent in her imperfect vocal prayer. Then she tastes the milk of faithful prayer. She rises above herself— that is, above the gross impulse of the senses—and with angelic mind unites herself with God by force of love, and sees and knows with the light of thought, clothing herself with truth.

—St. Catherine of Siena (d. 1380)[43]

COLLECT

Give strength, O Lord, to those who see you,
and continually pour into their souls the
holy desire of seeking you;
that they who long to see your face may not crave the
world's pernicious pleasure.
Amen.

—Mozarabic Sacramentary

Evening Prayer, Friday
(*Theme/Intent: True Discipleship*)

PREPARATION

You are the Holy One, image of the invisible God;
before all things, and in whom all things hold together.
Amen.[44]

GOSPEL SENTENCE

Our Lord Jesus Christ says: Enter by the narrow gate, since the road that
leads to destruction is wide and spacious, and many take it; but it is a
narrow gate and a hard road that leads to life, and only a few find it.

—Matthew 7:13–14

Silence

CONFESSION

Have mercy on me, O God, according to your loving-kindness;
  in your great compassion blot out my offenses.
Purge me from my sin, and I shall be pure;
  wash me, and I shall be clean indeed.
Make me hear of joy and gladness,
  that the body you have broken may rejoice.
Hide your face from my sins
  and blot out all my iniquities.

Create in me a clean heart, O God,
  and renew a right spirit within me.
Cast me not away from your presence
  and take not your holy Spirit from me.
Give me the joy of your saving help again
  and sustain me with your bountiful Spirit.
I shall teach your ways to the wicked,
  and sinners shall return to you.
Deliver me from death, O God,
  and my tongue shall sing of your righteousness,
  O God of my salvation.
Open my lips, O Lord,
  and my mouth shall proclaim your praise.
Had you desired it, I would have offered sacrifice,
  but you take no delight in burnt-offerings.
The sacrifice of God is a troubled spirit;
  a broken and contrite heart, O God, you will not despise.
Be favorable and gracious to Zion,
  and rebuild the walls of Jerusalem.
—Psalm 51:1, 8–19

FIRST READING

I shall take you from among the nations, and gather you from every land, and bring you to your homeland. I shall sprinkle pure water over you, and you will be purified from everything that defiles you; I shall purify you from the taint of all your idols. I shall give you a new heart and put a new spirit within you; I shall remove the heart of stone from your body and give you a heart of flesh.

—Ezekiel 36:24–26 (REB)

PSALM

Deus noster refugium

God is our refuge and strength,

    a very present help in trouble.

Therefore we will not fear, though the earth be moved,

    and though the mountains be toppled into the

    depths of the sea;

Though its waters rage and foam,

    and though the mountains tremble at its tumult.

The LORD of hosts is with us;

    the God of Jacob is our stronghold.

There is a river whose streams make glad the city of God,

    the holy habitation of the Most High.

God is in the midst of her;

    she shall not be overthrown;

    God shall help her at the break of day.

The nations make much ado, and the kingdoms are shaken;

    God has spoken, and the earth shall melt away.

The LORD of hosts is with us;

    the God of Jacob is our stronghold.

Come now and look upon the works of the LORD,

    what awesome things he has done on earth.

It is he who makes war to cease in all the world;

    he breaks the bow, and shatters the spear,

    and burns the shields with fire.

"Be still, then, and know that I am God;

    I will be exalted among the nations;

    I will be exalted in the earth."

The LORD of hosts is with us;

    the God of Jacob is our stronghold.

—Psalm 46

GOSPEL READING

Hear the Word of the Lord: Jesus said, "The lamp of the body is the eye. It follows that if your eye is clear, your whole body will be filled with light. But if your eye is diseased, your whole body will be darkness. If then, the light inside you is darkened, what darkness that will be! No one can be the slave of two masters: he will either hate the first and love the second, or be attached to the first and despise the second. You cannot be the slave both of God and of money. That is why I am telling you not to worry about your life and what you are to eat, nor about your body and what you are to wear. Surely life is more than food, and the body more than clothing! Look at the birds in the sky. They do not sow or reap or gather into barns; yet your heavenly Father feeds them. Are you not worth much more than they are? Can any of you, however much you worry, add one single cubit to your span of life?"

—Matthew 6:22–27

Silence

PRAYERS OF THE SAINTS

St. Elizabeth often had visions of heaven as she prayed. One day in Lent, she recounted: "I saw the heavens opened, and Jesus leaning toward me in the most kind way, showing me his loving face. I was filled with indescribable joy; and then when his face was gone from my sight, I mourned. Then, he must have taken pity on me, for his face returned before my eyes. He said, 'If you wish to be with me, I will be with you.' And I replied, 'I want nothing to ever separate me from you!'"

—St. Elizabeth of Hungary (d. 1231)

COLLECT

Blessed Father,

may we show ourselves to be faithful.

Our effort here is brief,

the reward eternal.

May the excitements of the world,

vanish like a shadow,

and not disturb us.

Amen.

—St. Clare of Assisi[45]

Morning Prayer, Saturday
(Theme/Intent: Redefining Family)

PREPARATION

Set your heart on the concerns of your Father.

Open your mind to the truth of your Brother.

Listen for the promptings of your Spirit.

Amen.

GOSPEL SENTENCE

Our Lord Jesus Christ says: I shall no longer call you servants, because a servant does not know the master's business; I call you friends, because I have made known to you everything I have learnt from my Father.

—John 15:15

Silence

CONFESSION

Have mercy on me, O God, according to your loving-kindness;

in your great compassion blot out my offenses.

Wash me through and through from my wickedness

and cleanse me from my sin.

For I know my transgressions,

and my sin is ever before me.

Against you only have I sinned

and done what is evil in your sight.
And so you are justified when you speak
    and upright in your judgment.
Indeed, I have been wicked from my birth,
    a sinner from my mother's womb.
For behold, you look for truth deep within me,
    and will make me understand wisdom secretly.
—Psalm 51:1–7

FIRST READING

For just as the body is one and has many members, and all the members of the body, though many, are one body, so it is with Christ. For in the one Spirit we were all baptized into one body—Jews or Greeks, slaves or free—and we were all made to drink of one Spirit. Indeed, the body does not consist of one member but of many. If one member suffers, all suffer together with it; if one member is honored, all rejoice together with it.
    —1 Corinthians 12:12–14, 26

PSALM

Laudate Dominum

Hallelujah!
    Praise God in his holy temple;
        praise him in the firmament of his power.
Praise him for his mighty acts;
        praise him for his excellent greatness.
Praise him with the blast of the ram's-horn;
        praise him with lyre and harp.
Praise him with timbrel and dance;
        praise him with strings and pipe.
Praise him with resounding cymbals;
        praise him with loud-clanging cymbals.
Let everything that has breath
        praise the LORD.
Hallelujah!
—Psalm 150

GOSPEL READING

Hear the Word of the Lord: He was still speaking to the crowds when suddenly his mother and his brothers were standing outside and were anxious to have a word with him. But to the man who told him this Jesus replied, "Who is my mother? Who are my brothers?" And stretching out his hand towards his disciples he said, "Here are my mother and my brothers. Anyone who does the will of my Father in heaven is my brother and sister and mother."

—Matthew 12:46–50

Silence

PRAYERS OF THE SAINTS

Blessed lover of humanity, bless all your people. Send into our hearts the peace of heaven, and grant us also peace in this life. Let no sin prevail among us. Deliver those who are in trouble. Set captives free. Give hope to the hopeless and help to the helpless. Lift the fallen, for you are the haven of the shipwrecked.

—Liturgy of St. Mark

Collect

O God, poured out in all of creation,
enlighten us by the splendor of created things.
Give eloquence to our dumbness
that we may praise you.
Open our eyes and alert the ears of our spirit
so that in all creatures we may see, hear, praise, love,
and worship you.[46]

Evening Prayer, Saturday
(*Theme/Intent: Redefining Family*)

PREPARATION

Know this: The LORD himself is God; he himself has made us, and we
    are his; we are his people and the sheep of his pasture.

—Psalm 100:2

GOSPEL SENTENCE

Our Lord Jesus Christ says: Blessed are those who hunger and thirst for
uprightness: they shall have their fill. Blessed are the merciful: they shall
have mercy shown them.

—Matthew 5:6–7

Silence

CONFESSION

Have mercy on me, O God, according to your loving-kindness;
    in your great compassion blot out my offenses.
Purge me from my sin, and I shall be pure;
    wash me, and I shall be clean indeed.
Make me hear of joy and gladness,
    that the body you have broken may rejoice.
Hide your face from my sins
    and blot out all my iniquities.
Create in me a clean heart, O God,
    and renew a right spirit within me.
Cast me not away from your presence
    and take not your holy Spirit from me.
Give me the joy of your saving help again
    and sustain me with your bountiful Spirit.
I shall teach your ways to the wicked,
    and sinners shall return to you.
Deliver me from death, O God,
    and my tongue shall sing of your righteousness,
        O God of my salvation.

Open my lips, O Lord,
  and my mouth shall proclaim your praise.
Had you desired it, I would have offered sacrifice,
  but you take no delight in burnt-offerings.
The sacrifice of God is a troubled spirit;
  a broken and contrite heart, O God, you will not despise.
Be favorable and gracious to Zion,
  and rebuild the walls of Jerusalem.
—Psalm 51:1, 8–19

FIRST READING

I therefore, the prisoner in the Lord, beg you to lead a life worthy of the calling to which you have been called, with all humility and gentleness, with patience, bearing with one another in love, making every effort to maintain the unity of the Spirit in the bond of peace. There is one body and one Spirit, just as you were called to the one hope of your calling, one Lord, one faith, one baptism, one God and Father of all, who is above all and through all and in all.

  —Ephesians 4:1–6

PSALM

Ecce, quam bonum!

Oh, how good and pleasant it is,
  when brethren live together in unity!
It is like fine oil upon the head
  that runs down upon the beard,
Upon the beard of Aaron,
  and runs down upon the collar of his robe.
It is like the dew of Hermon
  that falls upon the hills of Zion.
For there the Lord has ordained the blessing:
  life for evermore.

—Psalm 133

GOSPEL READING

Hear the Word of the Lord: Then the mother of Zebedee's sons came with her sons to make a request of [Jesus], and bowed low. She said to him, "Promise that these two sons of mine may sit one at your right hand and the other at your left in your kingdom." Jesus answered, "You do not know what you are asking." When the other ten heard this they were indignant with the two brothers. But Jesus called them to him and said, "You know that among the gentiles the rulers lord it over them, and great men make their authority felt. Among you this is not to happen. No; anyone who wants to become great among you must be your servant, and anyone who wants to be first among you must be your slave, just as the Son of man came not to be served but to serve, and to give his life as a ransom for many."

—Matthew 20:20–22, 24–28

Silence

PRAYERS OF THE SAINTS

I beg you, in the name of the Lord, to always include me in your holy prayers. I am your servant, lowly as I am, and with the sisters of San Damiano, we are devoted to you in prayer. May we all experience the mercy of Jesus Christ, now, and the everlasting vision of heaven, to come.

—St. Clare of Assisi[47]

COLLECT
Heavenly Lord,
bless us,
who follow in the footsteps of your Son, the Christ;
bless us,
who listen to the leading of your sweet Spirit;
bless us,
who, with you, are ever-renewing the Creation.
Amen.

✸ ✸ ✸

* III *
OCCASIONAL PRAYERS OF ST. CLARE

On the Loveliness of Christ

She is happy who clings wholeheartedly to Him:
whose tender touch and kindness,
whose ever fresh remembrance and fragrance,
whose radiant visage and clarity,
continually shares heavenly joy with her and all of the citizens
of the heavenly city.
She is happy who clings wholeheartedly to Him!
—Clare of Assisi[48]

On Faithfulness to Ideals

Father of Mercies,
may we strive to always imitate the way
of holy simplicity, humility and poverty,
shown us by our father, Francis, and in our conversion by Christ.
Spread the fragrance of a good name,
from those who live faithfully according to your will.
May we love one another with the charity of Christ.
May the love that we have in our hearts show itself in our actions.
And may our love and example increase
love of God and charity for one another in all places.
Amen.
—Clare of Assisi[49]

Three More Collects for Faithfulness[50]

Graceful God, to whom we have promised ourselves until death: Let us rejoice in the strenuous paths of virtue. Guide us on the path of faithfulness, so that, at the end of our earthly journey, we may be crowned by you with the laurel of life. Amen.

God of light, eternal and bright-shining, do not allow the noises and shadows of this fleeting world confuse us. Do not allow the deceptions of the world to muddle us. Give us strength to willingly bear and face the evil that we encounter, and do not allow your provident goodness to puff us up. The faith that you promised us, God, faithfully render it, and we will repay you. Amen.

O God, through your blessed son, our Savior Jesus Christ, heaven beckons us. Our Lord made the path on which we, too, will follow him into glory. We seek to love Jesus, who was crucified, with our whole heart, and never allow his memory to escape our minds. Remind us and show us how to meditate always on the mysteries of the cross and the anguish of the mother standing under it. Amen.

—Clare of Assisi

The Office of the Five Wounds of Christ [51]

Thomas of Celano's *Legend of St. Clare* tells us that Clare prayed these prayers, taught to her by St. Francis himself. We do not know their origin, and the earliest edition of the text is only as old as the sixteenth century. It is the method of these prayers, rather than the actual words of them, that communicate most profoundly how intimately Francis and Clare sought to identify with the life of Christ.

Each short prayer is addressed to the crucified body of Christ from right to left, hand to foot, and concludes with the wound in his side.

To the Right Hand

Precious Lord Jesus, by this sacred wound you have granted me pardon for my sins. Give me the grace to venerate your precious death and these sacred wounds as I should, and grant that by your holy help I may humble my body enough to thank you for this great gift. Amen.

To the Left Hand

Sweet Lord Jesus, I praise you for the sacred wound of your left hand. You have shown me your mercy; now, I plead, change in me whatever is not pleasing to you. Free me from my enemies and make me worthy of your glory. Amen.

To the Right Foot

Honeyed Lord Jesus, I praise you for the sacred wound of your right foot. Keep me, your humble servant, in your perfect will and deliver me from difficulty. When my life must end, I pray that you welcome me into eternal joy. Amen.

To the Left Foot

Tender Lord Jesus, I praise you for the sacred wound of your left foot. I plead with you, most holy Christ, that I may deserve to receive the Sacrament of your sweet Body and Blood, with an intimate confession and perfect penance, before the day of my death. Amen.

To the Wound in His Side

Kind Lord Jesus, I praise you for the sacred wound in your side. By your bitter death, you have cleansed me. Now, strengthen me so that I may love you as I should. May I please you perfectly, now and always. Amen.

For an Increase in Franciscan Spiritual Values

Father of our Lord Jesus Christ, we bend our knees and we ask that through the prayers of the glorious Virgin Mary, the holy mother of Christ, and by Father Francis and all of the saints, may Christ, who has given us bountiful beginnings, increase our efforts more and more, and guide us to persevere in that original spirit. Amen.

—Clare of Assisi[52]

Clare's Blessings

May You Reflect the Glory of the Lord

May you reflect the glory of the Lord. Place your heart in the divine substance through contemplation. Transform your being into the image that we reflect, the Godhead Itself. Then, you will feel what love is. Then, you will feel the sweetness that is revealed to us through the Spirit, what no eye has seen and no ear has heard, the love that God has for His lovers.

—Clare of Assisi[53]

A Blessing of St. Francis

Made famous in St. Francis's letter to Brother Leo, written on Mt. La Verna in 1224 just after Francis's stigmata experience, the original is still preserved in Assisi today. Francis was simply quoting the Torah (Num. 6:24–26) in his fatherly message for Leo.

The LORD bless you and keep you;
the LORD make his face to shine upon you, and be gracious to you;
the LORD life up his countenance upon you, and give you peace.

From Clare's Final Words

The Simple Blessing of St. Clare [To be said upon waking.]
Blessed be you,
God,
who created me.

The Benediction of St. Clare
Now, go calmly in peace,
for you have a good escort.
He who created you
has sent the Holy Spirit who guards
you as a mother does tenderly
love her child.
Amen.[54]

Clare's Last Wish
O daughters,
can you see the
King of Glory
that I see?

OTHER PRAYERS

Devotion to the Virgin Mary

Saint Clare was greatly devoted to the Virgin Mary for many reasons. The Blessed Mother was the virgin of all virgins, and the Mother of God. Also, like St. Francis before her, Clare always sought to understand how we are called to birth God in our lives. Both Francis and Clare embraced the Mother of Jesus with tremendous love, as Thomas of Celano says in his second *Life of St. Francis*, because she made the Lord of Majesty into our brother.[55] Finally, Clare's movement was born on that eventful Monday evening during Holy Week—when she fled her family home and joined Francis and the first friars—in the little chapel known as St. Mary of the Angels, or Portiuncula. When she knelt for Francis to cut her long hair as an entrance into the monastic life, Clare was kneeling before an altar devoted to Mary.

The Magnificat

This remarkable Song of the Virgin Mary, first said by her just after the Annunciation, has been precious to Christians of all backgrounds for two thousand years. Clare and the first Poor Clares would have prayed it aloud each day.

My soul magnifies the Lord, and my spirit rejoices in God my Savior,
for he has looked with favor on the lowliness of his servant.
Surely, from now on all generations will call me blessed;
for the Mighty One has done great things for me,
and holy is his name.
His mercy is for those who fear him from generation to generation.
He has shown strength with his arm;
he has scattered the proud in the thoughts of their hearts.
He has brought down the powerful from their thrones,
and lifted up the lowly;
he has filled the hungry with good things,

and sent the rich away empty.
He has helped his servant Israel, in remembrance of his mercy,
according to the promise he made to our ancestors,
to Abraham and to his descendants forever.
—Luke 1:46–55

The Memorare

Another popular, medieval prayer to the Virgin, the *Memorare* is often associated with St. Bernard of Clairvaux, but its author is actually unknown. *Memorare* is Latin for the first word, "remember."

Remember, O most gracious Virgin Mary,
that never was it known that anyone who fled to your protection,
implored your help, or sought your intercession
was left unaided by you.
Inspired with this confidence, I fly to you,
Mary, Virgin of virgins, Mother of Jesus Christ;
to you do I come; before you I stand,
sinful, sorrowful and trembling.
O Mistress of the World and Mother of the Word Incarnate,
despise not my petitions,
but in your mercy hear and answer wretched me
crying to you in this vale of tears.
Be near me, I ask you, in all my necessities,
now and always, and especially at the hour of my death.
O clement, o loving, o sweet Virgin Mary.
Amen.

Hail, Lady, Holy Queen

Thomas of Celano's second *Life of St. Francis* refers to the saint's love for the Virgin Mary because "she made the Lord of Majesty our brother." In other words, Mary is our mother too. In the second portion of this prayer of devotion, Francis summarizes some of the most popular medieval metaphors for the Virgin.

Hail, Lady, holy Queen,
holy Mother of God,
virgin made church,
chosen by the Father in heaven,
consecrated by His beloved Son,
through the Holy Spirit, the Paraclete,
in whom there was and always will be
grace abounding and all goodness.

Hail, God's palace,
God's tabernacle,
God's home,
God's robe,
God's servant!
Hail, God's Mother!

Francis's Psalm for Those Who Have Gone Before Us

In chapter 3 of his earliest Rule, St. Francis instructs his brothers on how and what to pray. Among other psalms, he asks them to say Psalm 130, or "Out of the Depths," along with the Our Father each day for the deceased. This psalm is a lovely, short, ancient psalm of David and an important piece of the Franciscan liturgical tradition. Reflecting upon death and the fleetingness of life, it is most appropriate to pray, "My soul waits for the LORD, more than watchmen for the morning, more than watchmen for the morning."

Out of the depths have I called to you, O LORD;
    LORD, hear my voice;
let your ears consider well the voice of my supplication.
If you, LORD, were to note what is done amiss,
    O Lord, who could stand?
For there is forgiveness with you;
    therefore you shall be feared.
I wait for the LORD; my soul waits for him;
    in his word is my hope.

My soul waits for the LORD,
   more than watchmen for the morning,
   more than watchmen for the morning.
O Israel, wait for the LORD,
   for with the LORD there is mercy;
With him there is plenteous redemption,
   and he shall redeem Israel from all their sins.

Francis's Song, "The Canticle of the Creatures"

Francis's most famous piece of writing bears repeating here for how it relates to Clare's life. Francis wrote this hymn, taught his friends to sing it, and then asked them to sing it to him on his deathbed. It is also important to realize that he composed the Canticle while visiting Clare at San Damiano. Francis was in pain, on his way to visiting a physician in the nearby town of Rieti, when he asked his brothers to take him to see Clare on the way. She prepared a comfortable place for him in the garden, and it is there that Francis wrote this song. It marks the beginning of our modern understanding of how earth and heaven join; it also speaks to how all are called to mediate justice and peace, curb the power of the world, and finally, embrace death as a natural part of life.

O most high, almighty, good Lord God,
   to you belong praise, glory, honor, and all blessing!
Praised be my Lord God with all your creatures,
   and especially our Brother Sun,
who brings us the day and who brings us the light.
Fair is he and shines with a very great splendor:
O Lord, he signifies you to us!
Praised be you, Most High, for Sister Moon and the Stars,
You set them in the heavens, making them so
bright, luminous, and fine.
Praised be my Lord for our Brother Wind,
and for air and cloud, calms and all weather
through which you uphold life in all creatures.
Praised be my Lord for our Sister Water,

who is very useful to us and humble
and precious and clean.
Praised be my Lord for our Brother Fire,
through whom you give us light in the darkness;
and he is bright and pleasant and very mighty
and strong.
Praised be my Lord for our Mother Earth,
who does sustain us and keep us,
and brings forth many fruits and flowers
of many colors, and grass.
Praised be my Lord for all those who pardon one
another for your sake,
and who endure weakness and tribulation;
blessed are they who peaceably endure, for you,
O most High, shall give them a crown.
Praised be my Lord for our Sister Death of the Body,
from whom no one can escape.
Woe to those who die in mortal sin.
Blessed are they who are found walking by your
most holy will, for the second death shall have no
power to do them harm.
Praise and bless the Lord, and give thanks to him
and serve him with great humility.

Short Prayer Poems of Jacopone of Todi

Jacopone of Todi was one of the most important Franciscan friars from the century after St. Francis. His songs of love are the essence of the early Franciscan spirit. In the years after St. Clare's death, Jacopone's verses galvanized the movement known as the "Spirituals"—those who taught extreme poverty and simplicity in imitation of Francis and Clare.

His *Laude* poems anticipate the personal, confessional, spiritual struggling of modern writers, and his long poem, *Donna del Paradiso*, portrays Mary the Mother of God with great sensitivity. The latter became the most loved Italian poem of the pre-Renaissance period.

Selections from Jacopone's Laude[56]

Song of the Ecstatic Soul
The activity of the mind
is lulled to rest;
    rapt in God,
        it can no longer find itself.

Being so deeply engulfed
in that ocean,
now it can find no place
    to begin.

Of itself it cannot think,
nor can it say what it is like:
    because transformed,
        it has another garment.

All its perceptions
have gone forth
    to gaze upon the Good,
        and contemplate Beauty which has no likeness.

Secrets of the Mystic Life
The doors are flung wide:
When we are joined to God,
    we possess
    all that is in Him.

We feel what has never been felt,
see what we have not known,
    possess what we did not believe,
    and taste, though not savor.

Since the soul is entirely lost
to itself,
 it possesses a height
 of unmeasured perfection.

Since it has not kept
in itself the mixture
 of any other thing,
 it has received in abundance.

Goodness Unimagined
Above all other language—love,
goodness unimagined,
 light without measure
 shines in my heart.

Song of a Soul
O why did you create me,
great God of Heaven above?
 Redeem me, and await me,
 through Jesus Christ my love.

See the Bloom
When Christ is grafted on the spray,
All the withered wood is cut away.
See the bloom springing from decay!
Changed into a wonderful unity.

And so, I live—yet not my self alone;
I am me, yet I am not mine own.
And this change, cross-wise, obscure, unknown—
Words cannot tell.

What Poverty Has
Poverty has nothing in her hand,
nothing craved, in sea, or sky, or land;
she has the Universe at her command.
In the heart of freedom ever-dwelling.

To Love
Born of fire divine,
spun of laughter,
wholly given,
never done.

Running over,
gently entering,
Thy table is
long and wide.

How welcome
we feel
who enter in.

Jacopone's verse prayers are always returning to the central themes of Sts. Francis and Clare. This one imagines that we, too, stand before the Nativity. The blessing promised in the last stanza is an example of the warmth of Franciscan spirituality.

Your Heart's Desire
All you sinners, erring throng,
serving evil lords so long,
come and hail the Infant Birth!

Even humble men, and innocent,
upright women, the diligent,
come before Him, come and sing.

Do not let Him in vain entreat,
come and kneel before His feet,
giving glory to the King.

You shall have your heart's desire,
tasting, with the heavenly choir,
feasts of Love eternally.

Stabat Mater Dolorosa

This prayer poem has been an important part of Franciscan spirituality since it was first written by Jacopone of Todi in the century after St. Clare's death. Both Sts. Francis and Clare consciously modeled their lives after Christ and his Blessed Mother; they not only had a devotion to Mary but they also sought to imitate her.

Stabat Mater Dolorosa[57]
The grieving mother stood weeping,
Near the cross her station keeping
Whereon hung her Son and Lord;
Through whose spirit sympathizing,
Sorrowing and agonizing,
Also passed the cruel sword.

Oh! how mournful and distressed
Was that favored and most blessed
Mother of the only Son,
Trembling, grieving, bosom heaving,
While perceiving, scarce believing,
Pains of that Illustrious One!

Who the man, who, called a brother.
Would not weep, saw he Christ's mother
In such deep distress and wild?
Who could not sad tribute render
Witnessing that mother tender
Agonizing with her child?

For his people's sins atoning,
Him she saw in torments groaning,
Given to the scourger's rod;
Saw her darling offspring dying,
Desolate, forsaken, crying.
Yield his spirit up to God.

Make me feel thy sorrow's power,
That with thee I tears may shower,
Tender mother, fount of love!
Make my heart with love unceasing
Burn toward Christ the Lord, that pleasing
I may be to him above.

Holy mother, this be granted,
That the slain one's wounds be planted
Firmly in my heart to bide.
Of him wounded, all astounded—
Depths unbounded for me sounded—
All the pangs with me divide.

Make me weep with thee in union;
With the Crucified, communion
In his grief and suffering give;
Near the cross, with tears unfailing,
I would join thee in thy wailing
Here as long as I shall live.

Maid of maidens, all excelling!
Be not bitter, me repelling;
Make thou me a mourner too;
Make me bear about Christ's dying,
Share his passion, shame defying;
All his wounds in me renew.

Wound for wound be there created;
With the cross intoxicated
For thy Son's dear sake, I pray—
May I, fired with pure affection,
Virgin, have through thee protection
In the solemn Judgment Day.

Let me by the cross be warded,
By the death of Christ be guarded,
Nourished by divine supplies.
When the body death hath riven,
Grant that to the soul be given
Glories bright of Paradise.

❋ V ❋

SOURCES FOR LITERARY AND HISTORICAL CONTEXT

A Very Brief Life of St. Agnes of Rome (d. 304)

Both St. Ambrose and St. Augustine, two of the Latin church fathers, speak of St. Agnes of Rome in their writings. They tell us that St. Agnes was only thirteen when she was martyred, probably in the year 304, during the hideous persecutions of the Roman emperor Diocletian. Hers is one of the first stories of a virgin martyr.

Early Christian tradition is replete with stories such as Agnes's, and these stories were terribly important to St. Clare and her own understanding of embracing Christ. Agnes spurned the offers of men who were drawn only by her physical beauty, and she opted instead for a "marriage" to Christ. Agnes's suitors were angered and humiliated by her refusals of marriage, and so they brought accusations against her for being a Christian to the local governor.

Father Alban Butler, the great eighteenth-century chronicler of saints' lives, recounts what happened next:

> The judge at first employed the mildest expressions and most seductive promises, to which Agnes paid no regard, repeating always that she could have no other spouse but Jesus Christ. He then made use of threats, but found her endowed with a masculine courage, and even eager to suffer torment and death. At last terrible fires were made, and iron hooks, racks and other instruments of torture displayed before her, with threats of immediate execution. The heroic child surveyed them undismayed, and made good cheer in the presence of the fierce and cruel executioners. . . .
>
> The governor, seeing his measures ineffectual, said he would send her to a house of prostitution, where what she prized so highly should be exposed to the insults of the brutal and licentious youth of Rome. Agnes answered that Jesus Christ was too jealous of the purity of His chosen ones to suffer it to be violated in such a

manner, for He was their defender and protector. "You may," said she, "stain your sword with my blood, but you will never be able to profane my body, consecrated to Christ." The governor was so incensed at this that he ordered her to be immediately led to the place of shame with liberty to all to abuse her person at pleasure.

Many young profligates ran thither, full of wicked desires, but were seized with such awe at the sight of the saint that they durst not approach her; one only excepted, who, attempting to be rude to her, was that very instant, by a flash, as it were of lightning from Heaven, struck blind, and fell trembling to the ground. His companions, terrified, took him up and carried him to Agnes, who was singing hymns of praise to Christ, her protector. The virgin by prayer restored his sight and his health.

[Then,] the governor . . . was highly exasperated to see himself set at defiance by one of her tender age and sex. . . . He condemned her to be beheaded. Agnes, filled with joy on hearing this sentence, "went to the place of execution more cheerfully," says St. Ambrose, "than others go to their wedding." The spectators shed tears to see this beautiful child loaded with fetters, and offering herself fearlessly to the sword of the executioner, who with trembling hand cut off her head at one stroke. Her body was buried at a short distance from Rome, beside the Nomentan road.

Less than fifty years later, a basilica was erected on the site of Agnes's burial site in Rome, under the supervision of Constantina, daughter of the first Christian Roman emperor, Constantine. The fame of Agnes spread rapidly. She was recognized as a martyr/saint throughout the Middle Ages. Her feast day is January 21.

The heroic story of St. Agnes of Rome inspired many early Franciscan women. Clare's sister was given the name Agnes, and when she joined Clare sixteen days after Clare's own conversion, Agnes, too, became a Franciscan. Similarly, the disciple with whom Clare often corresponded, Agnes of Prague, took St. Agnes as her patron saint and was, in turn, herself canonized in 1989 by Pope John Paul II.

SISTER CLARE
A "Little Play" by Laurence Housman

Laurence Housman lived one hundred years ago and wrote dozens of one-act plays about events in the life of St. Francis of Assisi. They were published singly beginning in 1922, and then eventually in three small volumes. This collection was called *Little Plays of Saint Francis: Complete Edition* (1935) and included the play that follows, *Sister Clare*.

The freshness and vitality of *Sister Clare* remains unaltered today. The play captures the simplicity and joy of the early Franciscan movement in ways that are not possible in either contemporary biographies or medieval texts. Francis and Clare play the key parts in the drama, but Brother Juniper also offers some spontaneous and characteristic moments of foolishness. The result is a timeless and moving portrait of what may have happened on that first night of Clare's joining the friars at Portiuncula. I have only slightly modernized the language of the original, and I have cut the length by approximately one quarter.

SISTER CLARE
By Laurence Housman

THE SETTING: In a bare, stable-like interior, Brother Juniper sits by a fire of glowing embers, his head dropping with sleep. To one side of the fire is a rough bench, to the other a recessed corn-bin with half-doors, the upper of which stands ajar. Opposite the fireplace, stairs lead up to a hayloft. Beside the staircase is a door into another chamber; the outer door is at the back. From within comes Brother Bernard carrying a light, and stands for a moment watching Brother Juniper's jerky efforts to keep awake.

BERNARD: Why aren't you in bed, brother?

JUNIPER: The father said I was to wait up.

BERNARD: Oh? Where is he?

JUNIPER: Gone into the forest to fetch wood.

BERNARD: At this time of night? What for?

JUNIPER: Brother Fire sent him for it. I heard 'em talking. The father said: "Brother Fire, it's late. Won't you go to sleep?" "No," said Brother Fire, and stuck out his tongue. "I won't." "What, you're staying awake?" said the father. "I am," he said, and again stuck out his tongue. So Brother Fire got his way and the father's gone to fetch wood for him.

BERNARD: Has he been gone long?

JUNIPER: If I've been sleeping, he perhaps has. [He turns toward the fire.] May you end!— sending the father out like that, on a cold night!

BERNARD: If the father doesn't mind, why should you?

JUNIPER: If we waited all minding until the father did, we might never mind anything!

BERNARD: Very true, brother. But why did you have to stay up after all the others?

JUNIPER: He said we had a friend coming, and if he wasn't back, Brother Fire and I were to be here, to make things comfortable.

BERNARD *[smiling]*: So Brother Fire had a reason?

JUNIPER: Sure! I never thought of it. There! *[To the fire:]* I forgive you, then! *[He puts on the last log.]* Oh! When Father Francis comes back, he'll find me sitting up in spirit, maybe, but in the body I will be—*[a snore comes from the loft]*—like the rest of us up there.

[Falling to sleep, Juniper jerks, and is then awake again.]

BERNARD *[going toward the stairs]:*   God give you good sleep, Brother Juniper.

JUNIPER: Yes, if God sends it to me! But more times than not it seems to come from the Devil.

BERNARD: Why do you say that?

JUNIPER: Because when I'm asleep, I dream of things I should not.

BERNARD: So do we all. But on waking, finding that they are not real, we forget them.

JUNIPER: Yeah? Do we? I wish I did. Oh, women are my mischief! I came here to be away from them. But Lord! When you go to sleep there's generally one waiting for you.

BERNARD: Come, come, brother.

JUNIPER: It is so! Have you heard, brother, how one day, just through lying asleep on his side—or his back, maybe—Adam got loose of a rib and it turned into a woman?

BERNARD: Surely.

JUNIPER: So that's how sin came into the world—all because of Adam's sleeping.

BERNARD: God caused him to sleep, brother.

JUNIPER: Did he? But he didn't wake when God called him. "Mother Eve," Brother Elias told us her name was; and a good name too, if it stands for evil. Oh, women are the root of all mischief. You know that yourself, Brother Bernard.

BERNARD: I have known it, brother. God rest you to peace, and keep us all from temptation. *[He goes upstairs, and for a few moments you see his light over the partition. Then, the light goes out and from above comes only the restful sound of slumber.]*

JUNIPER: Temptation? Oh, I don't mind temptation, when it's what you call reasonable. But it's the unreasonableness of it that takes me where I'm weakest. Lord! If a temptation of that kind were to come here now, I couldn't answer for myself—nor for her either. *[To the fire]* Well, are you keeping awake, or must I? There's no reason for the two of us doing it. So long as I wait up, that's all he told me . . . "Wait up," he said, "wait up." But when the weight of waiting gets on your eyes, it's like saying "Up!" to a dead donkey, for all the heed they give to you. *[And so, gently admonishing himself, he drops off to sleep, while from the loft above come the peaceful snores of the brothers.]*

[Then, the door opens. Cloaked and hooded, a young girl enters. There, with all the fresh beauty of saint or sinner, stands Sister Clare, as, from this day on, she is destined to be known. Advancing, she then stops and looks at the sleeping Juniper.]

CLARE: Brother, may I come in and be with you?

[Juniper wakes with a start, turns, stares at the apparition, crosses himself with both hands, springs convulsively to his feet, and runs in haste to the corn-bin. He jumps in and closes the door.]

[Unamused and unperturbed, Clare stands looking after him, then moves to the fire and, stretching out her hands, crouches to warm herself. But almost at once, her hands fall from weariness. With a deep sigh of exhaustion she sinks down and lets her head fall back on the bench.]

[Brother Juniper, after a while, peeps out, and not looking low enough believes that she is gone. He cautiously puts forth a leg. In doing so, he upsets a stool. Clare opens her eyes and turns. Juniper whips back into hiding. Quietly but resolutely, without any movement or speech, she begins to dig him out.]

CLARE: Brother . . . brother . . . brother.

[Unable to resist, Juniper puts out his head, and stays fixed by the stronger will.]

CLARE: Come back, brother. I would like to speak with you.

JUNIPER *[Very gradually, emerging]*:   What are you doing here?

CLARE: Resting.

JUNIPER: What are you resting here for?

CLARE: Because rest is here.

JUNIPER: Not for the likes of you, though. God forbid!

CLARE: God hasn't forbidden it yet, brother.

JUNIPER: What are you calling me "brother" for? I'm no brother to a temptation like you! Oh Lord! Where's Father Francis!

CLARE: In the forest, gathering wood.

JUNIPER: Oh? You knew that, did you? So you thought you'd catch me alone. *[He starts to cross himself.]* Oh God, be merciful to me a sinner! God be merciful to me a sinner! God be merciful to me a—

CLARE: Once is enough, brother. He hears you.

JUNIPER: When I've seen you go, I'll believe it!

CLARE: If you tell me to go, I will go.

JUNIPER: Surely it's not reasonable of you to say that. But if I don't tell you to go, it's not because I want you to stay.

CLARE: Why shouldn't I stay, brother?

JUNIPER: "Brother" again! What was it that brought you here?

CLARE: A rough road, a dark night, and feet that, in God's keeping, did not fail.

JUNIPER: Oh Lord! Am I waking, or am I sleeping? *[In saying so, he mounts the stairs to the sleeping chamber in great haste, and begins to rouse the brothers.]*

Brother Bernard . . . Brother Bernard, wake for the love of God! Brother Giles! Brother Elias! Brother Angelo!

BERNARD: What is it, brother?

JUNIPER: Get the others to wake up! When we are all awake, I will tell you.

ELIAS: We are awake, brother.

JUNIPER: Are you sure you're awake? I wish I could be sure that I was!

BERNARD: Tell us, brother: What is the matter?

JUNIPER: Down below is a temptation, brother, waiting for all of you. The Lord save you from it—and me—and all of us! Come! *[The brothers begin to follow]* Strike a light, and one of you hold me by the hand, for down there it is dark. *[A light is struck; together the brothers descend the stairs, Juniper leading them.]* Wait now! Cross yourselves; then I'll show it to you. Look . . . over there!

[The brothers see dimly through the faint light that there is a woman, young and fair, stretched out asleep before the fire.]

ELIAS: How did this happen, brother?

JUNIPER: God only knows. I was asleep. When I woke up, she was there.

BERNARD: What shall we do, brothers?

GILES: Wait until the little Father returns.

ELIAS: We cannot wait here, brother.

ANGELO: Let us pray, brothers, that we flee from temptation.

ELIAS: Yes, but here *is* temptation.

GILES: I think that the temptation is asleep, and will not awaken.

ELIAS: In sleep, Brother Giles, does the worm die? In sleep is the fire quenched? Come, let us go!

GILES *[making the sign of the cross over Clare]:* The Lord bless thee, little sister, and give thee peace. *[They go to the door, and opening it encounter Francis, who enters carrying wood.]*

FRANCIS: Where are you going, brothers?

JUNIPER: We were going for a walk, father, away from what is over there. *[He points to the sleeper. Francis goes over and looks at her.]*

FRANCIS: Sweet Sister Charity, come at last! . . . Why leave, brothers? *[The brothers stand looking a little ashamed of themselves.]*

BERNARD: We were afraid, father.

FRANCIS: Of what?

ELIAS: Of temptation.

FRANCIS: Where, brothers?

BERNARD: In our own hearts, father.

FRANCIS: Come, then, let us sit down, that in our hearts we may find reason. Our little sister is weary and will not wake up.

JUNIPER: Father, was she the friend that I was to wait for?

FRANCIS: Yes, brother.

JUNIPER: But why didn't you tell me, father, that it was a woman!

FRANCIS: Why should I? You could see that for yourself.

ELIAS: Father, if you knew that she was coming, why did you go and leave us?

FRANCIS: Because with Brother Juniper you were safe.

JUNIPER: With me? The Lord save us!

ANGELO: Why has she come, father?

FRANCIS: God sent her.

GILES: To be one of us, father?

FRANCIS: Yes! If we have brothers, why can't we have sisters, as well? Are we to say, "Go away," to any that have heard the voice of Love say, "Come"?

ELIAS: But what can she do, father?

FRANCIS: Bring others. Work as we do. Give service. Love poverty. Find freedom. Have joy!

ELIAS: But . . . what will the world say, father?

FRANCIS: I don't know, brother. Must we wait until we know what the world will say? What God says we know already. For had God not called her, she would not have come.

BERNARD: Who is she, father?

FRANCIS: A little sister, named Clare. *[He puts more wood on the fire, and covers Sister Clare with a cloak.]* Let us go to bed, brothers; it is late. You, Brother Fire, will sit up with her, and you, Sister Cloak, will keep her warm. Goodnight, little sister, sleep well.

JUNIPER: Father, you tempt me into thinking that there is no such thing in the world as a temptation.

FRANCIS: It's a good thought, brother. Play on it, and some day it may come true.

JUNIPER: If only Father Adam could have thought that!

FRANCIS: What then, brother?

JUNIPER: Then the Tree wouldn't have tempted him.

FRANCIS *[happy to be so instructed]*: No! . . . no! This is true, brothers. Juniper is always right.

GILES: Little Father, he always is!

[Elias makes a quick move of protest, crosses the room, takes up the candle, and stands waiting. The rest of the brothers one by one pass quietly back to bed. Elias follows them. Francis crosses, turns, and motions to Juniper.]

FRANCIS: Come, Juniper! *[And together they all go to the loft to sleep.]*

END

❄ THREE ❄
Brother Juniper,
the Protomartyrs,
and St. Anthony of Padua

Love God in Humility

IV

OCCASIONAL PRAYERS FOR FOOLS

V

FOUR STORIES OF BROTHER JUNIPER
FROM *THE LITTLE FLOWERS*

VI

THE STORY OF THE PROTOMARTYRS,
TOLD IN THE STYLE OF *THE LITTLE FLOWERS*

VII

ST. ANTHONY CONVERTS HERETICS
BY PREACHING TO FISH

INTRODUCTION
IT IS GOOD TO BE A FOOL

This third part of *Lord, Make Me an Instrument of Your Peace* centers on prayers from early Franciscans that focus on humility, service, and holy foolishness—not a quality many of us readily associate with praying or praying well.

Much of what we encounter here centers on Brother Juniper, whom we met in the story that concluded the last section of Part Two. We also meet the Protomartyrs—six friars who died on January 16, 1220 trying to preach the gospel in Seville and Morocco. *Proto* means "first." These six are recognized as the first martyrs of the Franciscan movement. And we meet and pray with St. Anthony of Padua, another friend of Francis and Clare, who is, after them, the most loved of Franciscan saints. Anthony was inspired to join Francis and Clare when he witnessed a solemn procession of the Protomartyrs' bodies traveling from Morocco back to Italy, through his native Portugal. He saw them, heard their witness, and saw their way of life, then left his monastery behind to become a friar. Anthony died five years after Francis and was canonized by the same Pope Gregory IX.

There are many strands of holy foolishness in Christian tradition, not all Franciscan. In the early sixteenth century, for example, St. Ignatius of Loyola—with profound devotion to St. Francis of Assisi—taught what he termed *agere contra*, or "acting against," as a way of combating fears and overcoming what holds us back from being our true spiritual selves. "Do the opposite" was Ignatius's advice in *agere contra*. If you are afraid of speaking in front of people, find the largest group of people you can find, and preach a sermon! This is just one example among hundreds.

There are holy fools and holy foolishness outside Christianity too. Some early Jewish Hasidic masters, for instance, did and said things that resemble the actions and sayings of early Franciscans. I once gave a talk on St. Francis and prayer at a synagogue in Boulder, Colorado, and was joined on the dais afterward by Rabbi Zalman Schachter-Shalomi, the most important figure in Jewish Renewal and an expert in early Hasidism, to discuss these similarities. That night Reb Zalman said,

Brother Juniper in early Franciscan days was the butt of all the jokes. He couldn't do anything right. But every time somebody had to learn a virtue Francis would send them to Juniper. And they'd just watch and learn how.

Reb Zusya of Hanipol was like him. One day the disciples—this was not too long after the time of the Baal Shem Tov (the Hasid founder)—were trying to figure out the saying that a person should accept bad happenings in the same spirit as they accept good happenings and say a blessing about this. They asked the master and he sent them to Reb Zusya. Everybody looked at Reb Zusya as a person who couldn't learn, who didn't know even the most well-known things. But the master had said to, so they went. "Reb Zusya," they said, "how is it that in the same manner as you are supposed to say a blessing over the good you are supposed to say a blessing over the bad?" And he said, "What's bad?" You see?[1]

Zen Buddhism, too, is full of holy fools. There are Zen masters who have stood up to give a talk or preach a sermon only to hear birds sing or see flowers swaying in breezes, and say, "*There* is your sermon," or "*That* is the message." In one particularly famous example, "The Flower Sermon," the Buddha transmitted *prajñā* (wisdom) to his disciples by holding up a white flower as his "sermon," and one of the disciples showed that he understood the message simply by smiling. This simplicity is easy to grasp, especially when we're children. I used to go outside at age six or seven after summer rainstorms to save earthworms from drying in the sun on our asphalt driveway. Rain would flood them from their holes, and onto the driveway they'd find themselves, unable then to get off that hot surface before drying up, once the sun returned. It felt to me then like the most important work I could possibly do in the world.

There are also stories of Zen masters earnestly trying to teach their students how the world is illusory, that what has ultimate meaning is outside of experience. Sometimes a master would face students who said they had absorbed these teachings, but he knew they really hadn't; only when the teacher contrives to cause some form of personal disaster in a student's life (losing a job, becoming implicated in a scandal) does the student throw up his or her hands and say, "Where's the meaning in this world?" Then the master knew he'd succeeded in transmitting the wisdom.

Above all else, Franciscan holy fools—and every other sort of fool in any religious tradition—live counter to the culture. St. Anthony the Great, one of the first saints of the desert, who intended his life to show disdain for the culture of Roman cities, said, "A time is coming when people will go mad, and when they see someone who isn't mad, they will attack him, saying, 'You are mad! You are not like us.'"[2] This aspect of foolishness is everywhere in the teachings and example of early Franciscans. It is another way in which they emphasize that prayer is a practice, not just words, and that this practice is necessary for making progress in a spiritual life. To pray with foolishness can be to discover who we are and what we have to do.

First, a Story . . .

About Me, My Daughter, and Gene Kelly

I will always remember the day I decided to introduce my preschool-age daughter to one of my favorite movies, *Singing in the Rain*, starring Gene Kelly, Donald O'Connor, and Debbie Reynolds. We sat and watched it together on the couch. She didn't wiggle much and laughed at the right places. I knew she was enjoying it.

But then we got to the title song and dance number. There was Gene Kelly, blissfully enjoying a rainstorm. You probably remember how he runs back and forth across a city street at nighttime in the pouring rain, singing at the top of his lungs, tap-dancing by stomping in puddles, grinning at a cop on patrol, becoming completely drenched in his business clothes. He is wearing a suit—and even gives away his umbrella!

As my daughter and I watched, I laughed out loud and was grinning ear to ear. That's what I always do when I watch that scene. She watched carefully, and was smiling, but to my surprise, she then turned to me in the middle of the scene and said, "That's kind of stupid, Dad."

She was only four at the time, but I was sort of offended. I don't know for certain why. Forget that she said the word "stupid" for a moment; we'll deal with that another day. Why was I bothered by her reaction? It isn't as if the movie has anything intimately or immediately to do with *me*, but I wanted her to like it as I did. "Why?" I implored. Then I suddenly realized that I probably knew what she meant by what she said. So I revised. "Do you mean . . . because he's getting all wet?"

"Yeah," she replied, still smiling, looking at the screen. The puddle-stomping continued even as we talked, and she was still trying to figure out the meaning of the scene. "But he's being kind of stupid," she added, yet again.

How do I answer this? I thought. *How do I get her to understand what this means?*

Adults easily understand that what Gene Kelly is doing is anything but stupid. But can his spirit be communicated in words? I at least gave it another try. "Not *stupid*, honey," I said. "Maybe he's just being . . . *foolish*?"

Maybe.

***

A child can't really appreciate what "foolish" means, nor how being a fool can be a virtue, a really good thing. Nor can she appreciate how foolishness might be a healthy sign that something good is happening, or able to happen, in your life. After all, how could someone who is still innocently carefree most of the time—without real responsibilities or stress—understand the absolute delight that can come when we allow ourselves to "let loose" others' expectations? That's what Gene Kelly is doing by singing and dancing in the rain: allowing his joy to overcome his decorum. We adults know this, and that's why we love watching him do it. Probably, we are wishing, deep down, that we could do that too.

G. K. Chesterton wrote in *Orthodoxy*, "Angels can fly because they can take themselves lightly."[3] We'd all like to fly like angels—or at least like Gene Kelly.

I might have communicated better with my daughter that day as we watched the movie together if I'd said that Gene Kelly was being "crazy." She sometimes likes to be "crazy" with her friends. They seem to know and appreciate that word for its sense of nonconformity and playfulness. But as an adult, *crazy* is a word that doesn't seem appropriate. I know how it means a lot of things, some clinical, and how sometimes it might be perceived as an insult, or at least out of place. That's why I quickly decided it wasn't the way to go when I was trying to explain why singing in the rain isn't necessarily "stupid."

I used the word *fool* instead, but then again, *fool* is also an insult to many. The word was even used that way—as a kind of insult—in the Hebrew Scriptures, as we will see in a second. But to many Christians throughout history, foolishness has been a goal, a spiritual occupation, even a badge of honor. They have gone out of their way to earn the name *fool*, even when they knew that those who were saying it never intended it as a compliment. They have been "fools for Christ's sake," to quote St. Paul, who says it like this:

> Here we are, fools for Christ's sake, while you are the clever ones in Christ; we are weak, while you are strong; you are honored, while we are disgraced. To this day, we go short of food and drink and clothes, we are beaten up and we have no homes; we earn our living by laboring with our own hands; when we are cursed, we answer with a blessing; when we are hounded, we endure it passively; when we are insulted, we give a courteous answer. (1 Cor. 4:10–13)

Otherwise, they're known as *holy fools*.

This can be confusing, and for good reasons. Even the Bible seems to contradict itself about fools. A fool for Christ's sake is altogether different from the kind of person the psalmist describes when he or she begins, "The fool says in his heart, 'There is no God.' They are corrupt, their deeds are vile; there is no one who does good. The Lord looks down from heaven on all mankind to see if there are any who understand, any who seek God. All have turned away, all have become corrupt; there is no one who does good, not even one" (Ps. 14:1–3). That's not a foolishness to emulate!

Nevertheless, St. Paul's foolishness is one to emulate. The Bible speaks about both kinds of fool—good and bad—but for the most part, the good sort has been lost.

The Good Fool

In her rich book *Jesus: The Holy Fool*, Elizabeth-Anne Stewart uncovers a variety of sources and inspirations for holy foolishness in the Christian tradition.[4] This section explores and expands on many of these, as well as others that are native to Francis and the early Franciscans.

The foolishness praised by St. Paul is a way of living out Jesus's teachings in the Beatitudes. *Beatitude* comes from a Latin word that means "happiness." The Beatitudes are ways to true happiness, and of course they aren't what you might expect. Who is blessed? The poor in spirit, the meek, the hungry and thirsty, people who are peacemakers—not the powerful. Even the "pure of heart"—and the phrase means pretty much what it implies, which is those who are simple or willingly naive—are singled out as blessed. Do you want to sign up for this sort of blessedness, this happiness? Not many do.

A Christian can point to Jesus's foolishness as the exemplar, just as Jesus sometimes pointed to the Hebrew prophets as his inspiration for defying others' expectations. Like Jeremiah, Jesus dressed simply. Like Isaiah, Jesus often walked around barefoot, and he didn't know where he was going to sleep at night. Contrary to what religious leaders thought appropriate, Jesus chose a strange mix of people as his followers and friends (women, the poor, despised tax collectors, the untouchable sick). Occasionally, he went against societal norms and theological expectations with an attitude of naivete. No matter if someone thought he was "dumb."

Even Jesus's own family thought he was a fool at times—and not the good kind. The Gospel of Mark says that, just after Jesus appointed his twelve disciples, "he went home again, and once more such a crowd collected that they could not even have a meal. When his relations heard of this, they set out to take charge of him; they said, 'He is out of his mind'" (Mk. 3:21). In twenty-first-century language, that sounds like they staged an intervention! They wanted to set him straight. Perhaps he was embarrassing the family.

Later, when Jesus was teaching Torah—good rabbi that he was—he invariably shocked his listeners, ratcheting up the expectations of God on those who seek to truly follow him. He said, for example, "You have heard how it was said, You shall not commit adultery. But I say this to you, if a man looks at a woman lustfully, he has already committed adultery with her in his heart" (Matt. 5:27–8). Seriously? What was once a law of Moses, easy to track in one's life, just got a whole lot tougher. Who would even know if one was observing a law such as this? The religious leaders of the day thought Jesus was nuts.

Jesus was a holy fool in the way he did not worry about the outcome or result of his teaching. Most important of all, he was a holy fool for allowing himself to be misunderstood and, later, mocked. He didn't defend himself when the meaning and purpose of his life was questioned by Pontius Pilate. He was willing to stand physically humiliated before crowds. In these ways, without any other agenda, there have been saints throughout history who have sought to imitate our foolish Lord.

> I give you the end of a golden string;
> Only wind it into a ball,
> It will lead you in at Heaven's gate,
> Built in Jerusalem's wall.
> (William Blake, from *Jerusalem: The Emanation of the Giant Albion*)[5]

There is a perfect line, an uncut thread, "a golden string" throughout history that connects the foolishness of Christ with holy fools who have lived in every generation since his death and resurrection. They all have understood how being reviled can be a sign of blessedness or holiness, a true mark of God's Spirit alive inside of someone. When people witnessed this foolishness in Francis of Assisi eight hundred years ago, they called him *pazzo*. That's Italian for "crazy"—so, I guess, we can't avoid the term! The adjective, however, made Francis happy, in the sense that he knew: if they call you crazy or a fool, you must be doing something right!

The first instances of the crazy foolishness in Francis were outpourings of the Spirit in him. They are difficult to explain if you use only rational or pragmatic ways of understanding: One example is when he stripped naked in front of a crowd in order to give everything back to his father that was rightfully his. Or when he began preaching to birds after people didn't seem to pay much heed to his words. Or when he scolded some of those birds for not listening carefully enough and chirping too loudly during Mass. Or when he joined a friend and disciple in deliberately humiliating himself—Francis had punished his friend by holy obedience (he was, by then, the friend's religious superior)—for refusing to preach the Good News. The punishment was to go and preach, then, in his underwear. But a few minutes later, Francis chastised himself for being too severe—and decided to repent by stripping down to his breeches himself and joining the friend in the pulpit.

Why would someone do these things? They don't exactly make sense, do they? And yet, somehow, they did, and do.

Here's another bit of context. At the time that Francis and Brother Juniper, one of his closest friends and first followers, were becoming fools for Christ, there were professional fools—hired in noble and royal courts, as well as traveling from town to town—acting as entertainers but also as truth-tellers. They were often regarded as possessing a strange sort of wisdom come from being detached from the normal ways of the world. They never stopped reminding their audiences that the world will lie to you, deceive you with false appearances; that it may seem rational, but actually it is mad. You see such a troupe in Shakespeare's *Hamlet*, for instance (act 5, scene 1). They are the grave diggers who appear after Ophelia's suicide, bantering about death, love, and the meaning of life. Such fools, however, were often thought untrustworthy, since their profession was to trick people and play parts in a play. Many ordinary people were hesitant to trust Francis and the first Franciscans, too, linking them with this sort of fool. One early Franciscan history reads, "Someone among them remarked: 'I wouldn't care to invite them into my house; they would probably steal my belongings.' And because of this, any number of insults were inflicted on them in many places. Therefore they very frequently sought lodging in the porticos of churches or houses."[6]

But it was often the hired fool, dressed in motley silliness, juggling and telling stories, who could make jokes at the expense of the mighty. A common man or woman might not dare say things that a fool could say with impunity. A fool was one who flouted conventions, poked fun at niceties, and got away with it because he was either feebleminded or very clever. In the stories of Francis and Juniper, it is often difficult to tell the difference between these two, and one gets the impression that this was by design. It was in this sense that Malcolm Muggeridge, journalist and author of a beautiful book about St. Teresa of Calcutta, once said, "Only mystics, clowns and artists, in my experience, speak the truth, which, as Blake keeps insisting, is perceptible to the imagination rather than the mind. Our knowledge of Jesus Christ is far too serious a business to be left to theologians and exegetes alone."[7]

A rich tradition of holy foolishness similarly exists in Russian Orthodox Christianity, where the fool is called a *yurodivyi*, which means "fool for Christ," but always has a sense of combining insanity with righteousness. In both Western Christianity and Eastern Orthodoxy, overcoming the sin of pride by following the humility of Christ is essential for the holy fool. But among Russian saints, a fool is never feebleminded. He is instead meant to irritate, exasperate, and provoke others to see the errors of conventional understanding. A *yurodivyi* does this, sometimes, by doing the most unusual and unexpected things. The intention is to shock or provoke self-awareness in others who need some. A *yurokevyi* might consort with prostitutes, or walk around with a dead dog, or eat forbidden foods on fasting days—actions designed to make a point. A *yurokevyi* was thereby saying to the world that *it* is full of insanity. This tradition of foolish behavior has often served as a connection to the gospel—at times, such as the Soviet era, when it was difficult to obtain a copy of the New Testament in a Russian translation.[8]

Francis's foolishness shows some similarities to Russian *yurokevyi*, as, for instance, when Francis strips naked in front of a crowd in Assisi as part of a dramatic demonstration to show everyone (and God) that he would no longer owe anything to his greedy father. Or when he generally dressed in rags, in contrast to the fine silks of first years of adulthood. The foolish

Franciscans of the thirteenth century were often regarded, just as some of those clever court entertainers, as purveyors of prophetic wisdom, able to see or understand things that others could not. They would express this wisdom in most unconventional, contrary, shocking ways, such as when Francis and Brother Bernard preached in their underwear, or even in the ways that Francis and others attended to the needs of lepers. The third-generation tertiary Franciscan Blessed Angela of Foligno used to even taste the diseased sores of men and women in the leprosarium, saying it was to her like the Holy Eucharist. On a much simpler plane, Francis and Juniper appreciated the motley fools of courts and town entertainments, and they emulated them by becoming entertainers themselves—"Jugglers for God," in the language of Francis. He wrote songs that puzzled his contemporaries, adopted surprising tunes, and taught people to sing about spiritual matters. "Francis consecrated merry-making to God's service, so that the devil might not have all the good tunes. The *laudi* [praises] which he directed his *jongleurs* [traveling entertainer] to sing for the Lord are the songs of the troubadours transposed into a theological key but in form and melodic delight the same."[9]

Who Is the Real Fool?

The most famous fool in history is a literary one. His name is Don Quixote, the fictional character drawn in the imagination of sixteenth-century Spanish novelist Miguel Cervantes. There is no better example of holy foolery than the ways in which Don Quixote acts as a knight errant, or "wandering knight," in an era when knighthood has all but vanished. He is a champion of chivalry, and chivalry is symbolic of virtue—both values of the past. So when Quixote prepares for battles and saves ladies in distress, we don't quite know whether he does it because he is mad or because he refuses to be mad like the rest of the world that no longer does such things. And when he does things like tilt at windmills (imagining that they are giants), he seems to be really tipping the scales away from sanity. Yet the paradox of *Don Quixote* remains: one never knows if its main character is a fool on purpose or by accident and whether he is, ultimately, saner than all the rest of his contemporaries.

When Cervantes writes this of Don Quixote, it is clear that his fool is also heroic: "The truth is that when his mind was completely gone, he had the strangest thought any lunatic in the world ever had, which was that it seemed reasonable and necessary to him, both for the sake of his honor and as a service to the nation, to become a knight errant and travel the world with his armor and his horse to seek adventures and engage in everything he had read that knights errant engaged in, righting all manner of wrongs and, by seizing the opportunity and placing himself in danger and ending those wrongs, winning eternal renown and everlasting fame."[10]

The first Franciscan friars were just as foolish as that. I even wonder if Cervantes had friars in mind when he created *Don Quixote*. You only have to replace a few words in those lines just quoted to see what I mean. Francis might be Don Quixote:

> The truth is that when his mind was completely gone, FRANCIS had the strangest thought any lunatic in the world ever had, which was that it seemed reasonable and necessary to him, both for the sake of his honor and as a service to the WORLD, to become a FRIAR and travel the world with his POVERTY and his RULE to seek adventures and engage in everything he had read that SAINTS engaged in, righting all manner of wrongs and, by seizing the opportunity and placing himself in danger and ending those wrongs, winning eternal renown and everlasting fame.

People like Francis and Juniper and the Protomartyrs who died in Morocco in 1220 take the gospel seriously when the gospel asks those who want to follow Christ to "not store up treasures for yourselves on earth, where moth and woodworm destroy them and thieves can break in and steal. But store up treasures for yourselves in heaven, where neither moth nor woodworm destroys them and thieves cannot break in and steal. For wherever your treasure is, there will your heart be too. The lamp of the body is the eye. It follows that if your eye is clear, your whole body will be filled with light" (Matt. 6:19–22). The Protomartyrs died by the sword in prison in Morocco while under suspicion for being insane, for why else would a group of poor Christian friars sojourn in Muslim lands preaching their faith when they knew that doing so was both illegal and mad by any worldly standard? Similarly, one sees in the stories of Francis, Juniper, Giles, and other early Franciscans that when they follow Jesus as the first disciples were told to do, they are taking the Gospel seriously, and that seems outlandish to other people: "Take nothing for your journey, no staff, nor bag, nor bread, nor money—not even an extra tunic" (Lk. 9:3). But this was the first necessity in the Franciscan rule of life.

Fools Know the Truth

The trouble with the world as it is isn't that the world is bad, but that we allow it to tell us who we ought to be. The gospel is alternative, not mainstream. Remember the Beatitudes. How many people do you know who go seeking meekness, hunger, and peace instead of power? If we want to follow Jesus, those are the values we'll uphold. And we won't uphold them by being "normal" in this world that is committed to things as they are.

Those who know the truth sometimes have to be foolish in order to communicate it. This is why the prophet Isaiah walked naked and barefoot for years (Isaiah 20), why the prophet Hosea married a harlot in order to make a point about faithfulness (Hosea 1), and why Jeremiah smashed a clay pot—because God told him to forcefully make a point (Jeremiah 19). These are examples of being foolish in order to capture attention—or to subvert established authority. Neither Isaiah nor Hosea cared a wit about their reputations; they cared, instead, about changing minds.

They also understood that there is a Mystery that explains life—and that Mystery is never fully grasped through reason alone. Knowing the truth ultimately involves a kind of "letting go" of the way that our brain seeks to control our small world. To quote again G. K. Chesterton's *Orthodoxy* (the chapter "The Maniac" is required reading for all fools), "The whole secret of mysticism is this: that we can understand everything by the help of what we do not understand."[11] The holy fool can see more, can understand more, can grasp her connection to a world that is endless, but only by accepting its mystery. This time, to paraphrase Chesterton, the fool is sane because he's able to float easily in an infinite sea, whereas reason seeks to cross the infinite sea and to make it finite.

When being a fool involves humiliation, a holy fool doesn't mind that either. As the Spanish theologian Miguel de Unamuno wrote in his journal when he was realizing that learning was not the way to God, "One must seek for the truth of things, not their reason, and truth is sought in humility."[12] Perhaps only a Christian would be able to appreciate this fully, since Christians have as their prime example a God who emptied and then further humbled himself.

But as we've seen already, other religious traditions have holy fools too. Hindu religious men in India leave behind careers late in life to become what is called a *sadhu*, devoted to asceticism and wandering. The young look to them as spiritual teachers. In Buddhism, holy lunacy exhibits itself in laughter—deep, belly laughter. The notion is that only the person who has abandoned worldly cares and drunk deeply in the spiritual life is able to laugh in such a genuine way. Francis didn't quite abide laughter—not of this sort—because in the milieu of late medieval Europe, laughter was considered frivolity and idleness, and these were signs of mocking. *The Mirror of Perfection*, an early account of Francis's life and teachings, tells of him teaching the importance of being joyful, but then adding that he wouldn't want "this joy to be shown through laughter or even empty words. . . . He abhorred laughter and an idle word to an exceptional degree. . . . By a joyful face he understood the fervor and solicitude, the disposition and readiness of a mind and body to willingly undertake every good work."[13] At its root, this shows that Christian holy foolery has always had an important purpose that is never lost from sight.

Francis's single most important piece of writing, his "Canticle of the Creatures," was written in the year 1225, when the regard for physical Creation was as low as it has been at any time in history. In light of that understanding, Francis's Canticle astounds people today. Only now, with the benefit of the teachings of physician-priest Teilhard de Chardin, the poems of English-language poets such as Mary Oliver and Wendell Berry, and Pope Francis's encyclical *Laudato Si'*, has this incredibly foolish prayer—in which St. Francis praises and blesses the wind and stars and rain and sun and every sort of creature—from eight hundred years ago finally come of age.

We can't get away from the fact that our inspiration comes first and foremost from the example of Jesus during his passion. He was willingly mocked and humiliated on his way to the Cross. He could have arranged things differently. Why did he allow the stripping of his clothes, the scourging, being made fun of by the Roman soldiers, and the jeering of the crowds? He became a fool in order to make a point about humility. In the process, he demonstrated how like us he is. We easily feel foolish, and we spend so much time trying to avoid the experience. This is why a holy fool is taught actually to seek out humiliating moments as a kind of exercise, in order to teach us the kind of wisdom that comes only from overcoming the all-too-present self. (See, for example, the story "When Juniper Went Naked to Town" in the pages below.) Today, this is the rarest kind of Christian foolery, but it's a type of spiritual practice that I hope may be revived at least a bit with the encouragement found in this book.

Bringing It All Together

The purpose of these prayers and this witness is to encourage us to be fools for Christ and to provide some resources by which to do it. Let our words and actions run counter to what society expects, because in so doing, we might be most faithfully living the gospel.

You'll encounter plenty of Scripture to keep you focused, some of which I've already mentioned. There are passages from the Gospels, from the Prophets of the Hebrew Bible, and from St. Paul, who wrote a lot in defense of foolishness in one of his most popular letters, First Corinthians. You will encounter these teachings in the week's worth of prayer and inspiration below (see "Seven Themes for Seven Days," pp. 213–16).

Keep in mind that for people like Francis and Juniper and Anthony of Padua, being a holy fool is often more than a way of discipleship; it is an act of protest. The early Franciscans wanted people to see the truth, and sometimes we wear such thick blinders that we need to be shocked in order to see through them. Being a fool can be a way of finding a new source of confidence, away from what the world offers and values, in priorities that are known primarily to others who share in the foolishness. Kahlil Gibran expresses this in an early work when he writes, "I have found both freedom and safety in my madness; the freedom of loneliness and the safety from being understood, for those who understand us enslave something in us."[14] May this section of *Lord, Make Me an Instrument of Your Peace*, in some small measure, set you free.

LOOKING TO ST. FRANCIS AND BROTHER
JUNIPER FOR INSPIRATION

"Then he entered into the city of Assisi and began, as though drunk with the Holy Spirit, to praise God aloud in the streets and the squares." That is how the first-ever biography of Francis relays one of the saint's earliest public expressions of faith. The author who wrote that account, Thomas of Celano, knew Francis personally. The analogy to drunkenness—public drunkenness, no less!—was clearly deliberate. That's what many thought of Francis in those early days.

He wasn't drunk on alcohol, of course. But to extend the metaphor, he was tipsy, light-headed, even to the extent of being louder in public than is usually deemed appropriate. He wasn't acting like he was drunk; he was praising God aloud "as though drunk." There's a difference.

A holy fool *does* sometimes act a part. He will pretend to be something that he isn't to make a point, or to get a message across. For example, once when Brother Bernard went to Bologna, he sat in the piazza all day for days on end, looking like what soon came to be known as a Franciscan fool: unshaven, filthy, with patches on his clothing and an incongruous smile on his face. "Who are you? Why are you here?" someone finally asked Bernard. In response, he pulled from his pocket the radically simple rule of life that he and the first Franciscans lived by, and shared it with them. Within days there were novice friars in Bologna.

Brother Juniper did the same thing, over and over—allowing himself to be poked fun of, even deliberately humiliating himself, to express the spirit of his faith and commitments. There was the time, for instance, when Juniper wanted to make himself a laughing stock before others and stripped himself of all but his underwear (yes, this is something of a recurring theme!). He carried a bundle of his habit and other clothes into the city of Viterbo—walking half naked, right into the marketplace. This story is told in full below (see pp. 250–51). Many young people came by and believed that Juniper had lost his senses. They threw stones and mud at him and pushed him around, spitting words of insult. But Juniper stayed there most of that day, enduring it happily. As the day was coming to a close, he then went to sleep at the convent nearby.

When the other friars saw what he'd done, they were angry. One said, "Let's lock him up." Another responded, "He deserves worse that that!" And another declared, "He's caused a scandal to the whole Order." But Juniper with joy answered, "I deserve all these punishments, and far worse."[15] Such a response surely made the others pause.

But before this contrived foolery could take place, there was the unpretending kind—the "drunk with the Spirit" kind:

> It was in the days when Francis was still wearing his secular cloth-
> ing, even though he had begun to renounce the things of the world.
> He had been going around Assisi looking mortified and unkempt,
> wearing his penance in his appearance in such a way that people
> thought he had become a fool. He was mocked and laughed at,
> and pelted with stones and mud by both those who knew him and
> those who did not. But Francis endured these things with patience
> and joy, as if he did not hear the taunts at all and had no means of
> responding to them.[16]

Somewhere between these two kinds of prayerful foolishness comes the ability to laugh at the world when it places value on what is really without meaning.

***

St. Francis wasn't always a saint or a holy fool. Quite the opposite. In this description from before his conversion began, Thomas of Celano didn't mean the last part as praise: "Almost up to the twenty-fifth year of his age, [Francis] squandered and wasted his time miserably. Indeed, he outdid all his contemporaries in vanities and he came to be a promoter of evil and was more abundantly zealous for all kinds of foolishness."[17] But it was soon after his twenty-fifth year that God took hold of Francis's life and Francis began to seek more important things.

Quickly, Francis and the first friends who joined him in the new charism that would be called Franciscan—men like Brother Bernard and Brother Juniper—came to represent the most important example of holy foolishness in the history of the Christian West. Together they created a renaissance of this unique way of living and communicating the gospel. Through them, faith was invigorated with innocence and simplicity. Clericalism, dogmatism, and crusading had dominated the church for centuries, but they soon gave way and the church was transformed. Other religious orders at that time were focusing on theological teaching and doctrinal preaching. Francis, Juniper, and the others had a different mission. They wanted to be, for lack of a better word, simple.

Innocence is underrated today. Francis possessed it without even knowing that he did. That's of course the whole idea. I can't read these lines from *Don Quixote* without thinking again of the earnest young Francis: "His armor being now furbished, his helmet made perfect, his horse and himself provided with names, he found nothing wanting but a lady to be in love with."[18] Cervantes is referring to his knight-errant hero, but it might as well again be Francis, who walked just as boldly and foolishly on the uncertain path that was his early conversion. For Francis, that lady soon became "Lady Poverty," to whom he quixotically devoted his entire life and then told his friends all about it.

"What woman are you thinking about, Francis?" his old friends asked him one day, expecting the daydreaming or vain friend of their youth to answer. He shocked them when he replied:

"You are right! I was thinking about taking a wife more noble, wealthier, and more beautiful than you have ever seen." They laughed at him. For he said this not of his own accord, but because he was inspired by God. In fact, the bride was the true religion that he later embraced, a bride more noble, richer and more beautiful because of her poverty.[19]

It was early on that Juniper joined Francis, and Juniper possessed a kind of innocence that might even have been greater than the founder's. It often seemed that Juniper could see nothing but the ideals and goals of Christian life. Charity, for instance, led him to forget himself, and he was often rebuked, even by Francis, for running around without clothes on, since he'd given them all away. Humility was so much his focus that he often appeared ridiculous before others, to the point that his brother friars were embarrassed about him, as we've seen. Embarrassment is a tool of the holy fool, both for training himself and for instructing others. We rarely understand it, because we're caught up in it. A character in one of Iris Murdoch's novels states this when he says, "Our chief illusion is our conception of ourselves, of our importance which must not be violated, our dignity which must not be mocked. All our resentment flows from this illusion."[20]

"I wish that I had a whole forest of such Junipers!" Francis once punned, when confronted with Juniper doing something embarrassing, and with his friars responding negatively to it. Francis clearly took the opposite view.

Like all the holy fools in Christian history, Francis and Juniper were possessed with a different way of looking at the world. They were influenced by the Spirit in such a way that they saw a different world from other people. Pouring rain, for instance, not only didn't deter Francis when he was walking one day with Brother Leo on the road, but became something he genuinely (and annoyingly, to Leo!) wanted to experience fresh and anew. With a similar conversion of the senses, Francis once praised Juniper, who was cooking for his brother friars, for his ability to turn garlic into lavender. By "garlic," Francis meant the smelly, old food the brothers often received while begging for scraps. Contemporary Franciscan Father Murray Bodo has imagined Juniper's response to this as, "I never thought of it before, but it is true. I often used to smell lavender when the brothers would bring home scraps they had begged."[21] Anyone else would have smelled the awfulness.

They were foolish in another important respect, as well. They lived without certainties that most people take for granted. This is because they wanted to follow their Savior, who said, "Foxes have holes and the birds of the air have nests, but the Son of man has nowhere to lay his head" (Lk. 9:58). Francis and Juniper didn't want homes or a secure future or even roofs over their heads. This is an example of how holy foolishness can sometimes involve seeking "the peace of wild things," as it was recently stated by the poet and farmer Wendell Berry.

Unpredictability also becomes a virtue, since there is a grace and freedom in the created, wild world that human-made institutions and structures just can't quite match. "O Lord, how manifold are your works! in wisdom you have made them all; the earth is full of your creatures," the psalmist says (Ps. 104:25). In fact, pausing to notice or enjoy these things becomes more foolish all the time. Just imagine a man who talks to animals as if they were his brothers and sisters, or a woman who gathers wild, free-ranging dandelions and values them as the loveliest of flowers of spring. Francis of Assisi threw himself in the snow, preached to birds, walked carefully over stones, and refused most everyday comforts. He was probably the freest man the world has ever known.

Unpredictability reorders priorities, too. For example, Juniper was known to too-easily give away his clothes to the poor. They'd ask; he'd give. Sometimes he went about nearly naked, and it seemed scandalous to some of the friars. After a while, he was forbidden to give away his cloak with a vow of obedience. The result? The next time a poor man asked Juniper for his coat, Juniper said, "I'm not allowed to give it to you, but I won't yell if you take it from me."

***

The Sufi poet Rumi once told a story of a man who was confronted by a police officer. The cop believed he was drunk. The man was asleep, leaning up against a wall in town, when the officer approached and asked what he'd been drinking. "Whatever was in this bottle," the man responded. "What was that, exactly?" said the cop. "That which now fills me," said the accused. "Come on!" exclaims the officer, becoming upset. The officer was, Rumi used to explain, "like a donkey stuck in the mud."[22] "You can't see what intoxicates me," the man finally replied. That's the "holy" in holy foolery. "And if I were still unhappy and reasoning perfectly, I'd be sitting upright and lecturing with the sheikhs," he added. That's the "foolery"— and how its wisdom penetrates the cloudiness of everyday life.

For eight hundred years, there has been a way of prayer that's deeply rooted in the teachings of Christ but practiced mostly outside the walls of a church. To practice one's faith with foolishness in the ways that are particularly Franciscan is a spiritual gift (not so much a practice, but a gift). It didn't originate with the life and teachings of Francis of Assisi and Brother Juniper—holy fools trace their spiritual practice at least back to

Christ—but it was galvanized in their unique lives, in their particular time and place. They discovered a life of joy, simplicity, and wonder. Their gift for expressing God's joy and love involved being small not strong, avoiding positions of power altogether, thinking not about results but about virtue, and enjoying rather than avoiding moments of insecurity, fear, and awkwardness. These practices for being foolish in the eyes of the world were, for them, a sure way to discover the presence of God. That is what is available to anyone who chooses to walk the path of the gospel in these countercultural ways.

Don't get me wrong: the holy fool's way is too radical for most people. This is for the few, not the many. When the famous Renaissance monk Erasmus wrote his satirical *In Praise of Folly*, he didn't recommend anything like what Francis, Juniper, and their friends lived out. By Erasmus's time, there was no one more arrogant in the church than the mendicant orders, including the Franciscans, and they had largely exchanged their founding values and spiritual practices for others that were more in keeping with the world. Erasmus ripped them apart, exposing their hypocrisies. A holy fool's ways aren't easy. But in their foolishness, Francis and Juniper remind anyone of what is the heart and soul of Jesus's teaching. You can't learn the gospel simply in books. You have to put these things into practice. But I think you will find, maybe to your surprise, that this foolish way makes good sense, especially today.

✳ II ✳
HOW FOOLS MIGHT PRAY
—AT LEAST FOR A WEEK

A holy fool prays, probably more than most people, because she knows how much she is in need of what prayer accomplishes.

There is very little by way of speculative theology in fools' prayer. That's not the purpose of it. Instead, prayer is for praise, relationship, gratitude, even celebrating the paradoxes and mysteries of faith. Prayer is for thanking God and aligning the heart more with God's desires.

Mornings and evenings are good times to pray, or to practice praying—the two can be one and the same. Both mornings and evenings are times to mark the beginning of what is new. In the morning, these lines from William Blake (which also beautifully recall how heaven and earth are inextricably linked) are worth remembering:

> Awake the dawn that sleeps in heaven; let light
> Rise from the chambers of the east, and bring
> The honied dew that cometh on waking day.

There are fresh possibilities as we thank God for eyes and hearts that open with the rising sun. The day has come around again.

Evenings are different. Each evening we have the emotions of the day and usually the exhaustion, too, to bring to a close. We do this by remembering praise and by expressing desires for the next day. We also recall what has just happened; perhaps we ask forgiveness for what we've done or not done. And often we ask, with saints throughout the centuries, for the Lord to protect us through the silent hours of the night.

This is what we'll do for a practice week.

What to Expect Each Day

The sequence for each day of this special morning and evening liturgy is as follows:

A. PREPARATION (a very simple prayer of intention)

B. THE WORD OF GOD—usually a Gospel sentence or other line from the New Testament that is pungent with the theme of the day. The same one is used for both morning and evening each day. The brevity of these passages can be profound—and encourage memorization.

C. *Silence* (more than a moment; take a minute or more if you can)

D. SONG OF MY SOUL (the psalm selection)

E. A READING FROM THE PROPHETS (a canticle from the Hebrew Prophets)

F. NEW TESTAMENT READING

G. *Silence* (again)

H. AN EARLY FRANCISCAN SAYING

I. A SPIRITUAL PRACTICE (this is where the praying meets the living)

There are many ways that you may choose to use these morning and evening prayers in your life. They can function as a special energizer of prayer in your devotional life. Prayer needs sparks to keep firing. As you walk along with Francis and Juniper and pray into the themes that formed their spiritual lives, you will reinvigorate your own.

First, if you already have a prayer book that you use daily, there are ways to pray these days as a supplement to your usual practice. Perhaps you wish to focus your prayer time with Francis and Juniper on a special weekend or a weeklong spiritual retreat on holy foolery or a broader Franciscan theme.

The Divine Hours of prayer have, from their earliest beginnings in the ancient synagogue, been intended for group use; so you may wish, in addition to praying on your own, to pray these short liturgies together with others in a group devoted to learning more about Francis of Assisi, Brother Juniper, and the charism of early Franciscanism. Otherwise, as you pray alone, know that you are not truly alone. You join with thousands of others around the world both past and present who have prayed similar words, as well. For them and for us, daily prayer is a means of beginning anew each day.

Second, if you already have a prayer practice and a prayer book, this offering of a week of prayers may be a temporary substitute for your regular prayer practice. You may wish to make a special prayer week, finding some fresh inspiration by praying, exploring, and living into the themes of the holy fool. It is natural to come to these points in any prayer life, when something new is needed, which explains the necessity of works such as this one. Don't skip the spiritual-practice suggestions that come at the end of each morning and evening. These are derived directly from early Franciscan lives; without them it may be impossible to make full sense of Franciscan foolery and our relationship with God.

Third, while I hope that these prayers become a personal and daily prayer ritual for many, they may also appeal to those who may wish to pray in community, in study groups, or even in academic settings. There is no way to really understand the "poor followers" of Christ, as Francis and Juniper referred to themselves, without enjoining their spiritual lives, its themes, and the very words of their prayers.

Seven Themes for Seven Days

We will begin with seven themes—one per day—that emerge from the life and writings of and about St. Francis and Brother Juniper. These themes will provide a framework and subject for each of our seven days of prayer.

Day One—*There Is Wisdom in Foolishness (Sunday)* To quote William Blake again (he was a holy fool), "If the fool would persist in his folly, he would become wise." In other words, as in every aspect of the Christian life, there is *telos* to what we do and who we are. *Telos* is a Greek word used by Aristotle as well as by St. Paul. It means "purpose, goal." Know this now before you go any further: fools are fools not only because it is the way to follow Christ but also because it is the way to truth. The world can see a holy fool only as a tragic figure, crushed despite his goodness, but we know differently. The fool's way is the way to a blessed future as he or she is slowly becoming what has been promised and what we yearn for:

In days to come the mountain of the LORD's house shall be established as the highest of the mountains, and shall be raised above the hills; all the nations shall stream to it. Many peoples shall come and say, "Come, let us go up to the mountain of the LORD, to the house of the God of Jacob; that he may teach us his ways and that we may walk in his paths." For out of Zion shall go forth instruction, and the word of the LORD from Jerusalem. He shall judge between the nations, and shall arbitrate for many peoples; they shall beat their swords into ploughshares, and their spears into pruning-hooks; nation shall not lift up sword against nation, neither shall they learn war any more. (Isa. 2:2–4)

Day Two—There Is Strength in Powerlessness (Monday)   Essential to any spiritual practice of holy foolishness is acknowledging that the only lasting power and strength in the world and in our lives rests in God—the God who came as a baby in a manger. Is there any greater example of powerlessness than the human infant? Of all the ways for God to enter the world, that is the one God chose, demonstrating the theme for this day: there is strength in powerlessness. The theme is emphasized in the readings from the Gospels, showing that there is no greater holy fool than Jesus himself, as is clear not just in the birth of Jesus, but in his passion, too. He provides the ultimate example for our lives.

Day Three—There Is Joy in Forgiveness (Tuesday)   Holy foolishness cannot exist without a profound and radical sense of forgiveness in our lives—a true "letting go." This becomes a sense of relief that is sometimes powerfully experienced with tears and dancing and shouting when you repent of your sins. As one contemporary author who studied holy fools has cleverly put it, "As I continued to meet holy fools, I noticed that they viewed repentance as the essential curriculum for spiritual kindergarten, college, and postdoctoral studies."[23] Allow yourself to be open to experiences and emotions such as these on day three; they are familiar to holy fools of all Christian traditions. As St. Antony of Egypt once said, "Here comes the time when people will behave like madmen, and if they see anybody who does not behave like that, they will rebel against him and say: 'You are mad'—because he is not like them."

Day Four—The Humble Are Blessed (Wednesday) In the Gospels, several of the Beatitudes are teachings of Jesus that we don't—*can we admit this?*—readily or easily believe. I'm talking about "blessed are the meek," and so on. We think of them as somewhat irrelevant to daily life in the real world, or as something for a future age when the world has changed from what it is. But when St. Paul says, "The message of the cross is folly for those who are on the way to ruin, but for those of us who are on the road to salvation it is the power of God" (1 Cor. 1:18), he's making a point about what is real. It turns out that much of that "real world" stuff that we've been told we should preoccupy ourselves with is not, in fact, real at all. This is a day to pray on this theme and seek to create in our lives the absence of vanity and egotism that otherwise fill most of everyday life around us.

Day Five—The Pure in Heart Are Blessed (Thursday) This day is all about treasuring what is foolish because now we accept and realize that the fool is one who has come to see life as it really is. A fool is able to live life to the fullest because of what she understands and who she is becoming. No longer is human existence all about surviving or competition. The philosopher Friedrich Nietzsche grew to hate Christianity and what it taught when he fashioned ideas of the superman and will-to-power. He couldn't stand the Christian's willingness to be weak. He found it pitiable, not something to be imitated. But Nietzsche was wrong. The saints are right. As the Bible says, Christ "emptied himself" (Phil. 2:7) for our sake. That's our model, and that's what we try to do, in following him.

Along the way, we avoid self-delusion and chasing after things (stuff, people, love, reputation, fame)—these efforts that fill the will-to-have, will-to-be, and any other process by which people are taught to self-fulfill. The holy fool knows life more simply, closer to its real essence, and, as a result, more beautifully. One contemporary author sums this up nicely when she imagines the people who don't get it: "How foolish to be an unholy fool!"[24]

Day Six—Folly Is Another Name for Righteousness (Friday) Why is this theme essential? Because spiritual practice is never something we do just for us, in the quiet of our house or room. Our lives are inextricably intertwined with the lives of others naturally, but we also are supposed to deliberately connect them and help each other. Even (or especially!) holy foolishness can help the people around us.

Why is folly another name for righteousness? Because it is foolish in the eyes of the world to do what brings us no earthly reward. It is crazy to spend time and focus energy on what brings us no glory. That's because the world assigns meaning to what the holy fool knows is without meaning. When we are foolish, what we do begins to resemble art—with unexpected revelations of beauty, new perceptions of what's real. As Thomas Merton once appreciated in the playwright Eugene Ionesco, "If one does not understand the usefulness of the useless and the uselessness of the useful, one cannot understand art."[25] And as St. Paul once said, "Since in the wisdom of God the world was unable to recognize God through wisdom, it was God's own pleasure to save believers through the folly of the gospel" (1 Cor. 1:21).

Day Seven—True Wisdom Brings Peace and Justice (Saturday) This is difficult, and that's why it comes last. It is difficult because a holy fool tries never to be self-righteous. Concerns for oneself undermine anything else that a holy fool might do. Still, a holy fool is often a prophet, and deliberately so—so the line is narrow to walk. As you grow in wisdom, remember the book of Wisdom and how the people complain about the "righteous man": "Let us lie in wait for the righteous man, because he is inconvenient to us and opposes our actions; he reproaches us for sins against the law, and accuses us of sins against our training. He professes to have knowledge of God, and calls himself a child of the Lord" (Wisd. 2:12). The righteous one is not wrong—doing what is right even when it's uncomfortable is the epitome of holy foolishness. We have to remember who we are serving. Also, a holy fool knows the truth of what poet Wendell Berry has recently said: "A change of heart or of values without a practice is only another pointless luxury of a passively consumptive way of life."[26]

A HOLY FOOL'S DAILY OFFICE

Morning Prayer, Sunday
(Theme/Intent: There Is Wisdom in Foolishness)

PREPARATION

Heavenly Father, I am your child.

That I know, not because we are alike,

but because in the morning I look to you.

In my sometimes feeble, fumbling ways,

you are all I seek. Amen.

THE WORD OF GOD

Here we are, fools for Christ's sake.

—1 Corinthians 4:10

Silence

Song of My Soul

The heavens declare the glory of God,

   and the firmament shows his handiwork.

One day tells its tale to another,

   and one night imparts knowledge to another.

Although they have no words or language,

   and their voices are not heard,

Their sound has gone out into all lands,

   and their message to the ends of the world.

In the deep has he set a pavilion for the sun;

   it comes forth like a bridegroom out of his chamber;

   it rejoices like a champion to run its course.

It goes forth from the uttermost edge of the heavens

and runs about to the end of it again;

   nothing is hidden from its burning heat.

.ect and revives the soul;

. LORD is sure

the innocent.

. LORD are just and rejoice the heart;

.dment of the LORD is clear

.ght to the eyes.

. of the LORD is clean and endures for ever;

the judgments of the LORD are true

and righteous altogether.

More to be desired are they than gold,

more than much fine gold,

sweeter far than honey, than honey in the comb.

—Psalm 19:1–10

A READING FROM THE PROPHETS

The days of punishment have come, the days of recompense have come;
Israel cries, "The prophet is a fool, the man of the spirit is mad!" . . . The
prophet is a sentinel for my God.

—Hosea 9:7–8a

NEW TESTAMENT READING

For it seems to me that God has put us apostles on show right at the end,
like men condemned to death: we have been exhibited as a spectacle to the
whole universe, both angelic and human. Here we are, fools for Christ's
sake, while you are the clever ones in Christ; we are weak, while you are
strong; you are honored, while we are disgraced. To this day, we go short
of food and drink and clothes, we are beaten up and we have no homes;
we earn our living by laboring with our own hands; when we are cursed,
we answer with a blessing; when we are hounded, we endure it passively;
when we are insulted, we give a courteous answer. We are treated even now
as the dregs of the world, the very lowest scum.

—1 Corinthians 4:9–13

Silence

AN EARLY FRANCISCAN SAYING

Blessed is the one who knows how to keep and hide the revelations of God, for there is nothing hidden that God may not reveal when it pleases him.

—Brother Giles of Assisi

A SPIRITUAL PRACTICE

Today, alone, somewhere outdoors, try preaching to the birds. If it happens to be winter and there are no birds to be found where you are, preach to the squirrels. Begin by speaking silently, if you prefer, in your mind. But stand before them and express yourself from your heart. Record how it felt. Do it again tomorrow.

Evening Prayer, Sunday
(Theme/Intent: There Is Wisdom in Foolishness)

PREPARATION

Holy One, I am following
in your path.
When I don't understand what's next,
I am comforted to know that
you do.

THE WORD OF GOD

Here we are, fools for Christ's sake
—1 Corinthians 4:10

Silence

Song of My Soul

I will bless the Lord who gives me counsel;

   my heart teaches me, night after night.

I have set the LORD always before me;

   because he is at my right hand I shall not fall.

My heart, therefore, is glad, and my spirit rejoices;

   my body also shall rest in hope.

For you will not abandon me to the grave,

   nor let your holy one see the Pit.

You will show me the path of life;

   in your presence there is fullness of joy,

   and in your right hand are pleasures for evermore.

—Psalm 16:7–11

A READING FROM THE PROPHETS

Thus says the LORD, your Redeemer, who formed you in the womb: I am the LORD, who made all things, who alone stretched out the heavens . . . who frustrates the omens of liars . . . who turns back the wise . . . confirms the word of his servant, and fulfills the prediction of his messengers.

—Isaiah 44:24–25

NEW TESTAMENT READING

Jesus said, "Do not store up treasures for yourselves on earth, where moth and woodworm destroy them and thieves can break in and steal. But store up treasures for yourselves in heaven, where neither moth nor woodworm destroys them and thieves cannot break in and steal. For wherever your treasure is, there will your heart be too. The lamp of the body is the eye. It follows that if your eye is clear, your whole body will be filled with light."

—Matthew 6:19–22

Silence

AN EARLY FRANCISCAN SAYING

As you announce peace with your mouth, make sure that greater peace is in your hearts. Let no one be provoked to anger or scandal through you, but may everyone be drawn to peace, kindness, and harmony through your gentleness. For we have been called to this: to heal the wounded, bind up the broken, and recall the erring.

—Francis[27]

A SPIRITUAL PRACTICE

Are there decisions you make in your life based in your faith that cause you to seem somewhat foolish compared to others? If not, perhaps there should be. If there are, rather than telling others about them like a prophet might feel compelled to do, do you hold them silently? Others probably still notice.

Morning Prayer, Monday
(Theme/Intent: There Is Strength in Powerlessness)

PREPARATION

Holy One, I am here with nothing.
I am like a bird aloft, with only
you holding up my wings.
Keep your air under me today,
please.

THE WORD OF GOD

For the wisdom of the world is folly to God.
—1 Corinthians 3:19

Silence

Song of My Soul

Be merciful to me, O God, be merciful,

for I have taken refuge in you;

in the shadow of your wings will I take refuge

until this time of trouble has gone by.

I will call upon the Most High God,

the God who maintains my cause.

He will send from heaven and save me;

he will confound those who trample upon me;

God will send forth his love and his faithfulness.

I lie in the midst of lions that devour the people;

their teeth are spears and arrows,

their tongue a sharp sword.

They have laid a net for my feet,

and I am bowed low; they have dug a pit before me,

but have fallen into it themselves.

Exalt yourself above the heavens, O God,

and your glory over all the earth.

—Psalm 57:1–6

A READING FROM THE PROPHETS

Hear the word of the LORD, O nations, and declare it in the coastlands far away; say, "He who scattered Israel will gather him, and will keep him as a shepherd a flock." For the LORD has ransomed Jacob, and has redeemed him from hands too strong for him.

—Jeremiah 31:10–11

NEW TESTAMENT READING

Pilate then had Jesus taken away and scourged; and after this, the soldiers twisted some thorns into a crown and put it on his head and dressed him in a purple robe. They kept coming up to him and saying, "Hail, king of the Jews!" and slapping him in the face. Pilate came outside again and said to them, "Look, I am going to bring him out to you to let you see that I find no case against him." Jesus then came out wearing the crown of thorns and the purple robe. Pilate said, "Here is the man."

—John 19:1–5

Silence

AN EARLY FRANCISCAN SAYING

The sisters shall not acquire anything as their own, neither a house nor a place nor anything at all; instead, as pilgrims and strangers in this world who serve the Lord in poverty and humility. . . . Nor should they feel ashamed, since the Lord made Himself poor for us in this world. This is that summit of highest poverty which has established you, my dearest sisters, as heirs and queens of the kingdom of heaven; it has made you poor in the things of this world but has exalted you in virtue.

—Clare[28]

A SPIRITUAL PRACTICE

It is so ingrained in us to "overcome" our adversaries, to "stand up for ourselves" and for what's right. That, of course, is not what Jesus did before Pilate, and only a holy fool would follow his example, even in this way. Compose a short prayer today—it can be only one line long—speaking to God of your desire to be faithful even in this difficult way.

Evening Prayer, Monday
(Theme/Intent: There Is Strength in Powerlessness)

PREPARATION

Heavenly Father, I don't know where I'm going
or what I am necessarily supposed to do.
But I know that following you doesn't always
make sense, as I have learned what sense is.
So, I will listen with the ears of my heart.
Amen.

THE WORD OF GOD

For the wisdom of the world is folly to God.

—1 Corinthians 3:19

Silence

Song of My Soul

My heart is firmly fixed, O God, my heart is fixed;
  I will sing and make melody.
Wake up, my spirit; awake, lute and harp;
  I myself will waken the dawn.
I will confess you among the peoples, O Lord;
  I will sing praise to you among the nations.
For your loving-kindness is greater than the heavens,
  and your faithfulness reaches to the clouds.
Exalt yourself above the heavens, O God,
  and your glory over all the earth.

—Psalm 57:7–11

A READING FROM THE PROPHETS

Then David blessed the LORD in the presence of all the assembly; David said: "Blessed are you, O LORD, the God of our ancestor Israel, forever and ever. Yours, O LORD, are the greatness, the power, the glory, the victory, and the majesty; for all that is in the heavens and on the earth is yours; yours is the kingdom, O LORD, and you are exalted as head above all. Riches and honor come from you, and you rule over all. In your hand are power and might; and it is in your hand to make great and to give strength to all. And now, our God, we give thanks to you and praise your glorious name.

—1 Chronicles 29:10–13

NEW TESTAMENT READING

First thing in the morning, the chief priests, together with the elders and scribes and the rest of the Sanhedrin, had their plan ready. They had Jesus bound and took him away and handed him over to Pilate. Pilate put to him this question, "Are you the king of the Jews?" He replied,

"It is you who say it." And the chief priests brought many accusations against him. Pilate questioned him again, "Have you no reply at all? See how many accusations they are bringing against you!" But, to Pilate's surprise, Jesus made no further reply.

— Mark 15:1–5

Silence

AN EARLY FRANCISCAN SAYING

Brother Juniper once determined by himself to keep silence for a six-month period. He did it this way. The first month for the love of the Eternal Father. The second month for love of Jesus Christ his Son. The third month for love of the Holy Ghost. The fourth in reverence to the most holy Virgin Mary. And from then forward, he spent each day in silence in honor of one of the saints. So he passed six whole months without speaking.

—from *The Little Flowers of St. Francis*

A SPIRITUAL PRACTICE

How often do you defend yourself before others? The next time you feel slighted or misunderstood or worse, keep silent, being the fool that your Lord was before Pilate.

Morning Prayer, Tuesday
(Theme/Intent: There Is Joy in Forgiveness)

PREPARATION

Father, Son, and Holy Spirit,
I need You today.
Reveal to me whatever necessary.
Startle me. Surprise me!
Or just make it plain as day
where I need to forgive,
or be forgiven.

THE WORD OF GOD

Do not stifle the Spirit or despise the gift of prophecy.

—1 Thessalonians 5:19

Silence

Song of My Soul

I will exalt you, O LORD
because you have lifted me up
   and have not let my enemies triumph over me.
O LORD my God, I cried out to you,
   and you restored me to health.
You brought me up, O LORD, from the dead;
   you restored my life as I was going down to the grave.
Sing to the LORD, you servants of his;
   give thanks for the remembrance of his holiness.
For his wrath endures but the twinkling of an eye,
   his favor for a lifetime.
Weeping may spend the night,
   but joy comes in the morning.
—Psalm 30:1–6

A READING FROM THE PROPHETS

Seek the LORD while he may be found, call upon him while he is near; let the wicked forsake their way, and the unrighteous their thoughts; let them return to the LORD, that he may have mercy on them, and to our God, for he will abundantly pardon.

—Isaiah 55:6–7

NEW TESTAMENT READING

So [Jesus] told them this parable. "Which one of you with a hundred sheep, if he lost one, would fail to leave the ninety-nine in the desert and go after the missing one till he found it? And when he found it, would he not joyfully take it on his shoulders and then, when he got home, call together his friends and neighbors, saying to them, 'Rejoice with me, I have found my sheep that was lost.' In the same way, I tell you, there will be more rejoicing in heaven over one sinner repenting than over ninety-nine upright people who have no need of repentance."

—Luke 15:3–7

Silence

AN EARLY FRANCISCAN SAYING

The brothers should always be careful that, no matter where they are, whether in a hermitage or any other place, not to appropriate any place as their own, or even to possess it instead of another. And whoever may come to them, either friend or foe, even thief or robber, they should receive all with kindness. And no matter where they are, they should spiritually and diligently show reverence and honor toward one another without complaints. And they should always be careful not to appear sad and gloomy on the outside, like hypocrites do, but show themselves to be joyful, cheerful, and gracious to others, in the name of the Lord.

—Francis[29]

A SPIRITUAL PRACTICE

Bring an unforgiven sin to God this morning. (Best of all, and if you are Catholic, take that sin to confession.) Or perhaps there is a sin you've already confessed but still haven't resolved with another person or within yourself. Do what you need to do to bring it to its full conclusion today and this week—for God's sake, for your sake, and to find the true joy of forgiveness.

Evening Prayer, Tuesday
(*Theme/Intent: There Is Joy in Forgiveness*)

PREPARATION

Holy Spirit,

I'm tired at the end of a long day,

but I'm dancing inside,

knowing that no matter what happens,

or happened,

you were with me in it! Amen.

THE WORD OF GOD

Do not stifle the Spirit or despise the gift of prophecy.

—1 Thessalonians 5:19

Silence

Song of My Soul

While I felt secure, I said, "I shall never be disturbed.

You, LORD, with your favor, made me as strong as

the mountains."

Then you hid your face, and I was filled with fear.

I cried to you, O LORD; I pleaded with the Lord, saying,

"What profit is there in my blood, if I go down to the Pit?

will the dust praise you or declare your faithfulness?

Hear, O LORD, and have mercy upon me;

O LORD, be my helper."

You have turned my wailing into dancing;

you have put off my sack-cloth and clothed me with joy.

Therefore my heart sings to you without ceasing;

O LORD my God, I will give you thanks for ever.

—Psalm 30:7–13

A READING FROM THE PROPHETS

They shall come and sing aloud on the height of Zion, and they shall be radiant over the goodness of the LORD, over the grain, the wine, and the oil, and . . . their life shall become like a watered garden, and they shall never languish again. Then shall the young women rejoice in the dance, and the young men and the old shall be merry. I will turn their mourning into joy, I will comfort them, and give them gladness for sorrow . . . and my people shall be satisfied with my bounty, says the LORD.

　—Jeremiah 31:12–14

NEW TESTAMENT READING

Always be joyful, then, in the Lord; I repeat, be joyful. Let your good sense be obvious to everybody. The Lord is near. Never worry about anything; but tell God all your desires of every kind in prayer and petition shot through with gratitude, and the peace of God which is beyond our understanding will guard your hearts and your thoughts in Christ Jesus. Finally, brothers, let your minds be filled with everything that is true, everything that is honorable, everything that is upright and pure, everything that we love and admire—with whatever is good and praiseworthy.

　—Philippians 4:4–8

Silence

AN EARLY FRANCISCAN SAYING

Sinners will come back to their God by humility, not by scolding. Christ tells us that those who are well do not need a physician, but those who are sick do.

　—Francis[30]

A SPIRITUAL PRACTICE

Some of us are simply not good at allowing joy to fill us. (I count myself in this camp, much of the time.) Perhaps we were taught to be more circumspect, not to easily show our feelings. For a few minutes, as long as you are able, stretch your arms wide and hold your palms facing out as if you might catch a huge beach ball that's about to be thrown in your direction. Close your eyes. Then, catch it!

Morning Prayer, Wednesday
(*Theme/Intent: Blessed Are the Humble*)

PREPARATION

Holy, Happy One!

I don't often think of you that way—

holy and happy.

But I hear your song in the morning

and I want to sing it with you,

today. Amen.

THE WORD OF GOD

Jesus said to them, "In truth I tell you, tax collectors and prostitutes are making their way into the kingdom of God before you."

—Matthew 21:31

Silence

Song of My Soul

Oh, how I love your law! all the day long it is in my mind.

Your commandment has made me wiser than my enemies,

    and it is always with me.

I have more understanding than all my teachers,

    for your decrees are my study.

I am wiser than the elders,

    because I observe your commandments.

I restrain my feet from every evil way,

    that I may keep your word.

I do not shrink from your judgments,

    because you yourself have taught me.

How sweet are your words to my taste!

    they are sweeter than honey to my mouth.

Through your commandments I gain understanding;

    therefore I hate every lying way.

—Psalm 119:97–104

A READING FROM THE PROPHETS

The wisdom of the humble lifts their heads high, and seats them among the great. Do not praise individuals for their good looks, or loathe anyone because of appearance alone. The bee is small among flying creatures, but what it produces is the best of sweet things. . . . Many kings have had to sit on the ground, but one who was never thought of has worn a crown.

—Sirach 11:1–3, 5

NEW TESTAMENT READING

God chose those who by human standards are fools to shame the wise; he chose those who by human standards are weak to shame the strong, those who by human standards are common and contemptible—indeed those who count for nothing—to reduce to nothing all those that do count for something, so that no human being might feel boastful before God. It is by him that you exist in Christ Jesus, who for us was made wisdom from God, and saving justice and holiness and redemption. As scripture says: If anyone wants to boast, let him boast of the Lord.

—1 Corinthians 1:27–31

Silence

AN EARLY FRANCISCAN SAYING

The brothers . . . should aim to maintain silence as long as God gives them the grace. They shouldn't argue among themselves or with others, but instead, should always be ready to humbly say, "We are worthless slaves!" They shouldn't be angry, for if you are angry you will be liable to judgement; if you insult, you will be liable to the council; and if you say, "You fool," you will be liable to the hell of fire. [Matt. 5:22]

—Francis[31]

A SPIRITUAL PRACTICE

Some of us desperately need to practice humility. There are many deliberately humiliating practices—such as those mentioned in the opening chapters from the Gospels and the lives of the Franciscan saints. They do us much good! Find a way to deliberately humble yourself today.

That said, others of us don't need any more humiliation. Circumstances and life events have already, and thoroughly, brought us low. Some of us only need to be reminded that the humility we are experiencing is a virtue with God. Such ones as these are like the poor whom Christ says will inherit the kingdom of God (Lk. 6:20). If this is you, know that you need to do nothing else to make yourself humble.

God sees each of us and knows who we are.

Evening Prayer, Wednesday
(Theme/Intent: Blessed Are the Humble)

PREPARATION

In the dark of this night,

watch over me,

O Lord,

as I attempt to watch for you.

Amen.

THE WORD OF GOD

Jesus said to them, "In truth I tell you, tax collectors and prostitutes are making their way into the kingdom of God before you."

—Matthew 21:31

Silence

Song of My Soul

I lift up my eyes to the hills;

from where is my help to come?

My help comes from the LORD,

the maker of heaven and earth.

He will not let your foot be moved

and he who watches over you will not fall asleep.

Behold, he who keeps watch over Israel

shall neither slumber nor sleep;
The Lord himself watches over you;
   the Lord is your shade at your right hand,
So that the sun shall not strike you by day,
   nor the moon by night.
The Lord shall preserve you from all evil;
   it is he who shall keep you safe.
—Psalm 121:1–7

A READING FROM THE PROPHETS

Woe to you who strive with your Maker, earthen vessels with the potter! Does the clay say to the one who fashions it, "What are you making"? or "Your work has no handles"? Woe to anyone who says to a father, "What are you begetting?" or to a woman, "With what are you in labor?" Thus says the Lord, the Holy One of Israel, and its Maker: Will you question me?
—Isaiah 45:9–11

NEW TESTAMENT READING

At this time the disciples came to Jesus and said, "Who is the greatest in the kingdom of Heaven?" So he called a little child to him whom he set among them. Then he said, "In truth I tell you, unless you change and become like little children you will never enter the kingdom of Heaven. And so, the one who makes himself as little as this little child is the greatest in the kingdom of Heaven. In truth I tell you, whatever you bind on earth will be bound in heaven; whatever you loose on earth will be loosed in heaven.
—Matthew 18:1–4, 18

Silence

AN EARLY FRANCISCAN SAYING

Brothers, who is so noble that he wouldn't carry a basket of manure from St. Mary's all through town, if he were given a house of gold? Why don't we want to endure a little shame in order to gain eternal life?
—Brother Juniper[32]

A SPIRITUAL PRACTICE

Kneel to pray tonight, even if you haven't kneeled for decades. Do it even if it feels odd. Do it especially if it feels odd! You aren't kneeling to please God; you are kneeling because your body can teach your soul something important.

Morning Prayer, Thursday
(Theme/Intent: The Pure in Heart Are Blessed)

PREPARATION

Show me today, Lord,
the beauty of your foolishness,
how yours are the ways that
lead to bliss.
I want bliss. I want you.
Amen.

THE WORD OF GOD

Blessed are the pure in heart: they shall see God.
—Matthew 5:8

Silence

Song of My Soul

O Lord, I am not proud;
  I have no haughty looks.
I do not occupy myself with great matters,
  or with things that are too hard for me.
But I still my soul and make it quiet,
like a child upon its mother's breast;
  my soul is quieted within me.
O Israel, wait upon the Lord,
  from this time forth for evermore.

—Psalm 131

A READING FROM THE PROPHETS

Morning by morning he wakens—wakens my ear to listen as those who are taught. The LORD God has opened my ear, and I was not rebellious, I did not turn backward. I gave my back to those who struck me, and my cheek to those who pulled out the beard; I did not hide my face from insult and spitting.

—Isa. 50:4a–6

NEW TESTAMENT READING

Blessed are the peacemakers: they shall be recognized as children of God.
Blessed are those who are persecuted in the cause of uprightness:

the kingdom of Heaven is theirs.

Blessed are you when people abuse you and persecute you

and speak all kinds of calumny against you falsely on my account.

Rejoice and be glad, for your reward will be great in heaven; this is how

they persecuted the prophets before you.

—Matt. 5:9–12

Silence

AN EARLY FRANCISCAN SAYING

The brothers should all strive to follow the humility and poverty of our Lord Jesus Christ, and remember that we deserve nothing else in the whole world except what the apostle says: "if we have food and clothing, we will be content with these" [1 Tim. 6:8]. Similarly, they should rejoice when they have an opportunity to talk with people who are easily despised, with the poor and the weak, with the sick and lepers, and with anyone who begs in the streets.

—Francis[33]

A SPIRITUAL PRACTICE

Good athletes and good musicians will tell you that there is a secret to their success that most coaches fail to teach: getting out of the way. An athlete gets out of the way of her teammates so that they can make the shot or run with the baton. A musician takes himself out of the way and allows the instrument to shine, since that's what really matters. Look for ways today that you might get out of the way.

Evening Prayer, Thursday
(*Theme/Intent: The Pure in Heart Are Blessed*)

PREPARATION
I need nothing tonight but you,
Lord.
Your presence.
Not your protection (but I'll take it)!
I need your love.

THE WORD OF GOD
Blessed are the pure in heart: they shall see God.
    —Matthew 5:8

Silence

Song of My Soul
The LORD is my shepherd; I shall not be in want.
He makes me lie down in green pastures
    and leads me beside still waters.
He revives my soul
    and guides me along right pathways for his Name's sake.
Though I walk through the valley of the shadow of death,
I shall fear no evil; for you are with me;
    your rod and your staff, they comfort me.
You spread a table before me in the presence of those
who trouble me;
    you have anointed my head with oil,
    and my cup is running over.
Surely your goodness and mercy shall follow me all the days
    of my life,
and I will dwell in the house of the LORD forever.
    —Psalm 23

A READING FROM THE PROPHETS

The Lord GOD helps me; therefore I have not been disgraced; therefore I have set my face like flint, and I know that I shall not be put to shame; he who vindicates me is near. Who will contend with me? Let us stand up together. Who are my adversaries? Let them confront me. It is the Lord GOD who helps me.

—Isaiah 50:7–9

NEW TESTAMENT READING

You are salt for the earth. But if salt loses its taste, what can make it salty again? It is good for nothing, and can only be thrown out to be trampled under people's feet. You are light for the world. A city built on a hill-top cannot be hidden. No one lights a lamp to put it under a tub; they put it on the lamp-stand where it shines for everyone in the house. In the same way your light must shine in people's sight.

—Matthew 5:13–16

Silence

AN EARLY FRANCISCAN SAYING

The spirit of the Lord desires for our flesh to be humiliated, lower, denied, considered by us as less worthy. The spirit of the Lord desires humility and patience, pure simplicity and peace of mind. It desires, above all, righteous fear, holy wisdom, and the divine love of the Father, Son, and Holy Ghost.

—Francis[34]

A SPIRITUAL PRACTICE

Most of our parents taught us to do the opposite of what Francis instructs in his Rule in the passage above. We are supposed to take good care of ourselves, and to present ourselves well in front of others. That's how we stay healthy and succeed. So, is Francis wrong? I don't think so. And our mothers weren't wrong either—unless they taught us that we should *always* be in charge, or *always* seek our own way. Tomorrow, practice some small way of deliberate humility in your bearing, your appearance, your self-presentation. Ask God to show it to you. Maybe even have fun with it. As you do, reflect on how you are serving the Lord in such a countercultural way.

Morning Prayer, Friday
(Theme/Intent: Folly Is another Name for Righteousness)

PREPARATION

I don't know what I'm doing
half the time, Lord,
but I know right now that I
want to do for you, today,
whatever I am supposed to do.
Show me, please.

THE WORD OF GOD

The message of the cross is folly for those who are on the way to ruin, but for those of us who are on the road to salvation it is the power of God.

—1 Corinthians 1:18

Silence

Song of My Soul

Hallelujah!
Give praise, you servants of the LORD;
  praise the Name of the LORD.
Let the Name of the LORD be blessed,
  from this time forth forevermore.
From the rising of the sun to its going down
  let the Name of the LORD be praised.
He takes up the weak out of the dust
  and lifts up the poor from the ashes.

He sets them with the princes,
  with the princes of his people.
He makes a woman of a childless house
  to be a joyful mother of children.
—Psalm 113:1–3, 6–8

A READING FROM THE PROPHETS

Let justice roll down like waters, and righteousness like an ever-flowing stream.
—Amos 5:24

NEW TESTAMENT READING

As scripture says: I am going to destroy the wisdom of the wise and bring to nothing the understanding of any who understand. Where are the philosophers? Where are the experts? And where are the debaters of this age? Do you not see how God has shown up human wisdom as folly? Since in the wisdom of God the world was unable to recognize God through wisdom, it was God's own pleasure to save believers through the folly of the gospel.
—1 Corinthians 1:19–21

Silence

AN EARLY FRANCISCAN SAYING

Unworthy servants of Christ as we are, may we sing a new song in the presence of your holy presence before your very throne, and follow the Lamb of God wherever he goes.
—Clare[35]

A SPIRITUAL PRACTICE

Simply to be a healthy human being, we have to laugh at ourselves. A holy fool does more than laugh: she tries never to take herself too seriously. Try clowning around this week, even if it doesn't feel comfortable at first. Learn to tell a joke. Wear something ridiculous. Smile at an inopportune time.

Evening Prayer, Friday
(Theme/Intent: Folly Is Another Name for Righteousness)

PREPARATION

Is it possible, God,

that my life has

something to do with yours?

I'm tired, and tonight, I don't know.

Is it okay for me to say just that?

But I want to know.

Amen.

THE WORD OF GOD

The message of the cross is folly for those who are on the way to ruin, but for those of us who are on the road to salvation it is the power of God.

—1 Corinthians 1:18

Silence

Song of My Soul

LORD, you have searched me out and known me;

you know my sitting down and my rising up;

you discern my thoughts from afar.

You trace my journeys and my resting-places

And are acquainted with all my ways.

Indeed, there is not a word on my lips,

But you, O LORD, know it altogether.

You press upon me behind and before

And lay your hand upon me.

Such knowledge is too wonderful.

—Psalm 139:1–5

A READING FROM THE PROPHETS

Thus says the LORD: "Do not let the wise boast in their wisdom, do not let the mighty boast in their might, do not let the wealthy boast in their wealth; but let those who boast boast in this, that they understand and know me, that I am the LORD; I act with steadfast love, justice, and righteousness in the earth, for in these things I delight, says the LORD."

—Jeremiah 9:23–24

NEW TESTAMENT READING

We are preaching a crucified Christ . . . a Christ who is both the power of God and the wisdom of God. God's folly is wiser than human wisdom, and God's weakness is stronger than human strength.

—1 Corinthians 1:23–25

Silence

AN EARLY FRANCISCAN SAYING

When we arrive and we're soaked by the rain and chilled to the bone, completely drenched with mud and very hungry, and we ring at the gate and the brother on duty says, "Who are you? Go away!," and we have to show patience and humility and charity with someone whom God has made to say what he says just to test us, write it down, brother: that's the source of our joy!

—Francis, speaking to Brother Leo[36]

A SPIRITUAL PRACTICE

Most of us feel we're too busy to play. Today is different. Do something you haven't done in ages, whether it's finding a swing set, playing catch, or rolling down a hill. See what playing can do for you (other than grass stains—don't worry about those; clothes can be washed), and see what it can do in your relationships with spouse, kids, neighbors, friends. Families, neighborhoods, and religious orders are not built on rules alone; they are built on friendships—and friendships are deepened when we are real, even awkward, with each other.

Morning Prayer, Saturday
(Theme/Intent: True Wisdom Brings Peace and Justice)

PREPARATION

I want to serve you, God,
and I think I know what to do.
What I need is courage, persistence,
and a touch of folly
to get it done.
Make me conscious of you at my
side today. Amen.

THE WORD OF GOD

As scripture says: He traps the crafty in the snare of their own cunning
and again: The Lord knows the plans of the wise and how insipid they are.
—1 Corinthians 3:20

Silence

Song of My Soul

Show us your mercy, O LORD,
   and grant us your salvation.
I will listen to what the LORD God is saying,
   for he is speaking peace to his faithful people
   and to those who turn their hearts to him.
Truly, his salvation is very near to those who fear him,
   that his glory may dwell in our land.
Mercy and truth have met together;
   righteousness and peace have kissed each other.
Truth shall spring up from the earth,
   and righteousness shall look down from heaven.
—Psalm 85:7–11

A READING FROM THE PROPHETS

Shower, O heavens, from above, and let the skies rain down righteousness; let the earth open, that salvation may spring up, and let it cause righteousness to sprout up also; I the LORD have created it. Woe to you who strive with your Maker, earthen vessels with the potter! Does the clay say to the one who fashions it, "What are you making"? or "Your work has no handles"?

—Isaiah 45:8–9

NEW TESTAMENT READING

He has given us an even greater grace, as scripture says: God opposes the proud but he accords his favor to the humble. Give in to God, then; resist the devil, and he will run away from you. The nearer you go to God, the nearer God will come to you. Clean your hands, you sinners, and clear your minds, you waverers. . . . Humble yourselves before the Lord and he will lift you up.

—James 4:6–8, 10

Silence

AN EARLY FRANCISCAN SAYING

The word of God belongs not to the one who hears or speaks it, but to the one who does it.

—Brother Giles of Assisi

A SPIRITUAL PRACTICE

A holy fool loves extravagantly. What does that mean? A fool doesn't measure risks when giving to a homeless person. A fool doesn't forgive with caveats someone who has slighted him. Search your heart today for someone you know who is in need, or who needs to know that you forgive them. Show him or her your love in an extravagant way.

Evening Prayer, Saturday
(Theme/Intent: True Wisdom Brings Peace and Justice)

PREPARATION

O Lord, I want
your kingdom,
on earth as it is in heaven.
I want it now, in my lifetime,
which means that I want
to help you bring it about
today. Amen.

THE WORD OF GOD

As scripture says: He traps the crafty in the snare of their own cunning
and again: The Lord knows the plans of the wise and how insipid they are.
    —1 Corinthians 3:20

Silence

Song of My Soul

Sing to the LORD a new song,
    for he has done marvelous things.
Sing to the LORD with the harp,
    with the harp and the voice of song.
With trumpets and the sound of the horn
    shout with joy before the King, the LORD.
Let the sea make a noise and all that is in it,
    the lands and those who dwell therein.
Let the rivers clap their hand,
    and let the hills ring out with joy before the LORD,
    when he comes to judge the earth.
In righteousness shall he judge the world
    and the peoples with equity.
    —Psalm 98:1, 6–10

A READING FROM THE PROPHETS

The whole of wisdom is fear of the Lord. . . . Better are the God-fearing who lack understanding than the highly intelligent who transgress the law.

—Sirach 19:20, 24

NEW TESTAMENT READING

The wisdom that comes down from above is essentially something pure; it is also peaceable, kindly and considerate; it is full of mercy and shows itself by doing good; nor is there any trace of partiality or hypocrisy in it. The peace sown by peacemakers brings a harvest of justice.

—James 3:17–18

Silence

AN EARLY FRANCISCAN SAYING

Humility seems to me to be like lightning. As lightning causes terrible flashes and nothing can afterward be found of it, so does humility dissipate every evil and is the foe of every sin, but leaves nothing behind.

—Brother Giles of Assisi

A SPIRITUAL PRACTICE

Where does God's love want to take you today, or in the near future? Each one of us, if we quiet our mind and listen, will eventually hear the Holy Spirit speaking in our heart. What is God saying to you? Where does your foolish love need to take you?

❈ ❈ ❈

OCCASIONAL PRAYERS FOR FOOLS

Christian spirituality, prayer, and liturgy are replete with the words of holy fools down through the centuries. These are like pearls so precious that if one discovered them in a field, one might go out and sell everything one owns to buy that field.

Some of these are words composed by Christians who were holy fools, while others are words that inspired holy fools then and continue to do so now. We are all on this journey, and certain prayers have a power to inspire, guide, challenge, and prod us along in a way that others don't as much. This short chapter is an offering of some of these, many of them Franciscan, organized in no particular order.

These first two prayers are slight variations on prayers in common use throughout Catholic and other Christian churches on the feast days of saints:

O God, who has brought us near to an innumerable
company of angels and to the spirits of just men and women made
perfect: Grant us during our earthly pilgrimage to abide in
their fellowship, and in our heavenly country to become
partakers of their joy; through Jesus Christ our Lord, who
liveth and reigneth with thee and the Holy Spirit, one God,
now and for ever. *Amen.*

O Almighty God, who by thy Holy Spirit has made us one
with thy saints in heaven and on earth: Grant that in our
earthly pilgrimage we may ever be supported by this
fellowship of love and prayer, and may know ourselves
to be surrounded by their witness to thy power and mercy.
We ask this for the sake of Jesus Christ, in whom all our
intercessions are acceptable through the Spirit, and who
liveth and reigneth for ever and ever. *Amen.*

This next one is the prayer that Francis is said to have prayed on the day he first heard God speaking to him. Francis was kneeling in the ruined church of San Damiano, outside the medieval walls of the hill town of Assisi, in silence, alone, when God said in such a way that Francis could understand: "Go and rebuild my Church." Francis responded in his usual, literal way: by gathering bricks in town and reconstructing that very church. This prayer later became Francis's prayer for himself, as well as the spirit of the Franciscan movement. It is textual tradition for it to be laid out as verse, since Francis is widely recognized as one of the first authors of poetry in the Italian vernacular. The crucifix before which Francis prayed is actually an icon; it is the image of the crucifix painted onto a twelve-centimeters-thick block of wood in the shape of a cross. It hangs in the Basilica of Santa Clara in Assisi to this day.[37]

> Most High,
> Most glorious God,
> Enlighten the shadows of my heart.
> Grant me a right and true faith,
> A certain hope, and
> A perfect charity, feeling, and understanding
> Of You,
> So that I may be able to accomplish
> Your holy and just commands.
> Amen.

This is the traditional priestly blessing, found in Numbers 6:24–26, used often by Francis and millions of other Christians throughout the ages:

> The LORD bless you and keep you;
> the LORD make his face to shine upon you,
> and be gracious to you;
> the LORD lift up his countenance upon you,
> and give you peace.

Sometimes a prayer is simply a frequent reminder of one's helplessness and need for God.

Lord,
without your hand
I can do nothing.
—Brother Juniper

O my most sweet Lord Jesus Christ,
have pity on me and on my Lady Poverty,
for I burn with love for her, and without her
I cannot rest.
O my Lord, who did cause me to love her,
you know that she is sitting in sadness,
rejected by all.
—Francis, in the paraphrase of Blessed Frederick Ozanam (1813–1853)

Almighty, eternal, just, and merciful God,
grant to us miserable ones the grace to do
for you what we know you want us to do.
Give us always to desire what pleases You.
Inwardly cleansed, interiorly illumined and
enflamed with the fire of the Holy Spirit,
may we be able to follow in the footprints of your
beloved Son, our Lord Jesus Christ, and attain
to you, Most High, by your grace alone, who
in perfect Trinity and simple Unity lives
and reigns and is glorified as God almighty,
forever and ever. Amen.
—Francis[38]

Anthony of Padua, although a tiny man in stature, was known to be a fiery preacher, as well as a convincing theologian. When he first began teaching the friars theology, Francis was concerned. Francis wrote Anthony to say, "I am pleased that you are now teaching sacred theology to our brothers providing one thing: As it says in our Rule, please see that you do not squelch the spirit of prayer and devotion in them."

A few years after that, after St. Francis died, it was Anthony who was the one to carry on the tradition of preaching to the fishes! (See pp. 257–58, below.)

God, Give Me the Words

As the apostles "spoke as the Spirit gave them the gift of speech,"
    we are happy when our words issue from the Spirit
    and not from ourselves!
O God, help me to speak only the words given by You,
    whenever and wherever I happen to be.
I can do this and still confess the faith.
I stand in the blazing splendor of the saints,
    looking always toward God the Father, Son,
    and Holy Spirit.
Amen.
—St. Anthony of Padua[39]

✳ V ✳

FOUR STORIES OF BROTHER JUNIPER FROM *THE LITTLE FLOWERS*

We tend to know the key stories about Francis and Clare. Or at least, they are easily obtainable. Brother Juniper is less known. Stories from his life are always colorful, countercultural (even as compared to his contemporary friars), and they deserve to be better known. Here are four of them.

When Juniper Went Naked to Town

One day, Brother Juniper wished to completely humiliate himself. So, he stripped his body of its clothes. Completely naked and exposed, Juniper put his underwear like a hat upon his head and tied his friar's habit with its cord around his neck, like a scarf. Done up in this way, he walked into Viterbo, straight into the town market, anxious to be mocked.

There in the marketplace he sat, in his nakedness, for only a few minutes before some young people saw him and decided he was surely insane. They began to throw rocks and mud at him, and they insulted him in every way they could think of. They even began to push him around.

Juniper smiled at them, and his smiles only seemed to enflame the boys' worst behavior.

After more than an hour of this, Juniper was a mess, and also a bit hurt. He decided to leave the city center and walk back to the friary that was already in that town.

When the other friars saw him, they were shocked and concerned, but they were also angry with Juniper for embarrassing the friary before the whole town, as he had done.

"Let's lock him up!" one of them said, referring to how Francis had once written that a heretical friar could be locked up in a prison in the friary, if necessary, before sending him away for religious discipline.

"He should actually be hanged!" another friar yelled, surely in half-jest, but also demonstrating how upset they all were with their brother.

"Maybe even burned at the stake!" added another, in the same spirit.

"No penalty is too great for how this man has betrayed our blessed Order! He has proven to be a shocking example of what it means to be a friar of God in this town," someone said.

Brother Juniper was sitting quietly and smiling while listening to this barrage. When they were all done, they demanded an answer from him. What led him to do such a thing in Viterbo? Finally, he smiled and answered them all, with joy and humility.

"All of you are right," he said, "I deserve everything you say, and even more for what I have done."

This was all to the glory of Christ. Amen.

When Juniper Cooked for the Friars

There was once a time when Juniper was the only friar staying behind in the friary. All the other friars were heading out for the day. The guardian said to him, "Brother, will you please prepare some food for the friars, so they can eat upon their return?" "I'll be happy to do so," Juniper replied. Then, the other friars went out.

Juniper began to think about the task at hand. *What a shame it is*, he thought to himself, *that every day one of the friars must occupy so much time with cooking instead of praying. I think I will cook enough today to last the friars for two weeks!*

And so, Juniper went into town and began to beg. He needed pots for cooking, and he wished to have eggs, meat, and some vegetables. On his way back to the friary, he also stopped to gather some firewood.

He filled the pots with water and put them over a fire that he made. Then he placed everything he'd received into the pots: vegetables, uncut; chickens, still with their feathers; and dozens of eggs, in their shells. *Everything will cook together, all at once!* he thought.

Once everything was underway, one of the other friars came home early. Juniper let him in, and together they sat by the roaring cook-fire. This other friar was one who loved Juniper for his simple ways, but he began to ponder what was in the pots and to observe what Juniper had underway. The big pots were so hot that he didn't dare go near them;

in fact, he covered up so as not to get burned from the heat they were throwing off. Juniper, meanwhile, remained busy stirring the contents and adding wood to the fires. A few hours later, all the friars returned to the friary. "Brother Juniper is definitely preparing a feast for us!" said the first friar to all of the others.

Juniper rang the bell for supper, and the brothers filed into the refectory. Juniper's face was red from the heat and exhaustion; he said, "Eat well, brothers, and then let's go pray. And no one should have to cook again for two weeks!"

The friars sat and stared at the food put before them. They were dumbfounded, and refused to eat. Juniper picked up a boiled chicken with its feathers still on, and ripped off a bite of the most offensive-looking portion, saying, while choking on it, "This is good!"

The friars sat and stared at Juniper. They were amazed. Then the guardian began to scold him for his wastefulness and foolishness. "Don't you know . . . ," he began to say. But then Juniper threw himself onto his knees and began to confess his sins to the gathering, chronicling nearly every sinful thing that he had said, done, and intended over the course of his life. "I have wasted so many good things of God and this order!" Juniper moaned. And he wouldn't stop repenting.

Finally, the guardian said to the friars, "I wish that Juniper would waste every day what he wasted today, if we would then receive this sort of edification. His simplicity and charity made him do what he did here today."

Why Juniper Played on a Seesaw in Rome

It was several years after Brother Juniper had joined the Franciscans, after his reputation was already well established, that he went to stay for a while in Rome. He already had a reputation for holiness, and there were some Romans who knew he was coming to their city, so they went out to meet him. Juniper saw these Romans on the road ahead, awaiting him, and he wanted none of their devotion. He began to ponder how to turn their expectations, and this greeting, on its head.

At about that moment Juniper saw two boys playing on a seesaw, which they'd made by setting a board of wood over the top of a log, with one of them sitting at either end upon it. He walked up to the boys and smiled at them and asked to join in their play. Soon, Juniper was taking a turn and seesawing on one end, a boy on the other. His arms were in the air, and he was laughing like a child himself.

The crowd of expectant Romans saw this, and they began to come closer. They wanted to take Juniper into the city, to honor him, and to show him where a man of holiness could lie down and rest after such a journey. But Juniper kept on playing.

The people were gobsmacked. As Juniper laughed and waved his arms, the people were trying to reverence and greet him as the holy man they knew he was supposed to be. But Juniper wanted to turn their reverencing into mocking and scorn.

"He's a fool," one of the Romans then finally said. Others were not sure. But as Juniper kept on playing with the boys on the seesaw rather than listening to the crowd that had come to greet him, after a little while all of the Romans slowly wandered away, disappointed. It was only then that Brother Juniper stopped seesawing and eventually made his way, quietly and on his own, to the friary in Rome.

How Juniper Became Rapt with Ecstasy One Day at Mass

Juniper was not a priest. He never said Mass, but he always listened to the Mass with close attention. At Mass, he was always devout within himself and composed in the presence of others.

But one day, when Juniper was at Mass at St. Mary of the Angels—the Portiuncula—he slowly became rapt with a kind of ecstasy. The look on his face showed that he had been transported, as if to another place. His brothers saw this and realized he had become unresponsive, so when the Mass came to an end they left him in the chapel.

After a long while, Juniper returned to his usual senses. Realizing that he was still kneeling in the corner of the Portiuncula, he rose and went to find his brothers outside. He was excited, bursting with his usual exuberance.

"Brothers!" he called as he approached them. They saw that he had returned from his state.

"Who in this life of ours is so noble that he wouldn't carry a basket of pig manure from St. Mary's all through the town of Assisi in order to earn a basketful of gold?" he said.

They smiled. Everyone would.

"In the same way," Juniper went on, for this is what he heard from God on his knees, "why don't we all want to endure brief moments of shame to gain life eternal, which is better and lasts longer than any gold in the world?!"

THE STORY OF THE PROTOMARTYRS, TOLD IN THE STYLE OF *THE LITTLE FLOWERS*

This is the story of the holy martyrs of our order, Vitalis, Accursius, Adjutus, Berard, Otto, and Peter, and how they came to glorify God with their witness of faith.

Our father Francis, almost from the moment of his conversion to religious life, felt a calling to meet, understand, and even convert people of the Muslim faith. He expressed a desire to take himself to Muslim places, which were then far from Assisi and St. Mary of the Angels, in the Levant and across the Sea.

Preaching to Muslims was unheard of, then, but was a passion of brother Francis. He and some other brothers attempted to go one year, but had to turn back, due to storms at sea. When they finally did make it to the Holy Land [in 1219], and there met with the Sultan, Francis confounded the Sultan with the truth of the Gospel, and left that righteous non-believer with a sense that he had met his first Christian. Upon returning to Assisi, brother Francis taught us in his holy Rule: "Those brothers who feel inspired to go among the Muslims or other non-believers must seek the permission of their minister, and the minister should not grant such permission unless the brother is fit and prepared for this ministry."[40]

It was also after his return from Egypt that Francis gave his blessing to six of our brothers to go without him to preach to Muslims in the west. Brother Vitalis led the group, but he took ill on the journey and died along the way. So Brother Berard was left in charge of the remaining five who headed west. Berard was fluent in many languages and had learned even to speak Arabic. They sailed across the sea in secular clothes, for it was against the law in the land they were going to, to appear as a Christian. But when they arrived in Seville, they changed back into their holy habits and walked directly toward the chief mosque, where they began to preach.

The crowd was astonished at their presence, and by their witness. Some among the crowd began to strike the friars and to beat them. It was against the law to preach any faith other than Allah and his prophet Muhammad, and Berard and the other friars knew that they were in personal danger. They showed by their actions and words that they were unafraid. Like their father Francis, they wanted to please God with a faith that is unafraid of martyrdom.

Brother Berard and the others presented themselves to the local magistrate as Christian friars, ambassadors of the King of Kings. They were immediately arrested. Then they were told to leave Seville, and so they walked south, onto the African continent [which was then part of the same Muslim-controlled kingdom], and they preached in Morocco just as they had preached the Gospel to the people of Seville. They were arrested again, and thrown into prison, where they were beaten for their holy witness. On January 16, 1220, by the hand of the Sultan himself, these first holy martyrs of the Franciscan Order were beheaded.

VII

ST. ANTHONY CONVERTS HERETICS
BY PREACHING TO FISH

The following is a condensed version of the story as originally told in
The Little Flowers of St. Francis.

If you remember from the Old Testament, you will recall how God once used the mouth of an ass to rebuke the arrogant ignorance of the prophet Balaam. So, too, did God once use St. Anthony of Padua.

The event took place in Rimini,[41] a place that was home to many heretics who had left behind the true faith for falsehood. Anthony was there to preach to them, to show them the path back to faith in Christ. But they were a hardhearted people. They refused to listen to him.

Inspired by God, Anthony went to the place in Rimini where the river meets the sea, and standing there, he began to call out to the fishes in the water.

"You, fish," he yelled, "listen to me! Listen to the Word of God! Faithless human beings refuse to hear God's Word, but you, you listen to what I have to say."

Anthony then paused and watched as fish large and small began to gather along the riverbank. They held their heads slightly out of the water. They looked up at Anthony. The sizes of the fish, from enormous to tiny, and their colors, every shade in the sea, were astonishing to witness. These creatures meekly awaited the saint's next words of exhortation. Then, Anthony continued.

"My brothers," he said, just as his father Francis had called many different types of creatures his brothers and sisters, "give thanks to God your Creator who has given you such a beautiful place in which to live. You are able to travel like pilgrims wherever you desire in the sea, and you have food abundantly for all your needs."

"Consider," Antony went on, "how your Creator protected you during the time of the Flood. Only you and your seagoing species were perfectly safe when other creatures were perishing. It was your own who protected the prophet Jonah until the third day, depositing him back on land to do his work for God. You were even the food for the blessed Jesus Christ during his time on earth, before he died, and then again, quite mysteriously, after his resurrection."

The fish remained there, transfixed, listening to Anthony's every word. They began to open their mouths slightly, as if they were offering praises to God.

"Blessed be God, for the fish of the waters offer him more praise than do the heretics among us humans!" Anthony shouted. And then, he kept on preaching. The gathering of fish grew with every minute that Anthony preached, until the riverbank was overflowing into the sea.

People in Rimini had followed Anthony to the seashore. They had watched what was taking place to their astonishment. When they heard his words, and witnessed the response of the fish, their hearts began to soften. They felt sorry for their previous obstinacy. In time, Anthony offered a concluding benediction, and the fish dispersed. It was then that the people offered to listen to Anthony's message, and it is said that many of them were converted back to the true faith on that day.

FOUR
Lord, Make Me an Instrument of Your Peace

This prayer, surely the most recognized one that is attributed to St. Francis, was not actually written by him. It also doesn't derive from Francis's teachings at chapter meetings or any other oral tradition. Its author is in fact anonymous, and the prayer itself is only a century old. Throughout much of the twentieth century, it appeared in multiple collections of prayers, many of them bestsellers. It was printed on cards distributed to soldiers during both of that century's world wars. Since 1976, due to the work of Franciscan scholar Kajetan Esser, OFM, we have recognized that the words of "Lord, Make Me an Instrument of Your Peace," are not in fact those of St. Francis.

Some scholars have traced the origins of the prayer to 1912, in France.[1] It could be that its author was living at that time in that place, since it seems to have first appeared then in a French-language magazine called *La Clochette* (The little bell). A Vatican newspaper then published a translation in Italian four years later.[2] It wasn't long after that before it appeared in nearly every language on earth.

So why include it in this book at all? The answer is simple. Despite all the doubts surrounding the prayer's origins, it is no wonder that the words of "Lord, Make Me an Instrument of Your Peace" were so easily assumed to be those of Francis. The lasting influence of this prayer—also commonly known as "The Prayer for Peace"—is above all due to how closely it reflects the true spirit of the Poverello. For this reason, these beautiful lines endure as an essential part of Franciscan spirituality.

Many prayer books, including those published by the largest of Catholic publishing houses, still include among its most popular selections versions of what is often titled "The Peace Prayer of St. Francis," or more simply "The St. Francis Prayer." It has also been set to music on dozens of occasions, just as that authentic writing of Francis, "The Canticle of the Creatures," was from its beginning meant to be sung.

Bing Crosby, for instance, recorded a version of "Lord, Make Me an Instrument of Thy Peace" in 1954 to support the cause for canonization of

Junipero Serra. His recording lasted seven minutes and forty-three seconds. The discography in *Bing Magazine* reads, "Bing undertakes the recitation of 'Peace Prayer of St. Francis' to help raise funds for Catholic charities and his reading is sincere and effective. After his opening narration, the choir and a soloist take over until Bing returns to join them as the prayer is completed in dramatic fashion."[3]

More in tune with twenty-first-century tastes, perhaps, is the soaring version recorded by the Italian Franciscan Friar Alessandro. His debut album, *Voice from Assisi* (2012), includes a beautiful rendition by this incredible tenor. It is titled, "Make Me a Channel of Your Peace." Alessandro was born in Assisi in 1978.

At the other end of the popular spectrum, vocalist Singh Kaur made versions of the prayer part of her large set of music on peace, adding to St. Francis's popularity at ashrams and new-age festivals. Canadian singer-songwriter Sarah McLachlan put it to music in 1997. She even, oddly, copyrighted her version with a writer's credit. Catholic singer-songwriter John Michael Talbot has also performed and recorded his own version. The Irish Catholic–raised folk group The Burns Sisters made the prayer song popular at their concerts throughout the 1980s and 1990s, showing how its message can blend with Woody Guthrie–inspired folk and protest songs.

Catholic schools hang copies of the prayer on the walls and in their halls. The schools of the Archdiocese of Chicago, as recently as a few years ago, built a campaign to promote peace in their communities around praying and teaching the prayer. Their superintendent of schools was quoted saying, "We chose the Prayer of St. Francis because it calls us to become 'instruments' of God's peace. True peace begins within each of us, and every person has a responsibility to spread God's peace through word, action, and prayer. The Prayer of St. Francis encourages each of us to examine our own hearts, and calls us to foster peace to those around us."[4]

Whoever did write these words had taken to heart the true charism of Franciscanism:

❊

Lord, make me an instrument of your peace.
Where there is hatred let me sow peace;
where there is injury let me sow forgiveness;
where there is doubt let me sow faith;
where there is despair let me give hope;
where there is darkness let me give light;
where there is sadness let me give joy.
O Lord, grant that I may not try to
be comforted but to comfort,
not try to be understood but to understand,
not try to be loved but to love.
Because it is in giving that we receive,
it is in forgiving that we are forgiven,
and it is in dying that we are born to eternal life.

We need to be instruments of God's peace in our world. St. Francis, St. Clare, St. Anthony of Padua, Brother Juniper, Brother Giles, Blessed Protomartyrs, and all Franciscan saints, please pray for us.

NOTES

✳ ONE ✳
ST. FRANCIS
Begin a Life of Conversion

1 *Francis of Assisi: Early Documents,* vol. III, ed. Regis J. Armstrong, OFMCAP, J. A. Wayne Hellman, OFM CONV, and William J. Short, OFM (New York: New City Press, 2001), 311.

2 *Francis of Assisi: Early Documents*, vol. III, 311.

3 *The Little Flowers of Saint Francis*, trans. Raphael Brown (New York: Image Books, 1958), 186.

4 *Little Flowers of Saint Francis*, 175–76.

5 See *The Mirror of Perfection*, in *Francis of Assisi: Early Documents*, vol. III, section 97, p. 344. This is my rendering of the text.

6 This collect is based on Lk. 2:29–32, what is commonly known in Latin as *Nunc Dimittis*.

7 Remesiana is in modern Serbia. This prayer is the concluding portion of the ancient prayer *Te Deum laudamus.*

8 This prayer resembles Francis's "Prayer Before the Crucifix" originally prayed at San Damiano in Assisi early in the saint's religious life. See *Francis of Assisi: Early Documents*, vol. I, 40.

9 Guigo II, "Ladder of Monks," in Guigo II, *The Ladder of Monks, A Letter on the Contemplative Life, and Twelve Meditations*, trans. Edmund Colledge, OSA, and James Walsh, SJ (Kalamazoo, MI: Cistercian Publications, 1979), 73. Guigo was a Carthusian monk and prior of the Carthusian motherhouse, the Grande Chartreuse. He wrote the *Ladder of Monks* and *Twelve Meditations*, but if St. Francis knew these great works, he probably knew them as the work of either Bernard of Clairvaux or St. Augustine, to whom they were often mistakenly attributed in the decades and early centuries after Guigo's death in 1188.

10 See "The Sacred Exchange Between St. Francis and Lady Poverty," in *Francis of Assisi: Early Documents*, vol. I, 529–54.

11 This collect is based on Phil. 1:9–11.

12 *On the Song of Songs I*, trans. Kilian Walsh, OSCO (Kalamazoo, MI: Cisterian Publications, 1980), 140–50.

13 Adapted from his *Life of Saint Francis*, vol.II, ix.

14 From *Evangelical Doctrine*, chap. 15.

15 Francis of Assisi, "Prayer for the Conclusion of the Offices," in *The Complete Francis of Assisi: His Life, the Complete Writings, and The Little Flowers*, ed. and trans. Jon M. Sweeney (Brewster, MA: Paraclete Press, 2015), 255.

16 From the Gelasian Sacramentary.

17 From *The Lauds*, lxxxvi. See the original Italian and literal prose translation in George T. Peck, *The Fool of God: Jacopone da Todi* (Tuscaloosa: University of Alabama Press, 1980), 161.

18 From the Mozarabic Sacramentary.

19 Slightly adapted from *The Letters of Hildegard of Bingen*, vol. 1, trans. Joseph L. Baird and Radd K. Ehrman (New York: Oxford University Press, 1994), 183.

20 From Pope Gregory IX's 1228 document proclaiming Francis of Assisi a saint.

21 Adapted from Francis's first Rule, chap. xxii, 27–32, as well as John 4:23–24.

22 Augustine, *Confessions*, trans. Henry Chadwick (New York: Oxford University Press, 1991), 17–18.

23 From the Mozarabic Sacramentary.

24 From "The Sacred Exchange Between St. Francis and Lady Poverty." See *Francis of Assisi: Early Documents*, vol. I, 553.

25 This collect is based on Galatians 5:16.

26 *The Rule of St. Benedict*, ed. Timothy Fry (Collegeville, MN: Liturgical Press, 1981), 48–49.

27 From the Mozarabic Sacramentary.

28 See *St. Francis of Assisi: His Life and Writings as Recorded by His Contemporaries*, trans. Leo Sherley-Price (New York: Harper & Brothers, 1960), 166.

29   *The Franciscan Prayerbook* (www.franciscan-archive.org) titles this prayer "Prayer for Final Perseverance." This version is a combination of their public domain translation and the one found in *Francis of Assisi: Early Documents*, vol. I, 120–21.

30   Paul Sabatier, *The Road to Assisi: The Essential Biography of St. Francis*, ed. Jon M. Sweeney (Brewster, MA: Paraclete Press, 2003), 136–37.

31   This version from the Book of Common Prayer, from the first edition (1549) in the Church of England to the most recent in the Episcopal Church in the United States (1979), is used throughout the Anglican Communion.

32   Peter Hunter Blair, *Roman Britain and Early England 55 B.C.–A.D. 871* (New York: W. W. Norton, 1966), 212.

33   *Francis of Assisi: Early Documents*, vol. II, ed. Regis J. Armstrong, OFMCAP, J. A. Wayne Hellman, OFM CONV, and William J. Short, OFM (New York: New City Press, 2000), 314.

34   Frances A. Yates, *The Art of Memory* (Chicago: University of Chicago Press, 1966), 57–58.

✳ TWO ✳
ST. CLARE
Listen for God's Leading

1   Evelyn Underhill was an Anglican laywoman and scholar who wrote groundbreaking books about mystics and mysticism in the early twentieth century. In a 1904 *Baedeker* for central Italy, Clare barely received one sentence of description in the midst of only one paragraph about the basilica built in her honor in Assisi in 1257. But, interest in Clare has galvanized, and several important manuscripts have been discovered, including *The Acts of the Process of Canonization* in 1920 (important for understanding her biography and influence), and various editions of Clare's important, last *Testament*, as recent as the 1980s. Scholars have studied her life from every direction, although there remains to be published a major critical biography of her. The closest would be Ingrid J. Peterson's *Clare of Assisi: A Biographical Study* (Quincy, IL: Franciscan Press, 1993).

2   From the essay "St. Clare of Assisi," in Father Cuthbert, OSFC, *The Romanticism of St. Francis and Other Studies in the Genius of the Franciscans* (New York: Longmans, Green, 1915), 83–84.

3   Linda Bird Francke, *On the Road with Francis of Assisi: A Timeless Journey Through Umbria and Tuscany, and Beyond* (New York: Random House, 2005), chap. 6.

4   G. K. Chesterton, *Saint Thomas Aquinas: The Dumb Ox* (New York: Sheed and Ward, 1933), 3.

5   Translated and quoted in Catherine Mooney's *Gendered Voices: Medieval Saints and Their Interpreters* (Philadelphia: University of Pennsylvania Press, 1999), 58.

6   Evelyn Underhill, *The School of Charity* (New York: Longmans, Green, 1934), 19.

7   Luke 2:34–35; Thomas of Celano, *The Legend of St. Clare*, chapter xxviii.

8   See "A Very Brief Life of St. Agnes of Rome" on pages 178–79.

9   Some scholars question the authenticity of Clare's letter to Ermentrude. Also, there is plenty of debate as to who authored *The Legend of St. Clare* in the mid-thirteenth century soon after her death, as part of the process of building the case for her canonization. Some have claimed that it was Brother Mark, the Brother Minor who was chaplain to the sisters at the time of Clare's death. Many other names have also been put forward, particularly in the last century, when Franciscan studies entered the modern era. In both cases, there are equally strong arguments for accepting Clare as author of the letter, and Thomas as author of *The Legend,* and so we will.

10 *Clare of Assisi: Early Documents*, rev. ed. and trans. Regis J. Armstrong, OFM CAP (New York: New City Press, 2006).

11 M. Dominica Legge, *Anglo-Norman Literature and Its Background* (New York: Oxford University Press, 1973), 258.

12 Modernized translation my own. See *The Book of Divine Consolation of the Blessed Angela of Foligno*, trans. Mary G. Steegmann (New York: Cooper Square, 1966), 160.

13 Pierre Teilhard de Chardin, *The Prayer of the Universe* (New York: Harper & Row, 1973) 122.

14 The *Works of Bonaventure, I*, trans. Jose de Vinck (Paterson, NJ: St. Anthony Guild Press, 1960), 214.

15 Patrick Boyde, *Human Vices and Human Worth in Dante's* Comedy (Cambridge: Cambridge University Press, 2000), 102.

16 S. of S. 1:2–3 and 3:4.

17 Ps. 45:10–15.

18 Celano, *Legend of St. Clare*, chapter 5.

19 1 Cor. 1:26.

20 2 Cor. 8:9.

21 Chapter 37 of Thomas of Celano's *Life*.

22 Phil. 1:9.

23 *Clare of Assisi: Early Documents*, 54.

24 Abhishiktananda, *Ascent to the Depth of the Heart: The Spiritual Diary (1948–73) of Swami Abhishiktananda (Dom Henri Le Saux)*, selected and introduced by Raimon Panikkar, trans. David Fleming and James Stuart (Delhi, India: ISPCK, 1998), 33.

25 1 Pet. 2:21.

26 This prayer is derived from the fourth paragraph of Clare's second letter to Agnes. It also makes reference to Lk. 10:42 and Rom.12:1 (as does Clare in that paragraph).

27 From *The Flowering Light of the Godhead*, book II, part 2.

28 Derived (and words only slighted changed) from Clare's second letter to Agnes, paragraph 5.

29 Derived from Angela of Foligno's "Sixth Consolation of the Passion of Jesus Christ," in *The Book of Divine Consolation of the Blessed Angela of Foligno*, trans. Mary G. Steegmann (New York: Cooper Square, 1966), 215–18.

30 Derived from Gal. 1:15–16.

31 Macrina was the sister of Sts. Basil of Caesarea and Gregory of Nyssa. This prayer is taken from the *Life of Macrina*, written by Gregory of Nyssa.

32 According to scholars, this canticle was written at about the same time as "The Canticle of the Creatures," when Francis was ill at the end of his life and Clare and the sisters were worrying about him. It is one of the "last words" from Francis to the sisters. See *Francis of Assisi: Early Documents*, vol. I, ed. Regis J. Armstrong OFM CAP, J.A. Wayne, OFM CONV, and William J, Short, OFM, et al (New York: New City Press, 1999), 115. Slight changes have been made for this translation.

33 This collect is very loosely based on one from the traditional Capuchin Office of St. Clare.

34 From St. Benedict's *Rule*, the prologue. The two Scriptures quoted are Rom. 13:11 and Ps. 95:7–8.

35 Derived loosely from Clare's third letter to Agnes, paragraph 3.

36 This collect incorporates language from Clare's fourth letter to Agnes, paragraph 4, and phrases from the apocryphal book Wisdom of Solomon 7:24–27.

37 This collect is inspired by Gal. 1:15–6, and also incorporates Francis's famous statement about preaching.

38 Derived from the *Testament* of Clare, paragraph 20.

39 Inspired by, and using phrasing from, Evagrius Ponticus's *Praktikos* 61. See *The Praktikos: Chapters on Prayer*, trans. John Eudes Bamberger (Spencer, MA: Cistercian Publications, 1970), 65.

40 From "Prayer to the Holy Cross."

41 This collect incorporates language from Clare's fourth letter to Agnes, paragraph 1, as well as phrases from Rev. 14:3–4.

42 Derived from Gal. 1:15–16.

43 From a letter of St. Catherine to Sister Eugenia, Catherine's niece. This title and translation © Jon M. Sweeney.

44 Derived from Col. 1:15, 17.

45 Derived from the letter to Ermentrude of Bruges, second paragraph.

46 Inspired by, and using phrasing from, a passage from St. Bonaventure's *Soul's Journey into God*. See *Bonaventure: The Soul's Journey into God, The Tree of Life, The Major Life of Saint Francis*, trans. Ewert Cousins (New York: Paulist Press, 1978), 67–68.

47 Derived from the first letter to Agnes of Prague, last paragraph.

48 Derived from the fourth letter to Agnes of Prague, paragraphs 9–14.

49 Derived from the *Testament* of Clare, paragraph 15.

50 These three collects are derived from the first three paragraphs of Clare's letter to Ermentrude of Bruges. Various editions.

51 See *Clare of Assisi: Early Documents*, 422–24, for the most complete explanation of these prayers. My rendering of them is a shortened version of what appears there and may, in fact, be closer to the version prayed by Francis and Clare.

52 Derived from the last two paragraphs of Clare's *Testament*.

53 This blessing is derived from paragraph 5 of Clare's third letter to Agnes. It also includes references to 2 Cor. 3:18 and 1 Cor. 2:9.

54 These words were spoken by Clare on her deathbed, speaking to her own soul. In Thomas of Celano's *Life*, Clare says to one of her sisters that she is speaking to her own soul.

55 Thomas of Celano, *Second Life*, paragraph 198.

56 These translations are adaptations of those first published in Evelyn Underhill's 1919 study, *Jacopone da Todi, Poet and Mystic: A Spiritual Biography*. The translations for that volume were done by Mrs. Theodore Beck, and have been shortened and revised in the renderings that follow. Underhill viewed Jacopone as one of the most important poets of mystical union with God, which comes through clearly in the first two. In the others, it is also easy to see the way in which the core themes of Franciscan life were carried on by the great poet's songs and verses. The first three poems are derived from *Laude*, xci, and the remaining five are from *Laude*, xcviii, lx, lx, lxxxi, and lxiv, respectively.

57 Translation by Abraham Coles.

❊ THREE ❊

BROTHER JUNIPER, THE PROTOMARTYRS,
AND ST. ANTHONY OF PADUA
Love God in Humility

1 I am quoting from written notes Reb Zalman shared with me after the event, August 24, 2013.

2 I have adjusted the translation slightly, for inclusive language. St. Anthony the Great, *The Sayings of the Desert Fathers: The Alphabetical Collection*, trans. Benedicta Ward (Collegeville, MN: Cistercian Publications, 1984), 6.

3 G. K. Chesterton, *Orthodoxy*, 1908, various editions.

4 See Elizabeth-Anne Stewart, *Jesus the Holy Fool* (Kansas City: Sheed & Ward, 1999).

5 William Blake, *Jerusalem: The Emanation of the Giant Albion* (1804–1820), plate 77, 1–4.

6 From "The Anonymous of Perugia," in *Francis of Assisi: Early Documents*, vol. II, ed. Regis J. Armstrong, OFMCAP, J. A. Wayne Hellman, OFM CONV, and William J. Short, OFM (New York: New City Press, 2000), 43.

7 *The Very Best of Malcolm Muggeridge*, ed. Ian Hunter (Vancouver, BC: Regent College Publishing, 2003), 226.

8 Oliver Ready, *Persisting in Folly: Russian Writers in Search of Wisdom, 1963–2013* (New York: Peter Lang, 2016), 10.

9 John Saward, *Perfect Fools: Folly for Christ's Sake in Catholic and Orthodox Spirituality* (New York: Oxford University Press, 2000), 88.

10 Miguel de Cervantes, *Don Quixote*, trans. Edith Grossman (New York: Ecco, 2005), 21.

11 Chesterton, *Orthodoxy*. In this quote, may GKC forgive me, I've altered his masculine pronouns to make the message more universal.

12 Miguel de Unamuno, *The Private World: Selections from the Diario Intimo and Selected Letters 1890–1936*, trans. By Martin Nozick with Allen Lacy (Princeton: Princeton University Press, 1984), 3.

13 *The Mirror of Perfection*, in *Francis of Assisi: Early Documents,* vol. III, ed. Regis J. Armstrong, OFM CAP, J.A. Wayne Hellman, OFM CONV, and William J. Short, OFM (New York: New City Press, 2001), 343.

14 From *The Madman: His Parables and Poems*, first published in 1918. See Kahlil Gibran, *The Collected Works* (New York: Everyman's Library, 2007), 5.

15 Paraphrased from an account in *The Little Flowers of St. Francis*. This story does not appear in my book, *The Complete Francis of Assisi: His Life, the Complete Writings, and The Little Flowers* (Brewster, MA: Paraclete Press, 2015).

16 Brother Ugolino, comp., *The Little Flowers of Saint Francis*, arranged chronologically and rendered into contemporary English by Jon M. Sweeney (Brewster, MA: Paraclete Press, 2016), 5.

17 Thomas of Celano, *First Life*, 2; Habig, *Omnibus*, 230.

18 Miguel de Cervantes, *Don Quixote*, trans. Charles Jarvis, ed. Lester G. Crocker (New York: Washington Square Press, 1970), 5.

19 From "The Legend of Three Companions," in *Francis of Assisi: Early Documents*, vol. II, 72.

20 Iris Murdoch, *Henry and Cato* (London: Triad/Granada, 1977), 154.

21 Murray Bodo, *Juniper: Friend of Francis, Fool of God* (Cincinnati: St. Anthony Messenger Press, 1983), 12.

22 Other than this quote, I'm paraphrasing the fable; but see "The Policeman and the Drunkard, on Spiritual Intoxication," in A. J. Arberry, *Tales from the Masnavi* (London: George Allen and Unwin, 1961), 152–53.

23 Mathew Woodley, *Holy Fools: Following Jesus with Reckless Abandon* (Carol Stream, IL: Saltriver/Tyndale House, 2008), 63.

24 Stewart, *Jesus the Holy Fool*, 32.

25 Eugene Ionesco, quoted in Thomas Merton's essay, "Rain and the Rhinoceros," in *Raids on the Unspeakable* (New York: New Directions, 1966), 21.

26 Wendell Berry, *In the Presence of Fear: Three Essays for a Changed World* (Great Barrington, MA: The Orion Society, 2001), 13.

27　From "The Legend of Three Companions," in *Francis of Assisi: Early Documents*, vol. II, 102.

28　From Clare's Rule, para. 8, in *Francis and Clare: The Complete Works*, trans. Regis J. Armstrong, OFM CAP, and Ignatius C. Brady, OFM (New York: Paulist Press, 1982), 219–20.

29　Francis of Assisi, The Original Rule, para. 7. See Sweeney, *Complete Francis of Assisi*, 213.

30　From *The Little Flowers*, in Sweeney, *Complete Francis of Assisi*, 336.

31　Francis of Assisi, The Original Rule, para. 11, slightly modified. See Sweeney, *Complete Francis of Assisi*, 216.

32　My translation from *The Little Flowers*, not included in Sweeney, *Complete Francis of Assisi*.

33　Francis of Assisi, The Original Rule, para. 9. See Sweeney, *Complete Francis of Assisi*, 214.

34　Francis of Assisi, The Original Rule, para. 17. See Sweeney, *Complete Francis of Assisi*, 220.

35　From the fourth letter that Clare wrote to Agnes. First appeared in slightly different form in *The St. Clare Prayer Book* (Brewster, MA: Paraclete Press, 2007), 112.

36　Slightly adapted from *The Little Flowers*. See Sweeney, *Complete Francis of Assisi*, 341.

37　Slighted adapted from Sweeney, *Complete Francis of Assisi*, 205.

38　Taken from *The St. Francis Prayer Book: A Guide to Deepen Your Spiritual Life* (Brewster, MA: Paraclete Press, 2004), 126.

39　Derived from one of his Sunday sermons. The quotation just before this, from Francis's letter to Anthony about teaching theology, may be found in full in Sweeney, *Complete Francis of Assisi*, 236.

40　This is from the last chapter of the Later Rule of 1223, written from experience, after Francis's trip to see Sultan al-Malik al-Kāmil during the Fifth Crusade at the Nile Delta in Egypt in 1219. This is my rendering. The word "Saracen" was used by Francis for Muslim, but in the thirteenth century in Italy, Saracen meant simply that.

41　Rimini is in northeastern Italy, on the Adriatic coast.

❖ FOUR ❖

LORD, MAKE ME AN INSTRUMENT OF YOUR PEACE

1 Adrian House, *Francis of Assisi: A Revolutionary Life* (Mahwah, NJ: HiddenSpring, 2003), 171.

2 Patricia Applebaum, *St. Francis of America: How a Thirteenth-Century Friar Became America's Most Popular Saint* (Chapel Hill: University of North Carolina Press, 2015), 71.

3 The recording session took place November 4, 1954. "A Bing Crosby Discography," *Bing Magazine*, accessed May 29, 2019, http://www.bingmagazine.co.uk/bingmagazine/crosby1bDecca.html.

4 Jim Rigg, quoted in Kathleen Manning's "What Do We Know About St. Francis, America's Most Popular Saint?," USCatholic.org, October 2, 2017, http://www.uscatholic.org/articles/201710/what-do-we-know-about-st-francis-americas-most-popular-saint-31161.

ABOUT PARACLETE PRESS

Who We Are

As the publishing arm of the Community of Jesus, Paraclete Press presents a full expression of Christian belief and practice—from Catholic to Evangelical, from Protestant to Orthodox, reflecting the ecumenical charism of the Community and its dedication to sacred music, the fine arts, and the written word. We publish books, recordings, sheet music, and video/DVDs that nourish the vibrant life of the church and its people.

What We Are Doing

BOOKS | PARACLETE PRESS BOOKS show the richness and depth of what it means to be Christian. While Benedictine spirituality is at the heart of who we are and all that we do, our books reflect the Christian experience across many cultures, time periods, and houses of worship.

We have many series, including *Paraclete Essentials*; *Paraclete Fiction*; *Paraclete Poetry*; *Paraclete Giants*; and for children and adults, *All God's Creatures*, books about animals and faith; and *San Damiano Books*, focusing on Franciscan spirituality. Others include *Voices from the Monastery* (men and women monastics writing about living a spiritual life today), *Active Prayer*, and new for young readers: *The Pope's Cat*. We also specialize in gift books for children on the occasions of Baptism and First Communion, as well as other important times in a child's life, and books that bring creativity and liveliness to any adult spiritual life.

THE MOUNT TABOR BOOKS series focuses on the arts and literature as well as liturgical worship and spirituality; it was created in conjunction with the Mount Tabor Ecumenical Centre for Art and Spirituality in Barga, Italy.

MUSIC | The Paraclete Recordings label represents the internationally acclaimed choir *Gloriæ Dei Cantores*, the *Gloriæ Dei Cantores Schola*, and the other instrumental artists of the *Arts Empowering Life Foundation*.

Paraclete Press is the exclusive North American distributor for the Gregorian chant recordings from St. Peter's Abbey in Solesmes, France. Paraclete also carries all of the Solesmes chant publications for Mass and the Divine Office, as well as their academic research publications.

In addition, Paraclete Press Sheet Music publishes the work of today's finest composers of sacred choral music, annually reviewing over 1,000 works and releasing between 40 and 60 works for both choir and organ.

VIDEO | Our video/DVDs offer spiritual help, healing, and biblical guidance for a broad range of life issues including grief and loss, marriage, forgiveness, facing death, understanding suicide, bullying, addictions, Alzheimer's, and Christian formation

Learn more about us at our website
www.paracletepress.com
or phone us toll-free at 1.800.451.5006

SCAN
TO
READ
MORE